Moral Theory

The Jones and Bartlett Series in Philosophy

Robert Ginsberg, General Editor

Ayer, A. J., *Metaphysics and Common Sense*, 1994 reissue with corrections and new introduction by Thomas Magnell, Drew University

Beckwith, Francis J., University of Nevada, Las Vegas, Editor, *Do the Right Thing: A Philosophical Dialogue on the Moral and Social Issues of Our Time*

Bishop, Anne H. and John R. Scudder, Jr., Lynchburg College, *Nursing Ethics: Therapeutic Caring Presence*

Caws, Peter, George Washington University, *Ethics from Experience*

DeMarco, Joseph P., Cleveland State University, *Moral Theory: A Contemporary Overview*

Gorr, Michael, Illinois State University, and Sterling Harwood, San Jose State University, Editors, *Crime and Punishment: Philosophic Explorations*

Haber, Joram Graf, Bergen Community College, Interviewer, *Ethics in the '90s*, a 26-part Video Series

Harwood, Sterling, San Jose State University, Editor, *Business as Ethical and Business as Usual: Text, Readings, and Cases*

Heil, John, Davidson College, *First-Order Logic: A Concise Introduction*

Jason, Gary, San Diego State University, *Introduction to Logic*

Minogue, Brendan, Youngstown State University, *Bioethics: A Committee Approach*

Moriarty, Marilyn, Hollins College, *Writing Science Through Critical Thinking*

Pauling, Linus, and Daisaku, Ikeda, *A Lifelong Quest for Peace, A Dialogue*, Translator and Editor, Richard L. Gage

Pojman, Louis P., The University of Mississippi, and Francis Beckwith, University of Nevada Las Vegas, Editors, *The Abortion Controversy: A Reader*

Pojman, Louis P., The University of Mississippi, Editor, *Environmental Ethics: Readings in Theory and Application*

Pojman, Louis P., The University of Mississippi, *Life and Death: Grappling with the Moral Dilemmas of Our Time*

Pojman, Louis P., The University of Mississippi, Editor, *Life and Death: A Reader in Moral Problems*

Rolston III, Holmes, Colorado State University, Editor, *Biology, Ethics, and the Origins of Life*

Townsend, Dabney, The University of Texas at Arlington, Editor, *Introduction to Aesthetics: Classic Readings from the Western Tradition*

Veatch, Robert M., The Kennedy Institute of Ethics, Georgetown University, Editor, *Cross-Cultural Perspectives in Medical Ethics: Readings*

Veatch, Robert M., The Kennedy Institute of Ethics, Georgetown University, Editor, *Medical Ethics*

Verene, Donald P., Emory University, Editor, *Sexual Love and Western Morality: A Philosophical Anthology*, Second Edition

Williams, Clifford, Trinity University, Illinois, Editor, *On Love and Friendship: Philosophical Readings*

Moral Theory
A Contemporary Overview

Joseph P. DeMarco
Cleveland State University
Cleveland, Ohio

JONES AND BARTLETT PUBLISHERS

Boston   London

Editorial, Sales, and Customer Service Offices
Jones and Bartlett Publishers
One Exeter Plaza
Boston, MA 02116
1-800-832-0034
617-859-3900

Jones and Bartlett Publishers International
7 Melrose Terrace
London W6 7RL
England

Library of Congress Cataloging-in-Publication Data

DeMarco, Joseph P., 1943–
    Moral theory : a contemporary overview / Joseph P. DeMarco.
        p. cm. -- (The Jones and Bartlett series in philosophy)
    Includes bibliographical references and index.
    ISBN 0-86720-954-2
    1. Ethics.   I. Title. II. Series.
    BJ1012.D45 1995
    171--dc20   95-3886
                                                  CIP

Acquisitions Editors: Arthur C. Bartlett and Nancy E. Bartlett
Production Editor: Anne S. Noonan
Manufacturing Buyer: Dana L. Cerrito
Editorial Production Service: Book 1
Typesetting: Seahorse Prepress/Book 1
Printing and Binding: Braun-Brumfield, Inc.
Cover Design: Hannus Design Associates
Cover Printing: New England Book Components, Inc.
Cover Photo: Peter LaTourrette

Printed in the United States of America
99 98 97 96 95   10 9 8 7 6 5 4 3 2 1

For Bonnie

Contents

Preface

Many philosophers teaching ethics today have moved toward an applied approach. This is surely a welcome move; a philosophical approach to ethics can, and has, helped us to become better at analyzing and solving moral problems. But the gains come because philosophers have, for centuries, proposed moral theories. The move toward an applied approach would be unwelcome if it encouraged us to jump into application while forgetting its base in theory.

This book provides a contemporary examination of moral theory. It learns from application; many philosophers recognize that highly abstract theories are not easily applicable. The turn has been toward positions, such as virtue ethics, that seem closer to concrete circumstances. This book examines the full range of theoretical positions, from extreme particularism to moral ideals. The challenge is both to identify the strengths and weaknesses of traditional, abstract theories and also to realize how these theories strengthen moral decision making.

My approach is eclectic. I view theories as attempts to order and guide moral experience. An eclectic view holds the promise of bringing coherence to moral experience. This view is certainly evident in the text, but the basic value of the text lies in its comprehensive approach, as the table of contents indicates. The student is exposed to many positions and invited to consider their strong and weak points.

In its organization, the text moves, more or less, from concrete positions to theories relying on abstract values and principles. Assuming that a concrete approach is more easily assimilated, students should find this comfortable even though the text is demanding. Refinements are explored, and end-of-section questions—an integral part of the text designed to amplify material and to point ahead to positions subsequently explored—are sometimes difficult. Questions considered especially taxing are labeled "For class discussion." Throughout the body of the text, the reader is asked parenthetical questions designed to encourage a careful and critical reading.

The first two chapters set the stage for an informed beginning. We need to start someplace, and starting with either abstract theories, such as Kant's, or with concrete positions that reject the use of principles, leaves the student without a critical base. Until we know a good deal about many positions, it is unrealistic to expect full understanding and informed critique. I deal with this by first exploring moral experience, its basic appeal and basic ingredients. I also make explicit some approaches to theory evaluation that philosophers typically implicitly employ. Following this, in Chapter 2, I survey basic approaches to moral theory. This chapter is meant to help students see the range of approaches before they concentrate, chapter by chapter, on specific systems. Some instructors might use these two chapters as preparatory reading, or as summaries, as theories are covered later in the text. However, I do recommend that class time be spent on the ways to evaluate theories; this should help the student to appreciate the probing techniques philosophers are accustomed to employ.

Although I start, after the first two chapters, with the more concrete positions, the text can be used in other ways. One could begin with the final chapter on metaethics, and Chapter 4, on subjectivity and relativism, after which several approaches can be fruitfully used—for example, first turning to moral values in Chapter 9. Many permutations would work. Here are two suggested alternate ways, listing chapter numbers: 1, 2, 12, 4, 8, 9, 6, 5, 7, 10, 3, 11; or 6, 8, 9, 10, 11, 3, 4, 5, 7, 12. Some instructors will begin where they believe the students will be most comfortable, say with moral rules in Chapter 6, while others will start with dominant theories, Kant and utilitarianism, in Chapter 8. The table of contents should help you to make the decision right for your style and views. In order to make the book flexible, I briefly reexamine some material within several chapters. This takes up few pages and should occasionally help students to understand relationships among topics covered.

Moral Theory includes many exciting, and controversial, topics usually overlooked in introductory texts: ideals, exemplars, norms, utopian thinking, role morality, conventions, casuistry, and feminist ethics. I also cover some basic material in political philosophy, such as liberalism, both contemporary and modern, and conservatism, and the multicultural challenge. These are covered quickly, but the added material helps to complete the sense that moral thinking should be involved in many types of decision making.

My attempt to bring moral experience to coherence finds value in many positions. This helps offset the sense students sometimes have that we have made no progress in moral thinking. Although a comprehensive approach can help students to understand the value we see in different basic positions, coherence in ethics has been rejected by many, probably most, philosophers. Even when rejected, I hope it provides an issue around, or against, which the value of other positions can be defended, strengthened, and explored. Our survey of moral theory succeeds when it not only covers the ground but also encourages good moral thinking.

The evolution of many of the ideas behind this text benefited from frequent discussion with Richard M. Fox and Samuel A. Richmond, both exceptional philosophers and colleagues at Cleveland State University. Thanks are also due to Robert Ginsberg and Art Bartlett, at Jones and Bartlett, who provided genuine encouragement and support. The suggestions of Eric W. Snider of the University of Toledo, Joram Graf Haber of Bergen Community College, and Hans Zorn of Roanoke College, reviewers for Jones and Bartlett, were very helpful in preparing the final draft. Finally, I would like to express appreciation to my ethics students at Cleveland State University and Tuskegee Institute; the form of presentation of the topics covered in this text was first developed through interaction with students during the last twenty years.

–J. P. D.

1

Introduction

Moral Experience and the Evaluation of Moral Theories

1.1 The Task Ahead

We are about to embark on a journey through moral theory. It's a fascinating trip: in presenting ethical theories philosophers have offered exciting responses to the dilemmas about the way we should organize and conduct our lives, morally speaking. Despite the sincerity, skill, and cleverness of moral theorists, no theory has yet to win a consensus among philosophers. Each theory seems, to different people, to include too much or to leave too much out. Some theories include too much by demanding actions thought to be clearly immoral, or else by demanding as moral obligations actions that people usually believe they are permitted not to do. Some theories fail to commend or reject actions that many people believe to be either commendable or morally forbidden. The problem is to find a theory that neither requires too much nor permits too much—a tall task—while providing clear and helpful advice about moral decision making.

In coming chapters, we try to clear the way toward constructing such a theory by examining basic, and very different, moral theories. We find that each is lacking and that each has strengths. This should not be surprising. The challenge is to properly identify both the strengths and the weaknesses. We try to do this. You should examine critically all the claims made in this and the following chapters, determining whether we understate strengths or take weaknesses to be strengths or strengths to be weaknesses. You may reason, against my judgment, that one of theories is in fact completely right, without any weaknesses.

If you agree with me that each theory has strengths and weaknesses, and take seriously the strengths and weaknesses I identify, even if you don't agree, then we have a genuine, perhaps Herculean challenge on our hands: to develop a theory that accounts for all the strengths and avoids all the weaknesses. At the end of the last chapter, I offer some suggestions about how a comprehensive, adequate theory can be formulated. You might want to read that chapter first, returning to it again when you critique other theories.[1] If you are intrigued by the task of putting together a sound, comprehensive, instructive, and coherent theory, I hope you take seriously how the different aspects of moral experience we examine can be mutually supporting.

To believe that anybody today has all the answers about moral theory is naive. We need good, reasonable debate on moral perspectives because we need, perhaps more than ever before, good and reasonable theories. In my view the best way to move toward an adequate theory is to study and debate the best theories produced so far. This is the intention of this book: although brief, it covers a wide variety of views, offers a critical perspective, yet attempts to respect and find value in many points of view. This is the basis, I think, of genuine debate: respect based on knowledge of the positions offered, coupled with critical inquiry.

In this chapter, we begin by claiming that moral experience is complex and that a theory that seems to exclude parts of that experience must explain either (1) that the excluded parts are not proper, or else (2) that the theory can explain, or account for, them. In this way, moral experience becomes the data for moral theory. Some philosophers reject this approach, viewing moral experience as too confused or even as too immoral to function properly in the evaluation of moral theories. So we offer several other methods, less dependent on moral experience, that may help us to evaluate moral theories. Although I believe that the most helpful approach is to use moral experience as the basic guide, I think it is wise to use, in our inquiry, all points of view on the way to developing and critiquing a theory. We must be critical, and we must have good ways to develop our critiques. This is crucial, at least for the beginning theorist. We not only have no consensus on the right theory, but we have no consensus on how to develop a theory, on the correct methodology to use, so the best response is to become as familiar as we can with all the main ways of offering a critique, and come to our own reasonable conclusions on the best method to use to locate the most adequate moral theory.

Aside from learning about influential moral theories, we aim to find what is right and wrong with each, move toward the endorsement of the best view, and establish the best way to evaluate a theory. Each of these aims offers a demanding, exciting, and rewarding challenge.

1.2 Judging Theories in Ethics

All of us make moral evaluations. If we encounter an adult mistreating a child, hear a news account about an abduction and murder of a high school student, find out about a totally neglected elderly person, or realize that a politician is taking graft, we call those things morally wrong. Such acts are serious, but even less serious events may elicit moral disapproval: a friend fails to keep a date, a student lies to a teacher to ensure an incomplete grade, a teacher repeatedly misses class, a parent is late with child support payments, someone litters in a national forest. Such events, serious and less serious, lead most people to make moral evaluations. A moral evaluation is a judgment about some event, action, person, state of affairs, or even another moral judgment. After any judgment, we may question whether it is proper, morally speaking. How can we defend moral judgments? Do we have ways to determine whether moral judgments are correct or incorrect? Are the moral judgments made by some people better than those made by others? Are all moral judgments simply matters of personal taste? Or are moral judgments objectively right or wrong, no matter what you or I believe? These are questions that moral theorists attempt to answer by developing moral theories.

This book is about moral evaluations, but often only indirectly. It surveys many of the basic ways to provide answers to these questions. When you finish this study, you should be able to debate responsibly the range of answers, and you will know many of the basic strengths and weaknesses of each. Hopefully, you will be able to use this knowledge to articulate and defend your own views.

Moral theorists in the West have developed positions in ethics for over two thousand years, producing almost every point of view or theory you can imagine: from an extreme denial of the validity of any moral judgments to dogmatic affirmation that every single action, no matter how insignificant, can be judged, objectively, as morally right or wrong. Much depends on our analysis of these positions; our theoretical commitments help determine how we evaluate moral judgments.

As we explore and debate different ethical theories, each supporting different basic outlooks on moral judgments, we profit by having some general way to evaluate them. Almost all the theories have strengths and all have weaknesses; moral theorists have not settled on a single position in ethics, and almost all theories are supported by some and rejected by others. In the following chapter we will briefly survey some basic positions in ethics.

The moral positions we are going to examine are theoretical; they do not supply direct answers to questions about whether a particular action, like breaking a promise to a friend, is morally proper; instead, they mainly speculate on how, in general, we may best resolve moral problems. Moral theories are about the ways we ought to understand and come to conclusions about moral obligations, permissions, and evaluations. Claiming that a person has a special obligation to give to the United Way, a moral judgment, is different from explaining *why* a person might have such an obligation. A moral theory attempts to explain why we have the obligations we have, and how we can decide what obligations we have. For example, a moral theory might hold that we have an obligation to help others. By then applying this general statement we may conclude that giving to the United Way best allows us to help others, and thus, according to the theory, we ought to do it.

Although some theories, say in logic or mathematics, may be thought of as self-contained and be judged by their consistency, elegance, and simplicity, practical theories in subjects from astronomy to zoology explain, organize, control, and predict their specific subject matter, and so are judged by their effectiveness in doing so. Does an economic theory do a good job at explaining how economies work, and does it allow us to function more effectively as economic agents? Does a theory in psychology permit us to understand personal relationships and dependencies, and does it help us to make accurate predictions about human behavior? We may judge an economic or a psychological theory by the way it performs its basic functions in relation to economic or mental experience. We also keep in mind that these theories are not merely used to understand what occurs but also to change or control our environment. We ask economists to provide theories that will help to guide public and private decisions in order to secure growth or avoid inflation, and we depend on psychologists to help us overcome emotional stress. Theories that cannot perform these functions may be evaluated negatively.

Ethics is not much different. Moral experience is part of our lives, and moral theory will be judged mainly in relation to that experience, on how moral experience is explained and ordered, and how we can use moral theory to guide actions. By *moral experience*, we mean the way people have viewed moral evaluations, obligations, permissions, rights, justice, freedom, respect, and a host of other things. Does a moral theory explain and organize our moral experience? Does it help us to control and guide our lives so that our lives become morally better? Does a theory help us to explain, organize, and even predict moral decision making?

Although we may judge moral theories in relation to moral experience, we can't be simplistic about the moral experience. Theories are public property. A theory in economics is not about your economic experiences or mine, but about *our* experiences. The more broadly we conceive "our" to be, the better the test of the theory. A psychological theory that is only about

New Yorkers, interesting as it may be, is too limited because it is not about general psychological experience.

Any moral theory that recommends actions that run counter to *our* moral experience should be suspect. Almost everyone believes that seriously harming another person without a good reason is morally wrong; any moral theory that seems to approve such harm will seem unacceptable because moral experience, broadly conceived, goes against it. A theorist may try to convince us that gratuitous harm is not morally wrong, but the theory will look weak because it conflicts with a widely shared basic moral conviction. To show that a theory is incorrect, we can appeal to strong moral convictions. Remember that theories are designed to help us make difficult moral decisions; a strong theory is one that does so.

Determining the value of a theory is not as easy as it first seems. So far we propose using experience to evaluate most theories. This is fine until we realize that the way something is experienced is likely to be influenced by theory. We all live within traditions—religious, cultural, political—that have developed under broad prospectives that may be interpreted as ethical theories. Our moral experience is largely molded by these theories. Now it starts to seem circular: we evaluate theory by moral experience, which itself is molded by theory! For example, a person from a religious tradition that strongly supports forgiveness as a key virtue will tend to believe that any moral theory not proposing adequate endorsement of forgiveness is weak.

Philosophers offer several answers to this question. We want to take these answers seriously and keep them all in mind when evaluating the viewpoints that we examine. As theorists, we don't want to restrict ourselves, at least at first. We want to be able to evaluate theories from a variety of perspectives. As we do this, we should become more skillful in determining which types of evaluation help us develop better moral theories—that is, theories that better guide, explain, organize, control, and predict in relation to moral experience. In the next section we consider different ways to move from moral experience to an evaluation of moral theories. Even though we have yet to examine a theory, we will learn some basic techniques to critically evaluate and defend them. We will use moral experience—perhaps a refined sense of moral experience—to determine what makes a theory valuable; with this in mind we can develop or adopt good theories and use them to help us make proper moral judgments.

Study Questions 1.2

1. Suppose a moral theorist claims that moral theory has nothing to do with moral experience—that is, what most people take to be morally right or wrong is irrelevant. Assuming you held this position, how would you defend the claim? (Here are some hints: You might claim

that moral experience is inconsistent, that all sorts of actions have some supporters. Or you might claim that morality comes from authority, say the authority of God or of local custom, or that it should be based on the experiences of some gifted individuals.)

2. Try to answer the arguments made by those who reject moral experience as a guide to evaluating moral theory. (You may want to proceed by offering a counterexample: for example, suppose morality depends on the wisdom of a gifted person and that person tells us that we should do some unspeakable action.)

3. Suppose that moral experience is inconsistent, with some people approving what others disapprove. Does this show that moral experience is ineffective as a guide in ethics? (Remember that one of the purposes of moral theory is to explain, order, and guide moral experience.)

1.3 Moral Experience and the Evaluation of Moral Theories

Moral experience is complex, partly because many different moral standards have been used to judge individual actions, rules, laws, institutions, and customs. The variety of opinions is sometimes overwhelming. One reason for developing a moral theory is to enable us to evaluate diverse and conflicting moral judgments. We use moral theory to evaluate moral opinions and judgments, yet many moral theories exist. So we also need to determine which are helpful or correct; in other words, we need to evaluate theories as well as judgments. In Section 1.2, we saw that moral experience can be used to help us judge moral theory, which in turn helps us refine and organize moral experience, but we will use moral experience to judge theories. This circularity suggests that we should refine our understanding of how moral experience can be used to evaluate moral theories. We now look at three ways to do this.

1. Ideal Observers

One way to evaluate a moral theory is to rely upon a "purified" sense of moral experience. We might attempt to discover what moral judgments would be like for perfect beings, and then use their sense of morality to judge moral theory. If a moral theory could not adequately explain the supposed moral decisions of perfect beings, it would not count as a correct theory.

But how do we determine what a being with a perfect moral sense would be like? One way is to omit from our own moral sense the factors that impede good moral judgments. (Before you read on, think of some factors that keep people from making good moral decisions. See if the ones you select are like those mentioned in the next sentence; if they are not, consider how a perfect moral decision maker should be defined.) We know that some people are overly self-interested, biased, unsympathetic, and not well attuned to what is going on around them. The judgments of such people count for little in evaluating basic positions. Instead we might think of a perfect moral judgment maker as one who is completely unbiased, disinterested, aware of relevant facts, and able to sympathize with all those involved in any situation. Even though no such perfect person actually exists, we could try to figure out what kinds of judgments such people would make if they did. Philosophers have called such a person an *ideal observer*.

Using the judgments of an ideal observer, we could discount part of moral experience and only rely on those judgments and evaluations that would be made under ideal conditions. Although this ideal observer does not exist, we may use these as guidelines for making proper moral judgments. For example, a racist judgment would be rejected by an ideal observer because it is biased; similarly, a judgment that advocates taking advantage of an uninformed person in order to make large profits would be rejected by a sympathetic disinterested observer, one who understands and appreciates all the perspectives involved. In this way, we could attempt to identify those moral judgments that appear unbiased, well-considered, and able to be supported from many perspectives. Then we can use these judgments, which we argue would be supported by an ideal observer, to test a theory. If a theory conflicts with these judgments, it is in trouble. If a theory conflicts with too many of these judgments, it is dead. The theory that supports many of these refined judgments, however, begins to look very promising.

This position evaluates a theory by way of counterexamples. A counterexample to moral theory is a judgment, clearly supported by the theory, that most people would reject; that is, most people would believe immoral something that the theory accepts as proper. Suppose we believe that punishing the innocent is wrong and that an ideal observer would agree. We may also maintain that the judgment is widely shared and easy to support under due and careful consideration. Any theory that violates this judgment is in trouble; it has some explaining to do. A theory might be able to overcome some problems; it might fail the test of one counterexample, but be so good at explaining and organizing other basic beliefs, including other judgments supported by our hypothetical ideal observer, that it holds its own despite this failure. It may even convince us that the counterexample is itself mistaken. Although a theory might withstand a few counterexamples, too many may lead us to reject it.

Using this approach, we get a sense of the judgments that a theory cannot violate in a wholesale way. But we need not depend on an ideal observer to develop a set of *refined judgments*, those, for example, that eliminate bias. We might look to the level of support judgments have; moral judgments supported by many people from different places may seem secure enough to count as refined judgments. As you go through the coming chapters, consider responses to these questions: How do we develop a set of carefully considered basic moral judgments to serve as the data of moral theory? Will this set be culturally dependent? Are the views of some people—such as those who are respected as morally wise—superior to the views of others? Are some basic moral concerns more objective than others, and should the expression of these concerns dominate the purified list of judgments? Using judgments as a way to evaluate theories becomes more potent when they can withstand critical scrutiny. As you work through the coming chapters, you should be able to refine and better defend the judgments you consider fundamental in evaluating moral theory.

2. Moral Coherence

The second way to evaluate moral theories is more holistic and embracing because it is unwilling to limit the moral experience. All aspects of moral experience count, even those that appear to be selfish or poorly considered. Under this view, the job of the moral theorist is to account for as much moral experience as possible without considering where it comes from; the job of a theory is to bring those diverse moral viewpoints into as full a coherence as possible. Diverse positions are said to cohere when some or all of the following are true: (1) they do not conflict; (2) one can be derived from another; or (3) they offer mutual support—that is, if we hold one, we are more likely to also believe the other. Point (1) is a weaker form of coherence, while (2) or (3) provides stricter, more helpful indications that the positions held do fit together comfortably.

    The coherence method searches for a theory that not only brings many or most of our moral views into coherence but also accounts for, guides, and orders more of moral experience. We do have conflicting views. Most believe that people should not lie and should not harm, but what about a harmful truth? A theory that gives an answer to such a question is doing its job: it is organizing moral experience. The best theory is the one that most successfully brings our moral experience, as broadly conceived as possible, to coherence. If we are against breaking moral rules, like the rule against lying, and we are also against harming others, a good theory will show us what to do in the case of a harmful truth. If a theory can resolve many such conflicts, conflicts at the base of moral experience, we may begin to believe that it is an especially good theory. So in evaluating a theory we keep in mind how well it can resolve moral conflict; how it orders moral judgments, showing us which is more basic or more important; and how it allows us to make not only consistent judgments, but judgments that give mutual support. For example, the judgements that parents are permitted to lie under appropriate conditions, but that their teenage children should never lie are consistent, but offer little mutual support. The judgments that everyone should work and that society has an obligation to provide opportunities are consistent *and* mutually supporting.

Now that we have two ways to judge a moral theory—how well does it bring moral experience to coherence, and how well does it support "ideal" judgments?—we can combine them and modify them. We may call for coherence, so that a theory includes and orders as much of moral experience as feasible, yet rank some aspects of that experience as more important than others by insisting that a theory support the "special" judgments of an ideal, or nearly ideal, observer. We can rely on the ideal observer for more than specific judgments by claiming that some broad principles, like the principle against harming, are so central in moral theory that no ideal observer would leave them out; thus we may require all theories to support those principles. Failure to bring the main ingredients of moral experience into coherence is a graver weakness than failure to take into proper account its less serious aspects. Even though some judgments and principles are given a special role, others less central or important might continue to have impact in this combined method of evaluation; several less serious judgments may overcome a better supported judgment. In the combined method, a theory tries to bring all judgments into coherence, but some judgments are considered more important than others.

As we explore moral perspectives in the coming chapters, we can begin to use the first two methods more fruitfully. We can develop better ways to argue that some judgments are crucial, that some rules are needed in any moral theory, or that some principles cannot be ignored. Our hope is that as we learn more about proposed theories, we can better use moral experience as a base to judge theory and can develop a better idea of which aspects of moral experience ought to be assigned greater weight in our deliberations.

3. Moral Reasonableness

A third way to evaluate moral theories puts moral experience into a secondary status by claiming that we can figure out, using our reasoning powers, which moral theories are best. Some moral views are not reasonable; they may be inconsistent or unrealistic, or they may fail to take into account basic facts about human nature or social life. With this method, a theory is judged not by how well it matches moral experience but by how reasonable it is. Nevertheless, moral experience may play a role; if a theory is too far from basic moral commitments, we may doubt that it is as reasonable as it claims to be. Since reasoning about how reasonable something is, is often tricky, we need controls on our speculation about reasonableness. (To help understand why "reasonableness" is itself difficult to evaluate, think of a case of disagreement between a parent and a child, where each side believes that its view is eminently reasonable.) Moral experience may help limit uncontrolled speculation about reasonableness. So even when reasonableness is the main guide to moral thinking, our moral experience may be called upon to play a role. (For example, the parent may claim that the child lacks responsibility while the child accuses the parent of restricting freedom; one side claims that being reasonable must include responsibility while the other insists on respect for freedom.)

We might decide that a reasonable theory allows each person to pursue his or her own interests as fully as possible. Since we value human reason, why not allow individuals to make their own choices whenever this does not conflict with the decisions of others? A theory that constrains people without good reason may be viewed as unreasonable. Under this view, a particular aspect of reasonableness—allowing people to pursue their interests—may be used to judge moral theories. How well does a suggested theory make it possible for each person to pursue his or her own life with the fewest constraints? A theory with too many rules may seem unacceptable under this viewpoint. Once again, as we develop a sense of moral reasoning and increase our knowledge about different moral theories, we will be better able to judge positions by their "reasonableness." For now, we should consider whether a theory is too restrictive or too permissive, consistently applicable, not self-defeating, and universal (applicable to all). All of these have been offered as reasonable standards that any moral theory must meet.

Sometimes this method of evaluating theories claims that it does not depend on, but strictly evaluates, moral experience. Actually it usually incorporates moral experience, at least surreptitiously. In the example given above, a reasonable theory may be one that allows us to pursue our own individual interests as fully as feasible, but what kinds of interests count? We may decide that what I want only really matters, morally speaking, when I choose it. If I am brainwashed, or ignorant about my own needs, my desires may appear self-destructive. We react negatively to coercion, even when a coerced person thinks that his or her decisions were freely made. Here the reaction against coercion may help us to define "reasonable," and so may help us to judge which theories are best; the reaction against coercion is itself a central part of moral experience. So although while this third method does not explicitly appeal to moral experience, it should be in line with fundamental aspects of morality, like the rejection of coercion.

Although moral experience plays an important part in evaluating theories, it must be used with care; we should keep in mind that our moral experience is influenced, explicitly or implicitly, by mistaken moral theories. And what we consider to be an entrenched part of moral experience may simply be a special view of ours. We may come to the study of moral theory with many views, believing that we already know how to determine right from wrong, but these views also need to be examined to be sure that they are supported by good reasons or else rejected. The three evaluation methods may help to determine whether our views can stand up to critical evaluation, and by comparing our views or theories with those of the philosophers presented in the following chapters, we should clarify the three methods, use them to judge our own views, and determine which positions, ours or others, best satisfy our tests. Moral experience, with its weaknesses, its conflicts, its compelling features, its wisdom, and its foolishness, may help us gain insight into the correct moral theory; nevertheless, our moral experience might guide us in arbitrary or haphazard ways. It might give us some insights, help us avoid some blunders, and point us toward what really matters, though it might not lead us to any final theory.

Our task is twofold: to find the best theory, and, in the search, to perfect the ways we make moral judgments and our reasoning about morality. I propose that in the following chapters we use all three ways to evaluate moral theories. In examining a theory we may need to combine several methods or, in some cases, we may use just one. In all three, a basic moral position is evaluated, at least in part, in relation to moral experience. The problem is to determine whether moral experience plays a dominant role or a minor one. Part of what we will do is to evaluate the role played by our moral experience as the data of moral theory; through the study of philosophical moral theories we should end up with a better sense of the strengths and weaknesses of current moral experience.

Study Questions 1.3

1. In the statement below, the philosopher Bernard Williams talks about the use of moral experience in developing a philosophical theory. By "a phenomenology of the ethical life," he means a description, without evaluation, of the way people make moral judgments and evaluations. Explain and evaluate his comment.

> There could be a way of doing moral philosophy that started from the ways in which we experience our ethical life. Such a philosophy would reflect on what we believe, feel, take for granted; the ways in which we confront obligations and recognize responsibility; the sentiments of guilt and shame. It would involve a phenomenology

of the ethical life. This could be a good philosophy, but it would be unlikely to yield an ethical theory. Ethical theories, with their concern for tests, tend to start from just one aspect of moral experience, beliefs.[2]

2. (For class discussion.) Do you agree that an ideal moral observer would be unbiased, disinterested, and sympathetic? What do these terms mean? Suppose people disagree about whether a judgment is biased. For example, suppose one person claims that abortion is wrong while another claims that it is permissible, and both think that an unbiased person would agree with them. Can this disagreement be resolved based on a definition of "bias"?

3. Present three or four judgments that you have good reason to believe an ideal observer would make, e.g., that breaking a promise is wrong. Argue for each by showing that it is unbiased and disinterested (as opposed to self-interested).

4. Suppose we believe that it is morally wrong to tell a lie, to harm another, and to interfere with the freedom of another. Consider the following case:

> Professor Stern is the adviser to a student, Eurica Learnwell, who wants to pursue graduate studies in philosophy. Stern believes that Eurica is unprepared, but knows that she will be hurt by his opinion. In order not to harm her, Stern tells her that she is now fully prepared for further study.

Do the values we hold conflict in this case? If so, present an argument in favor of giving one value priority over the others. For example, you might claim that avoiding a lie is more important than avoiding harm. Be careful in presenting your answer; although it might be clear when one is telling a lie, whether something harms a person or deprives him or her freedom is often not so obvious.

5. (For class discussion.) Suppose one theory is better able than another to balance the conflicts between moral rules (like "Do not lie") and moral principles (like "Do no harm" and "Do not violate the freedom of another person"). Present two arguments: one claiming that this makes little or no difference in evaluating the two theories and one claiming that, provided the theories are equally well constructed, the ability of one to balance widely held values makes it a superior theory. Present your reasons for supporting one of these arguments.

6. (For class discussion.) The notion of "reasonableness" is far from clear. It clearly involves consistency, but after that different philosophers defend different ingredients. Some believe that a reasonable theory is one that explains the necessity for having a good moral

theory. Many reasons could be given:
a. To help make society function more efficiently.
b. To interpret divine commands.
c. To allow people to be as free as possible.
d. To allow people to be as happy as possible.
e. To bring more that is morally valuable into the world: more courage, truthfulness, kindness, justice, and the like.
f. To help resolve interpersonal conflict.
g. To allow people to debate, interpret, support, and live by moral beliefs.

Can these seven conceptions of the purpose of moral theory be used to evaluate moral theories? Pick at least three of them, and use each to determine how a theory living up to the standards you selected would deal with the three values in question 4. For example, standard (d) would give priority to avoiding harm.
7. (For class discussion.) The well-known American philosopher W. V. Quine made the following remark in considering different scientific ways of organizing and conceiving the world around us:

> We may revise the scheme, but only in favor of some clearer or simpler and no less adequate overall account of what goes on in the world.[3]

Discuss what relevance, if any, Quine's remark has to methods for evaluating moral theories.

1.4 Moral Evaluation

To test a moral theory, we need a solid grasp of the ingredients in moral experience; this is the case no matter which standard we select. For example, in study question 1.3.6, we saw that our notion of reasonableness is influenced by the way we value various aspects of moral experience. In the rest of this chapter, we outline many aspects of moral experience, the sorts of things we value. The better we understand the ingredients involved in moral reasoning, the better we can determine the adequacy of a moral theory. We should get a better idea of what values an ideal observer would support, what things need to be brought to coherence, and what reasonableness will include. This should prepare us to understand the different positions presented in the next ten chapters, and also give us some ammunition for approving or rejecting a proposed view. We may be able to argue, on the basis of the items presented here, that some aspects of moral experience are more basic than others, that some are not really crucial in a moral theory, or that some are inconsistent with others. We might also see ways to argue that these ingredients are not inconsistent or that a theory must account for each of the items presented. My position, which will become clearer as we proceed, is that a theory is most valuable when it can order and guide all of the aspects presented. Most philosophers, including those we examine in this work, would disagree with that claim, arguing instead that one particular point of view takes clear dominance and that it is unnecessary to account for or to give a basic role to many aspects of moral thinking. Each theory we present is a challenge to the view that overall coherence is the proper test of a moral theory; if a less inclusive theory is selected as the proper one, we need to determine that one can argue, convincingly, that some parts of morality can be safely ignored or placed into a derivative role. Philosophers attempt to find the best ways to argue for a moral position so that we can have confidence that it is correct; knowing many positions, with their strengths and weaknesses, helps us to make those arguments stronger because we can have confidence that if any aspect of moral experience has been omitted, it has been done with adequate care.

We begin our survey by considering what is involved in making moral claims. As we will see, ethics is not simply a matter of considering some basic evaluations or judgments; it involves a variety of judgments about different subjects. In evaluating a moral theory, we want to know whether the theory has omitted some crucial part of moral experience when it claims that the part in question is not actually a moral concern. We should ask, "Which kinds of things are omitted by a theory?" Perhaps a theory correctly omits part of moral experience, or perhaps it leaves out too much; this is part of what we explore in the following chapters.

1.4a The Moral Domain

Morality involves evaluations, but not all evaluations are moral evaluations. The conclusions we reach in our evaluations, moral or otherwise, are not under consideration now; instead, we are considering what kinds of things are morally evaluated. We will call this the *domain* of moral experience. Many people evaluate animals, but most people do not evaluate animals *morally*; to say that a dog did a morally bad thing is odd (although if you knew my dog, you might be tempted to make such claims). We do punish dogs, and sometimes dogs are even legally put to death for harming a person. This does not mean that we evaluate dogs as morally good or bad, but rather that they are treated as dangerous or trainable. We don't morally judge natural objects, like a stone; even a beautiful sunset or the first spring day is not judged as morally good.

Many things, however, are morally evaluated. As we examine the moral domain, those things that are often thought to merit moral evaluation, we will keep in mind that any moral theory that omits much of the moral domain must do some explaining. If a theory is unable to offer evaluations for too many of the things that are, in fact, morally evaluated, we may believe that we are not given adequate instruction by the theory. In the following chapters, keep in mind the things that we do morally evaluate, and consider whether the theories examined are able to account for such evaluations.

The following list proposes candidates for admission into the domain of moral inquiry. You should carefully consider each to see if you agree that it is a proper subject of moral judgment.

(1) Actions Performed by Individuals   We frequently make judgments about acts done by individual people. Alice may be considering whether to drop out of college because her family needs money. If Alice does not take a full-time job, she may decide that she is acting immorally. This is a judgment about a single act, quitting college, performed by a single person, Alice. (Is this really a single action, or is it more properly a series of actions?)

Thus, we may judge a specific act done by an individual to be morally wrong. For example, we may judge that Sam was wrong to lie about attending the party last night. This is a judgment about a particular lie, told in a specific circumstance, by an identifiable individual. But we may make a more general judgment, that a *type* of action, lying, performed by *any* individual, is, in general, wrong. We may now say that any person is wrong to tell any lie. Sam's lie is an *instance* or *token* of a general type of action, lying, that people other than Sam may perform. We may believe that Sam is wrong to lie because lying, as a type of action, is wrong. On the other hand, we might not think that lying is generally wrong; instead we might claim that Sam was morally wrong for telling a specific lie, perhaps because it was harmful. As we will find out, some theories only permit judgments about concrete actions, while other theories insist that we primarily judge types of actions and only judge tokens as instances of those types.

The moral domain includes types of actions, so we may judge a moral rule, "Don't lie," as morally proper or morally improper. This is different from judging that a particular lie is wrong, although individual cases of lying are also judged and thus are part of the moral domain.

Some theorists believe that the only things that should be morally evaluated are acts by individuals, provided these are broadly construed to include all actions, even *counterfactual* actions (actions that might have been done but were not). For example, we can say that it would have been morally right for Ricardo to leave the meeting, even though he actually stayed. Even though actions can be broadly understood, a theory that only allows for the judgment of individual actions is a restricted theory. Restricting the moral domain to actions performed by individuals limits the utility of a moral theory. In moral theory, we need good reasons to limit the domain. If it turns out that people routinely make moral judgments about things other than individual actions, the burden of proof should be on a theory that restricts morality to judgments about individual actions, because such a theory seems to be unable to provide useful help in making other types of evaluations.

(2) Group Actions   We frequently evaluate the actions of groups of people. We may believe, for example, that the Senate acted immorally by failing to vote on a extension of an unemployment law, or that it acted immorally by increasing the income tax on the middle class. Or we may criticize a governing board for its decision to limit membership in a country club. Some believe that such evaluations boil down to criticisms of individuals, say, those who voted affirmatively, or those who voted, no matter how. But sometimes we criticize actions of a group even when we do not know who its members are, and we may hold any future members of a group responsible for its previous actions. Although we often evaluate what a group does as a indirect way to evaluate individuals, sometimes our intention is to judge the group action as such, perhaps as a way to criticize the rules and regulations under which the group was formed or the power a group has within an organization.

Whether we include group actions in the moral domain makes a significant difference in moral theory. Suppose we believe that group actions can be evaluated. We may decide that a particular group should be disbanded because membership in it leads to immoral action. We may decide to restrict membership in the group even if no actual immoral action has been performed because we believe that it is the type of group that leads to immoral actions. (Think of the kinds of groups that are not permitted on your campus.) A moral theory centering on moral rules, for example, may find it difficult to make such determinations because moral rules tend to center on types of actions done by individuals. We might conclude that judgments about group actions are properly omitted from moral theory, but we want to know, from theorists supporting such omissions, why decisions about group actions are not needed.

(3) Personality and Character Traits   We might judge that a gentle or a fair person is morally good simply because he or she is gentle or fair, and not because of the actions performed by that person. In this way, a judgment is made about a person's trait or personality. We may decide that some character traits are virtuous while other traits are morally improper. Philosophers doing *virtue ethics*, a type of moral theory, claim that character traits are not reducible to individual actions. Gregorio is considered fair not

simply because he acted fairly on several occasions, but because he has a tendency to act fairly and has good insight into whether a particular act is fair. He is not fair because he acts fairly, but he acts fairly because he is fair. Some theorists claim that basic judgments in ethics should not be about individual or group actions but instead about character traits or virtues, and only secondarily about actions performed by individuals. Once again, a theory that has no place for judgments about character traits has the burden of explaining why they are not a proper part of the moral domain.

(4) Institutions and Practices   When we listed group actions as part of the moral domain, we meant specific actions performed by a group, such as a particular vote taken by a particular governmental unit. Now we are moving to a higher level, a more broadly defined level. Within an institution, like a college, actions are performed by individuals and groups according to rules, regulations, and "institutionalized" patterns of behavior. These patterns together define the way things are done in the institution, although this might not be codified. For example, some institutions promote more friendly behavior than others, some are more secure or provide more freedom, and some are more bureaucratic. We may judge institutions, even judge them as morally proper or morally improper, and this judgment may or may not involve particular actions or personal character traits.

A *practice* is typically more broadly defined than an institution. A practice involves general patterns of behavior, rules, definitions, and procedures. The practice of medicine is bigger than the way care is provided at a particular institution, say a metropolitan hospital. Practices and institutions might include, for example, governments (local and federal), multinational corporations, the United Nations, the World Bank, the International Labor Organization, and Greenpeace.

Practices and institutions are frequently morally evaluated, and so it appears that they should be included in the domain of moral experience. Yet many moral theories do not attempt to evaluate them. Again, a theorist needs to present good reasons for limiting the moral domain, so we may evaluate a theory, in part, by considering whether it supports judgments about practices and institutions.

Judgments about the virtues of individuals may be extended to judgments about the virtues of groups, institutions, or practices. A practice or institution may be evaluated as fair, or just, or even kind or cold. Some theories—for example, some theories in virtue ethics—are not able to support such judgments. Since such judgments are commonly made, we should question how a theory will deal with the evaluation of virtues in institutions and practices. We will discuss institutions and practices in greater detail in Chapter 11.

(5) Moral Rules and Principles Morality is complex because its domain includes not only the areas discussed above, but also its criteria for making evaluations. We can see this by considering character traits; character traits, such as fairness, may be used to judge other aspects in the domain—for example, individual actions—but they may themselves be judged, for example, when we claim that acting from a sense of "honor" is morally improper. We saw in our consideration of individual actions that we frequently appeal to moral rules (such as "Keep your promises") and moral principles (such as "Do no harm"). As we shall see in Chapter 6, the list of proposed moral rules is long and controversial. Some people accept some moral rules and principles that others reject, such as the rule against eating animals. The point we want to make now is that moral rules, principles, and supposed virtues are morally evaluated. A rule like the prohibition of abortion is accepted by many, and rejected as immoral by many others. A moral theory may be used to determine whether a moral rule or principle is proper. Thus moral theory is complicated by the fact that aspects of morality used to judge features of the moral domain are themselves members of the domain.

(6) Ideals Ideals are distinguished by their supposed unattainable nature. Loving one's neighbor as oneself, a classless society, perfect equality, and a society led by a genuinely wise philosopher have all been proposed as ideals. Those who make the proposals usually believe that although full attainment is not possible, we should strive toward it insofar as feasible. Ideals may be used to judge, for example, whether one practice is better than another, depending on whether it is closer to the ideal. Ideals are often helpful in making moral evaluations, but some ideals may be foolish or harmful. (Can you think of any harmful "ideals"?) Ideals themselves may be morally evaluated, and so are part of the moral domain, just like rules and principles.

Although we could easily expand the list of the members of the moral domain (and I hope you try), we have enough to do the job. Remember that the job is to use moral experience as a challenge to moral theories. We want to know whether a particular theory omits part of the moral domain; if it does, we want a good reason. A theory should be judged, at least partly, on whether it can accommodate aspects of the moral domain—or successfully defend itself if it does not.

Study Questions 1.4a

1. Do the Ten Commandments limit the moral domain to individual actions? What about a moral theory that claims that you may do anything you want if it does not harm anyone (or anyone else)?

Suppose we believe that we should only do to others those actions we would permit to be done to ourselves (a paraphrase of the Golden Rule). Does this rule limit the moral domain to individual actions? (In answering this question, try to show whether these moral positions have anything to say about aspects of the moral domain other than actions of individuals. For example, can they be used to judge practices or ideals?)

2. (For class discussion.) Speculate on whether an entire ethical theory can be built around virtues. For example, suppose some people are known to be fair. Can this judgment help us to determine which practices are fair or which rules are fair? Does it help us to determine which types of acts are fair? One way is to ask the opinion of fair people. Is this an effective way to make moral judgments about actions, rules, or institutions?

3. Are we *likely* to judge that an institution is morally corrupt but that the individuals within the practice are virtuous? Is this a *possible* judgment?

4. Propose ways to criticize moral rules. (Give concrete examples of some moral rules you consider controversial, and carefully consider the reasons why you believe that they are controversial.) Can we use judgments about individual actions to criticize moral rules? (Hint: If a lie is proper under certain conditions, does that mean that the rule against lying is morally improper? But remember that rules may have exceptions and still be rules.) Are rules and principles different? What is the difference?

5. Consider some current debates: over abortion, civil rights, international aid, universal health care. Do debates over such issues contain appeals to ideals? If so, list the ideals involved. Do people morally evaluate these ideals? Explain how.

6. (For class discussion.) Explain, in terms of the domain of moral inquiry, the following statement by the contemporary moral theorist John Rawls.

> [M]any different kinds of things are said to be just and unjust: not only laws, institutions, and social systems, but also particular actions of many kinds, including decisions, judgments, and imputations. We also call the attitudes and dispositions of persons, and persons themselves, just and unjust. Our topic, however, is that of social justice. For us the primary subject of justice is the basic structure of society....[4]

Is a theorist always wrong when he or she limits the domain of a theory as Rawls does? (This question is really about whether some limitations are theoretically helpful, or if the limitations end up restricting further inquiry. Even if you know little about Rawls's view, your answer should be in terms of whether limitations are helpful. Keep in mind that a theorist cannot do all things at once.)

1.4b The Moral Range

The notion of a moral domain that we have presented has been copied from mathematics, where a domain limits of things a function works upon. When mathematicians specify a domain, they also specify a *range*. In mathematics a domain limits what goes into a function, and the range tells us what can come out. We could have a mathematical function that only deals with natural numbers, like 0, 1, 2, 3, etc., and that function may determine whether the number is odd or even. Natural numbers go in (the domain), and the answer comes out: odd or even. In this case, the range comprises the determinations "odd" and "even." The same happens in ethics: we consider things in the domain and evaluate them, and the moral range is the kinds of evaluation we may make. For example, we may consider all individual actions as the domain to determine whether they are morally obligatory; the range then consists of the determinations "obligatory" and "not obligatory."

Some moral theorists have argued that the moral range is simple, containing only one or two possible judgments. For them the only proper moral evaluations claim either that something is obligatory or that something is permitted. If we are only dealing with actions, this isn't too far-fetched. But if the domain contains character traits, the claim that traits are obligatory seems awkward; for example, we do not claim that being wise is obligatory because wisdom is something we cannot readily control. (Think about what else we might include in the range of a virtue theory.)

We will now list possible members of the range of moral inquiry, the kinds of moral judgments we can make. Although our list will not be complete, you can see that people make many different types of moral claims; any theory that fails to support or to tell us how to make such claims may seem too limited and so should be called upon to explain its limitations on the moral range.

(1) Obligatory or Prohibited We frequently hear that people have a moral obligation to keep their promises, to tell the truth, to take care of their children, to respect their parents. People also proclaim that many actions are prohibited: to steal, to murder, to harm without good reason, to neglect parents. As we will see, some theories only support judgments about what is obligatory or permitted; to make these judgments, these theories usually rely on rules or strict principles.

(2) Permitted   An action may be judged to be permitted yet not obligatory; this judgment may be the result of a moral inquiry. Most of us would judge that we are morally permitted to skip lunch, but that we are not obligated to skip lunch. Some moral theories have no room for permissions and are thus criticized as overly constraining.

(3) Recommended   A theory may hold that some actions are recommended, but not obligatory. This is different from being merely permitted. We might be morally neutral about permitted actions but not about recommended actions. When something is morally recommended but not obligatory, it is considered morally better than its alternatives. Many actions are recommended, but not in a moral sense; an adviser may recommend that a student seeking a job go to a convention. This sounds like a *prudential* recommendation, not a moral one. Prudential recommendations often involve individual interests, which many philosophers exclude from the moral realm. Nevertheless, the recommender believes that going to the convention makes it more likely that the student will get a job, and for this reason going is better than not going. Though we judge that going to the convention is good, we might not think the person deserves moral praise for doing so. A morally recommended action, similarly, is thought to be a better action than other permissible actions. If a person does a *morally* recommended action—say, giving to charity—then we may think that the person deserves moral praise.

(4) Morally Superior to   We often judge things in relation to each other. Donna is a better designer than Mark. Jimi is a better guitar player than Stevie Ray. These are not moral comparisons, but they are similar. Democracy is considered morally superior to dictatorship. Volunteering at a shelter is morally superior to going to the circus. Lying is morally superior to giving insult. People make such claims, though sometimes incorrectly, and we may look to theory to provide guidance about which are proper claims. Moral comparisons seem to be a suitable part of the moral range, and so any theory that is incapable of supporting them must show why they are unnecessary.

So far we have given an abstract list of things that a moral theory may evaluate and the types of judgments that may be made. Even though this is a basic and simple task, it gives us a way to begin to judge a moral theory. Theories that miss too many aspects of the moral domain and the moral range have the burden of proof because they need to explain why certain types of judgments are improper or why some things should not be judged. We may decide, for example, that if we want guidance about comparing one situation to another, we need to reject theories that are not comparative, that simply issue obligations and permissions.

As we proceed, we will be examining different basic theoretical positions in ethics; we should keep in mind, when evaluating theories, how each defines, implicitly or explicitly, its domain and range. Nevertheless, we should not use the range and domain as the ultimate way to judge a theory; this would be an overly simple test, which many theories may pass without telling us which is the best theory. And some theories may be improperly excluded. Say we believe that judgments about institutions should be included in the domain of a theory, but find that the only theories that include them end up violating our basic convictions, or the basic convictions of an ideal observer; we may, regretfully, decide that the moral domain should not include judgments about institutions, or that the best we can do is to support a theory that fails to make such an inclusion.

Ultimately, we are best able to judge moral theories when we know many theories well enough to compare their comparative strengths and weaknesses. In this work we will survey different basic moral positions. To help us to make some tentative claims about the positions we encounter in the first few chapters, we will outline in the following chapter some very basic moral points of view. As we go through them, ask whether these positions present a limited range and domain, and try to make some initial judgments about the merit of one view in relation to the next.

Study Questions 1.4b

1. (For class discussion.) Can you think of a theory that is composed only of obligations? Such a theory would not recommend actions or claim that one action is better than another. (At the minimum the theory would maintain that one type of action, and only one, is obligatory.) If so, how would you argue in favor of the theory? (You must show, at the least, that other parts of the moral range are not needed.) How would you argue against it?

2. Some theories appear not to leave room for the judgment that actions are permitted, by claiming that we are always obliged to take the morally best action. For example, a theorist could claim that we are always obliged to perform the actions that produce the greatest happiness. (Such a theory is called *act utilitarianism*.) Would this theory allow room for permitted actions? Would it allow room for actions that are permitted but not obligatory? Explain why the last two questions involve different considerations. If this theory does not allow for permitted actions, is this a weakness? Consider ways this weakness might be overcome. For example, the theorist might claim that often the best action is the one that a person wants to take, making obligations and permissions practically equivalent. Is this a good way

to overcome the limited range of the theory?

3. Can a well-formulated moral theory be developed that provides support only for making recommendations? What would such a theory be like?

4. If one action is morally better than another, are we morally obliged to take that action? Can one morally prohibited action be morally better than another? If not, why not? If so, give an example. Would the judgment that one morally prohibited action is better than another help us in making moral judgments?

5. (For class discussion.) Does a limited moral range restrict the moral domain? Why or why not?

Further Reading

Alexander Sesonske's *Value and Obligation: The Foundations of an Empiricist Ethical Theory* (New York: Oxford University Press, 1964) is a good, brief, but somewhat dated, overview of different types of moral judgments. He also provides a set of criteria, different than that found here, for evaluating moral theories. Perhaps the best brief introduction to ethics is W. K. Frankena's *Ethics*, 2nd ed. (Englewood Cliffs, N.J.: Prentice-Hall, 1973).

Endnotes

1. I have attempted a full statement of a coherence theory in *A Coherence Theory in Ethics,*Volume 10, Value Inquiry Book Series (Amsterdam: Rodopi, 1994).

2. Bernard Williams, *Ethics and the Limits of Philosophy* (Cambridge: Harvard University Press, 1985), p. 93.

3. W. V. Quine, *Ontological Relativity & Other Essays* (New York: Columbia University Press, 1969).

4. John Rawls, *A Theory of Justice* (Cambridge: Harvard University Press), p. 7.

2

Basic Approaches to Moral Theory

2.1 Moral Points of View

In this chapter, we are going to survey a variety of theories on how to make moral evaluations. This survey is sketchy; it only briefly summarizes basic positions. These summaries are meant as a kind of road map that will help you make your way from one position to another as each is presented in much greater detail in the coming chapters. These summaries are not meant to be comprehensive, so some things will not seem completely clear. As you finish the following chapters, you might want to return to the corresponding summary in this chapter; this should help to keep the details of several theories straight . Since these are summaries, they should be much more significant to you once you finish the appropriate chapters. We present them all at the beginning to give you an idea of what the first few theories we examine in detail are competing against and what they reject.

In Chapter 1, we stated that some things are judged to be obligatory or permitted, but not how this is done; moral experience does include ways to make proper moral judgments. People don't merely say, for example, that a parent is wrong not to take a child on a picnic today; they say that since the parent promised to take the child, it is wrong for the parent not to. An appeal is made to a moral rule: keep one's promises. Morally, we value keeping promises, and we look negatively on breaking them. This is a well-ingrained moral rule, so any theory that claims that promise keeping is not a good thing, or is an immoral thing, has some explaining to do. The theory may be correct, or may find a way to convince others that promises should not be made or should not be kept once made. But the burden of proof is on those theories that neglect or contradict our strongly held moral convictions.

Moral experience includes ways to distinguish right from wrong, which may be used to judge moral theories: can a theory account for well-established or strongly supported approaches to moral decision making? A theory that can, either by showing them wrong, or supporting them, is, other things being equal, superior to those theories that cannot.

We will establish a short list of basic ways philosophers have proposed to establish morally correct judgments. This section is a preview of much of what follows in the next ten chapters, and each of these positions will be carefully examined later. All these positions have significant strengths and significant weaknesses; they all seem, at first sight, to express a part of moral experience. The challenge of moral theory is to account, one way or another, for such moral points of view.

(1) Particularism

Particularism, which is discussed more fully in Chapter 3, is sometimes called *situation ethics.* A particularist rejects the use of moral principles, norms, or rules in making moral decisions. None of these offers proper moral guidance because genuine moral problems all have such a rich context that they overwhelm the simplicity of a moral rule or principle. (Consider the complicating factors that may be involved in deciding whether to lie to one friend to keep another friend from serious trouble.) Each case may involve dissimilar causes and consequences, as well as distinct locality, time, and economic circumstances. In short, each situation judged may be morally unique. For the particularist, broad ethical principles like "Do no harm" cannot be properly applied to particular cases. Should we avoid harm at the cost of doing real good? What if people voluntarily accept the risk of serious harm that a coach, in a sport like football or cross-country track, might inflict on an athlete? How is harm determined in a given case? These questions suggest that any one principle is inadequate. A single principle is too abstract to give effective guidance because it leaves out too many valid moral considerations. Using multiple principles—say, "Do good" and "Don't harm"—leads to conflict. What happens when we can only do good by doing some harm? Given a set of rules or principles rich enough to cover all basic moral concerns, conflicts will prevail in virtually every case. Since multiple rules or principles cannot give guidance, the particularist insists that we should face the fact that moral problems are solved one by one. Rules and principles might point us to relevant circumstances, direct our attention to harms caused, freedoms promoted, injustices, and so on, but once we notice these things, we need to make an essentially unique judgment about every case.

The particularist claims that using moral rules and principles is improper in making moral judgments. Since moral problems are contextual and complex, **all moral judgments must be made in reaction to individual cases, keeping in view all significant aspects of the case.** (Before going on, give some thought to the strengths and weaknesses of particularism.)

(2) Casuistry

Particularism raises significant questions. Does it invite biased reactions? Isn't it actually hostile to widely accepted moral standards in allowing each person to make up his or her own mind about things that have social consequences? What kind of moral guidance can it give? Shouldn't similar cases be decided similarly? Imagine a professor allowing a makeup test to one student who overslept and denying it to another by claiming some odd dissimilarity between the two, say that one is a little taller and may need more sleep! *Casuistry*, which is explored in Section 3.4, attempts to overcome some of these problems while acknowledging that cases can be quite complex and dissimilar. The casuist respects the guidance that moral rules may give, but insists that such guidance is proper only in the right kinds of cases. Casuists believe that the way to proceed is to identify *paradigm cases* of a proper application of a rule: cases that are uncontroversial and without complicating circumstances—for example, the brutal, unprovoked punishment of a child. When we deal with cases that are very much like the paradigm case, we know that the rule holds. The casuist also wants to give advice on dissimilar cases by examining variations on the paradigm cases: other cases that differ significantly yet have many of the same ingredients. The casuist tries to determine whether those differing cases are bound by the same rule or a different one. As the casuist deliberates on varied cases, the hope is that so many examples will be gathered that we can find an already solved case similar to our problem. The casuist believes that similar cases should be decided similarly and that we need the guidance of moral rules and wise observations. However, the casuist is contextual because he or she is willing to look at the background circumstances of a case and requires that good judgment be applied; no simple application of a rule can solve a moral problem. The hoped-for result is a catalogue of cases wisely judged with the help of rules. These cases become the models, or precedents, for future moral judgments.

The claim that casuistry is part of moral experience is not to be taken literally. We mean instead that casuistry is a theory that does correspond to a way we react, morally speaking. We do compare one case to another, and we often have in mind, perhaps only implicitly, a paradigm case. Under normal circumstances a parent would not leave a young child alone, and we react negatively to those who do. But we can all easily imagine circumstances where we believe that leaving a child is justified—for example, in an emergency. The casuist accounts for, and tries to systematize, the way one case differs from the next.

The casuist claims that **moral judgments should be made by comparing cases against judgments made in paradigmatic cases and in cases examined, by people of good judgment, that diverge, little by little, from paradigmatic** cases. When we find the proper fit between our problem and a problem already solved, we will be able to make the correct judgment.

(3) Virtue Ethics

I remember attending a lecture on Spanish painting, presented by the Spanish Club at my college. I confess to having had a greater interest in Spain than in fine art, but I was amazed at the way a skillful art critic could bring a painting to life. What first seemed to me to be the boring depiction of a religious person was, by the end of the lecture, exciting and thought provoking. An expert in any field is able to notice things that the uninitiated fail to appreciate. We may think of any capacity that allows us to function in an exceptional or excellent way as a *virtue*. The virtue of an art critic is to know good art, and a virtuoso diagnostician is able to spot unusual illnesses. Some practitioners are better than others, in art and in medicine, so we may say that some are more virtuous, in a nonmoral sense.

If it were enough to have simple rules or set routines to follow, all normally intelligent people could become equally good practitioners, but this is not the case. Some people have special insight and talent in accounting, law, philosophy, business, sports, art, teaching, communications, mathematics, or medicine, and their judgments are especially valuable in those areas. Based on their experience, their studies, and their special insight, these people become leaders and reformers in their fields.

Virtue ethics, which is covered in Chapter 4, concludes that the views of people of virtue, moral virtue, determine what is right and wrong. If we want to find out how to treat the poor, we should follow the lead of Mother Teresa, or some other virtuous person. We respect the opinions of others in law, mathematics, and medicine; we should similarly respect the moral opinions of morally virtuous people. Better yet, we should develop moral virtue for ourselves, but not merely to solve moral problems. Being virtuous is itself a good thing, so we should strive to be people of virtue for its own sake.

Virtue theorists claim that proper moral judgments follow not from moral rules but from opinions supported by people of genuine virtue. This is a form of particularism; the virtuous person makes judgments in the face of complex individual circumstances. We would not expect good lawyers, coaches, or physicians to make a difficult judgment without seeing things for themselves. The point is that people of virtue do not, ultimately, follow moral rules or principles, but through their virtue they establish the right thing to do or the right evaluation to make.

Virtue ethics is used in casuistry because casuists rely on the pronouncements of people identified as wise; the judgments of these people are expressed as simple rules governing paradigm cases. However, virtue ethics, in its pure form, does not include detailed analysis of paradigm cases.

Virtue theorists argue that **difficult moral judgments are properly made by people of virtue. If we do not have the appropriate virtues, we can find the correct judgment, even judgments about proper character traits, by consulting the views of a virtuous person.**

(4) Intuitionism

You may be wondering how a virtuous person, or a particularist, makes judgments. Rules may help, but a uniquely appropriate judgment is required. What is the basis for that judgment? Several traits may come to mind: a good moral judge might be better able to appreciate the interests of others, more sensitive and knowledgeable about consequences of actions, or better able to consider more facets of a case at the same time. A virtuous person might be able to ignore his or her own interests and concentrate better on the issues at hand.

Philosophers have gone a step beyond analyzing the traits standing behind good judgments. Some philosophers claim that particularism may be based on a special moral sense. In philosophy an *intuition* is an immediate awareness: knowledge we have without debate, inquiry, and reasoning. For example, I intuit my own sense of fear, or happiness, or the pleasantness of that first spring day. I don't need to persuade myself that I'm tired of the winter; I simply step out and immediately, almost as a surprise, realize the pleasantness of the first spring day. I react to a brutal act as immoral without requiring reasons for my judgment. If someone asked, "How do you know that it is a pleasant day?," I would be surprised; I experience the day as pleasant. Similarly, I experience the brutal act as wrong.

Under *intuitionism,* which will be discussed in greater detail in Chapter 12, rightness or wrongness is experienced much as the day is experienced as pleasant. Intuition is sometimes held to be the basis of moral judgments in particularism, casuistry, and virtue ethics. It is one way those theories can claim that judgments are not fixed by rules or principles. On the other hand, some philosophers have claimed that we may have intuitive knowledge of rules. We simply know that lying, in general, is wrong or that breaking a promise is generally a bad thing.

The intuitionist is right to claim that some events instill moral shock, and that we make many judgments with conviction and without argument or debate. The evening news frequently presents such events. We may feel that our reaction and judgment is right, even if we can't articulate a defense of the reaction. Sometimes our reactions break all the rules—for example, we may instinctively judge that the murder of an evil person was not morally wrong even though it was not in self-defense. Everything we previously believed might indicate that such an action is wrong, yet our immediate reaction may be that it is right. These reactions are thought to have moral standing; they are part of moral experience. To deny such judgments any standing at all seems to cut moral theory free from its base in actual experience and establish a moral dogmatism. But remember: intuitionism is the more extreme doctrine that *all* valid moral knowledge is based directly on intuitions.

Intuitionists claim that **we have a special moral capacity to judge right from wrong immediately, without moral argument; the best way to resolve a moral problem is to tune into our attentive reaction to the problem.**

(5) Relativism

People around the world do many things differently. They have different forms of government, customs, languages, and cultures. They also have different moral attitudes. Significant and morally charged activities, from raising children to sex role differences, vary in different places at different times. Practices considered crucial in one culture may seem absurd in another. This seems to deny the independent status of moral intuitions because our reactions to situations may themselves be culturally conditioned even though they are experienced as occurring immediately, without deliberation, and as self-evident or natural.

Undue criticism of different ways of behaving is a form of *chauvinism*: the view that one's cultural way of doing things is the only right way. Criticism may be based on a failure to appreciate, or a misinterpretation of, the significance of actions, or it may be a simple value disagreement, just as you and I may legitimately differ over whether Stevie Ray Vaughn was a better guitarist than Jimi Hendrix.

Cultural relativism, which we will study in Chapter 4, is the view that no absolute standards can be used to judge moral viewpoints, and that morality is relative to local codes and customs. The right thing for a person from Canada may be wrong for someone from Japan. Everyone should be morally judged by his or her own social codes, practices, conventions, and norms.

Once these observations are made, we may question whether criticizing our next-door neighbors, who act significantly differently from us, is morally proper. They may dress differently, have a different work ethic, view sexual relationships differently, and so on. They might not directly harm anyone else but just live a different style of life. If judging actions in other cultures is chauvinistic, aren't we equally wrong to judge the actions of people near us who adopt a different lifestyle? An *extreme ethical relativism* allows each person to determine a moral code for himself or herself.

Relativism, as a moral doctrine, contains a higher moral appeal. Relativists defend the right of cultures or individuals to establish their own morality by claiming that everyone has an obligation to be *tolerant*. Yet this seems to be an absolute demand: the one thing we cannot do is to establish for ourselves an intolerant moral view that attacks the morality of another.

Relativism is part of moral experience. Many react negatively to morally righteous people who want to tell others how to live their lives. People in Japan know best how the Japanese should live, and people in my house know best how we should live. This is part of moral experience, but only part. Many moral theories are universally oriented; they claim that everyone should live by the same rules and principles. This seems to make sense as well; even the relativist typically insists on the universal value of tolerance. A moral theory that can save what is right in relativism while establishing a way to defend universal moral claims would be a strong theory, other things being equal.

The ethical relativist claims that **moral problems are solved by applying culturally or individually relative moral standards. Each person is bound by a relative moral code, relative either to a culture or subculture or to a set of individually established standards.**

(6) Absolutism

The relativist's support for tolerance is often presented as an absolute because tolerance is supported even if some cultures are intolerant. This seems contradictory and so plays into the hands of the *moral absolutist*. A moral absolutist claims that there is one, and only one, proper moral code and that everyone ought to live by it. The code might not be known, but once it is discovered all are morally obliged to live under its direction. (Many of the theories we examine in the following chapters are examples of absolutism.) If we don't know the proper code, we are obliged to seek to discover the one objective, morally correct view. Many believe that the correct moral code is established by God because, whether we know it or not, God's code is the proper code. Others believe that an absolute moral code is based on our human nature, or the way we are as persons. Absolute moral codes may also be based on reasonableness, claiming that one code is more reasonable than all others. It may be based on a careful examination of the nature and meaning of morality itself, or an examination of what it means to be a morally good person.

Absolutists often believe that morality can be expressed in one principle, several principles, or a short list of moral rules that everyone should support. But rules and principles are not essential to absolutism; even a particularist can be an absolutist. (Can you explain how?)

Gratuitous harm seems to be wrong for everyone, and thus all people act immorally unless they avoid doing harm. This seems to be an absolute requirement. Even the relativist somehow argues in favor of the absolute value of tolerance. Absolutism, like relativism, is part of moral experience. Relativism and absolutism seem incompatible, which puts pressure on an inclusive view of morality. The ultimate test for a theorist attempting to account for as much of moral experience as is feasible may hinge on how well the debate between the relativist and the absolutist is handled.

An absolutist believes that **a moral decision is made by first determining the one correct moral viewpoint, and then applying that viewpoint to the issue at hand. That application may take into account differing circumstances, but the ultimate appeal is to some standard that obligates all people.**

(7) Moral Rules

A *moral rules approach,* explored further in Chapter 6, is one type of moral absolutism. Morality is often viewed as a public system that allows people to function effectively in a social, interdependent world. Morality is not a way to dominate our lives by telling us, for every occasion, which actions are better than others and which we must do. If I want to be a couch potato, as long as I don't interfere with others, nothing in a proper moral theory, one that is not overly restrictive, prohibits me from being one. Morality is a way to allow us to get along with each other, and to refine it further is to get carried away, morally speaking. All that is needed is a basic list of rules of good conduct; after that, we can do what we want.

Under this view, moral rules are basically negative because they direct us to avoid certain actions but do not tell us what we *should* do. We should not do things such as lying, stealing, killing, or breaking promises; when people break such rules, social life is threatened. This is a limited notion of morality that certainly leaves out much of the moral domain and range. This may be proper; for example, it might be that attempts to provide a more positive morality are disruptive or that they unfairly infringe on the moral rights of individuals. Any theory, including rule theory, that claims that its view of moral experience is the only right one should show why other views are mistaken. Rule moralists are correct in pointing out the need for some basic moral rules; moral rules are a part of moral experience, but we must question whether this view is wholly adequate.

Under the moral rules view, to make a moral decision about a certain action, **we should consider whether moral rules are violated. If not, the action is permitted, but if a rule is violated the action is prohibited.**

(8) Moral Principles

Moral rules govern such actions as lying, breaking promises, and stealing. *Moral principles* are less specific. They give us more general guidance: do good, avoid harm, do what leads to as much happiness as possible, treat others as you wish to be treated. Each principle takes into account a greater variety of actions than a rule. Thus, theorists believe, a principle can provide a proper account of all that is needed in moral experience. Unlike a rule theory, a view that emphasizes principles takes seriously the function of explaining, ordering, and guiding moral experience. Being able to account for much of moral experience in a few principles is one reason that many theorists accept a theory supporting a single principle or two or three basic principles.

Some moral principles look to consequences: always act to create the most good, to perfect your own character, or to satisfy your own desires. *Consequentialism* and *teleology* are theories based on producing good outcomes. Under these views, we should always do what produces the best results, depending on how "best" is defined, often in terms of happiness or the perfection of human traits.

Consequences are important in moral experience. But some things seem wrong, period. Sometimes we are best advised to judge a case on the issues at hand, without considering consequences. A theory that, at least in part, is willing to ignore consequences is called a *deontology*. (Consequentialism and deontology are examined in Chapter 8.) I remember grading a poorly done logic test, at the end of which the person taking the test had written: "At least I didn't cheat." If serious, such a claim may indicate a refusal to live by consequences. It is wrong to cheat, the student may be saying, no matter that the consequences of honesty involve a bad grade.

Both teleology and deontology are part of moral experience. Part of moral experience values principles that are not to be broken despite bad consequences, and part of moral experience emphasizes actions that produce good results. These two points of view establish a fundamental division among moral theorists. In Chapter 8, we will give examples of the main theories under each heading. For now, note that moral principles are part of moral experience and that teleology and deontology provide a way to divide theories into two sometimes hostile camps, each claiming that it best directs moral evaluation.

A theory supporting a principled approach directs us to **solve all moral problems by applying moral principles. These principles should be abstract enough to guide all moral decision making and able to account**

for all of moral experience or else to help explain why some parts of moral experience are safely rejected or ignored.

(You may want to look ahead to Chapter 8 on moral principles because the theories explored there have had a profound influence on moral thinking. They can be used as a kind of benchmark test: any theory must be at least as effective as the utilitarian and Kantian theories.)

(9) Substantive Ideals

Ideals (covered in Chapter 10) are sometimes used to make moral judgments. For example, in deciding whether you have an obligation to help your friend move into a new apartment, you might consider the ideal of loving your neighbor as yourself. This is called an ideal; it is ultimately unobtainable because it demands such thorough love of all those near us. Nevertheless, we can use the ideal to get guidance about what should be done, like helping a friend. Ideals are vague. They do not attempt to tell us exactly what to do, but they set the proper direction, give us a sense of how far from perfect things actually are, and tell us that one action—for example, the more loving action—is better than another.

For some theorists equality is a social ideal; others see perfect freedom as setting the proper political direction. Loving your neighbor, equality, and freedom are *substantive ideals* which will be explored in Chapters 9 and 10. A substantive ideal tells us, in broad terms, what we should be attempting to achieve. It gives us a goal, a *telos,* to keep in mind. Even though it may be unattainable, we do have some idea what a perfectly equal society would be like. Our understanding of equality, freedom, and love could have some guiding effect on our actions, even though the goal is elusive.

Moral experience includes substantive ideals, and such ideals often do have moral power. But ideals give limited guidance because too many of the details of everyday life are left out. Should we lie to avoid embarrassing a friend? How should housework be shared? Is it morally proper for an instructor to give a low grade to a student who is emotionally distressed? These issues may be poorly resolved by appeal to substantive ideals, yet other issues, say about raising taxes on the rich, may be resolved with the help of a substantive ideal, like that of equality.

We may use a moral ideal to make judgments about the sorts of actions, virtues, practices, and institutions that bring us closer to the ideal state. For example, in choosing from among alternative paths of action, a moral ideal instructs us to select the action that helps to bring our reality into better conformity with the ideal. Since helping our friend is more loving than going about our own business, helping the friend moves the world toward being a more loving place.

(10) Procedural Ideals

Procedural ideals are different from substantive ideals in that procedural ideals do not fix a goal. Instead, they tell us the ideal conditions under which we should make moral choices. We might, for example, imagine an ideal moral agent, a disinterested, rational, fully knowledgeable judge who is sympathetic yet not personally affected by his or her judgments. No such observer exists. But we can speculate on what judgments an ideal observer might make. Suppose you know a great deal about antiques and go to a yard sale held by an older, poorer person who knows nearly nothing about them. Say that person wants to sell for $5 an item that you know is worth $500. Are you morally permitted to buy it at $5 or should you share your information? Our opinion on this might be biased because we need the money, so we consider what an ideal observer would say. Procedural ideals do not emphasize beforehand whether it is wrong or right to buy at $5, but, if an ideal is defined richly enough, it gives us a way determine the right thing to do.

Appeal to an ideal observer is not the only procedural ideal. *Social contract theory* views proper moral beliefs as the result of a fair initial agreement. The conditions under which the initial agreement is made are ideal conditions, often conceived in terms of full equality, freedom, and knowledge. What kinds of moral rules and principles would informed, free, and equal people select in the initial choice situation? Whatever principles they select are the proper ethical principles.

When we reason under the guidance of a procedural ideal, the outcome of the deliberation is the morally proper path. In other words, the judgment that results from a serious application of the procedure is the morally correct opinion, whatever it involves.

Procedural ideals are abstract and so may not seem to be part of moral experience. But actually people do recognize that their moral judgments may be based on special interest and try to find ways to eliminate bias, perhaps by imagining what someone with a very different background would conclude. A biased moral theory is unacceptable, nearly by definition, so we look to a moral theory to protect against bias, whether about race, sex, national or ethnic identity, occupation, or self-interest. Some theories, like social contract theory and Kantian ethics, offer explicit ways to control partiality, and some—for example, act-utilitarianism—are presented as though unbiased judgments can be made without any attempt to discover covert or overt bias. (These theories will be covered in coming chapters.)

In this section we quickly scanned ten basic ways to make moral decisions. They all have value and each is used in moral deliberation. A good theory is able to explain away, or incorporate, each of these techniques.

Keep this in mind as we explore each theory in greater detail in the coming chapters.

Study Questions 2.1

1. How morally unique are individual cases? Consider two cases in the news—for example, two cases of assisted suicide. Do these cases have enough in common so that the same principles could guide our reasoning, or are they different enough that no rule or principle is equally applicable to both? Suppose a medical doctor claims that no medical rules or principles can effectively guide the treatment of a patient, using arguments like those given in favor of ethical particularism. Try to construct that argument. How strong is the argument in favor of medical particularism?
   Consider the moral domain of particularism. Does the moral domain contain aspects that the particularist leaves out?
2. Casuists have often been criticized as provincial and nitpicking. Using the above account, try to figure out why such charges are leveled. In answering, consider where the casuist's rules come from, who makes the wise judgments, and how cases may differ one from the other.
3. Is virtue required to judge who is virtuous? (You may want to compare judging virtue to judging other things. For example, do you need to be a good guitarist to judge who is good?) Is it likely that one person can adequately judge all the concerns listed in the moral domain? That is, is virtue limited so that a person may be virtuous in some moral ways and lack virtue in others? Can a virtuous person be biased? How free of bias does a virtuous person have to be?
4. Do people have the same moral intuitions under similar circumstances? Do people see the same thing when looking in the same direction? Do people from the same society, neighborhood, club, or family have similar moral intuitions? Suppose people have different intuitions; does this strengthen or weaken intuitionism?
5. In the section on intuitionism, the claim was made that it is dogmatic to deny any moral status to firmly held intuitions that violate all the rules. A *dogmatic view* is a view, uncritically held, that opposing views will not be considered. Moral intuitions that break the rules often challenge established theories. Is it really a form of dogmatism for a theorist to deny status to a moral intuition that goes against the theory? (Consider your answer in relation to a scientist who denies any status to the observations of people who sincerely claim that they have witnessed a UFO driven by a creature from outer space.)
5. (For class discussion.) What is the difference (if any) between claiming that all have the right to establish their own moral code and claiming

that all should be tolerant of the moral codes of others? Do moral codes differ depending on the social roles people occupy? For example, is there a different moral code for lawyers and for teachers? Does the relativist exclude any aspect of the moral domain?

6. Should absolute values be based on human nature, or is this an inconsistent view because it makes values relative to human nature? Can God change God's own moral code? If so, is God's moral code relative? Is tolerance really an absolute value, or is it merely the affirmation that all values are equally good? When we claim that absolutism is part of moral experience, we mean that many people believe that morality involves absolute judgments. Is this true?

7. List eight commonly accepted moral rules. Can moral rules conflict? Are the moral rules you listed culturally relative?

8. (For class discussion.) Are deontology and teleology incompatible? Should we consider a system of moral rules as a deontology or as a teleology? Can an intuitionist be a teleologist? Can a relativist be a deontologist? Which point of view, deontology or teleology, accounts for more of the moral domain?

9. (For class discussion.) Concepts like "love," "freedom," and "equality" are not precise. Try to offer a working definition of each. Suppose a society is "equal." What effect would this have, if any, on the ideals of freedom and love? Why are these held up as ideals? Is "self-reliance" held up as an ideal? Why or why not? Which aspects of the moral domain are best judged by ideals? For example, are institutions better judged by an equality ideal than acts by individuals?

10. (For class discussion.) Are procedural ideals part of the moral experience? Can we effectively make moral decisions based on procedural ideals? Can we make effective moral judgments by reasoning about what an ideal observer would decide? Suppose the nature of the ideal observer was defined to include many specific character traits. Would a clear conception of an ideal observer make it easier or more difficult to make moral judgments? Is a unanimous agreement among free and equal people a better test than the supposed opinion of a single ideal observer? What parts of the moral domain are left out by procedural ideals?

11. (For class discussion.) J. K. Austin has not done well lately. J. K. has been ill and out of work for five months, yet owes more than $1,000 in income tax. J. K. believes that filing a fraudulent tax return will bring a small refund. Select four of the above methods, and state how J. K. would use each to make a moral judgment about whether to cheat on taxes. Do all four methods come to the same conclusion? Which way of reaching a conclusion is best? Answering this question should show us that more than a simple statement of a position is sometimes

required to allow for informed moral decision making. For example, if you selected a procedural ideal as one of the four ways, you might soon conclude that a fuller explanation of how to proceed using that view is required. If this is the case, specify in your answer why a conclusion cannot be reached.

2.2 Conclusion

We have offered a survey of many things often considered to be in the moral domain and range, and ten basic ways moral decisions might be reached. We could have added other considerations, but you have read enough to realize that moral theory is filled with controversy. Different theorists have different opinions on all of these aspects of moral experience. Many theorists select only a few items on our list as important for moral deliberation, and the items selected differ from theorist to theorist. Some theorists believe that some aspects of moral experience are more fundamental than the others, or that some of the items we covered are not a proper part of morality. Still other theorists may take seriously, in some way, everything we mentioned but hold that all the rest can be derived from one consideration or a few considerations.

A moral theory explains, orders, and guides moral experience. It may do these things by rejecting part of moral experience, or by claiming that one aspect is dependent on, or derivable from, others. As students of moral theory, we want to determine whether such explanations work. If the explanation amounts to a simple, undefended rejection of a part of moral experience, then we can correctly claim that the theory is not doing its job because it is not adequately explaining, organizing, or guiding our moral experience. When a theorist discounts too many items, then we expect a compelling explanation. For example, if a virtue theorist is correct, virtues have an autonomous status; they cannot be derived from principles, rules, or anything else. So a theorist proposing nothing but moral rules must either show that virtues are an unneeded or unhelpful part of moral experience or else that our attitudes about virtues are best derived from other parts of moral experience. Insofar as we find that virtue theorists are correct in arguing that virtues are not derivable from rules or principles, we are unlikely to accept another point of view as adequate by itself. In this case, we will expect some independent role for virtues in moral theory. The same can be said for particularism, rule theory, deontology, and teleology.

In dealing with these theories, we want to ask, in the following chapters, how well they instruct us on moral experience. Do they give us an adequate account of moral experience? Do they leave out too much of what we consider to be crucial in making moral judgments? Can they order and explain (or explain away) parts of moral experience thought to be crucial? This is a way to test moral theories: how well do they deal with moral experience?

You may find it unlikely that any one of the ten types of theories we have presented can account for all the others. Many theorists argue against including many of the things we mentioned by claiming that people wrongly hold that those aspects are a proper part of moral experience. Other theorists attempt to show that many of these can be derived from a smaller number of central concerns, while other theorists argue that they all play some role in making moral decisions, but that these roles must be coordinated with each other. We want to be able to determine which of these basic positions is the most adequate at ordering, guiding, and accounting for moral experience.

We will examine the basic theories relating to the ten ways used to resolve moral problems, and consider arguments about the strengths and weaknesses of each. In the final section of Chapter 12, we examine some suggestions about how to formulate a theory that preserves the strengths of various views while eliminating the weaknesses. You may want to read that section now, before you examine individual theories. This may help you to make a better judgment about whether a theory should exclude part or a great deal of our moral experience, whether a comprehensive theory is helpful, or whether including too much adds unnecessary complexity and conflict. A simple theory, claiming that one aspect or another should dominate, has theoretical elegance and apparent ease of application. A more inclusive theory, one that tries to involve as much of moral experience as is feasible, may be more complete, and thereby more satisfying.

In examining each theory, we should consider what it omits, and how the omission might influence our moral deliberations, for better or worse. Take seriously the criticisms offered in the next few chapters, but also offer your good reasons to support or reject the views in this text. The decisions we make affect our lives as moral beings, and as philosophers we must reason in support of our decisions.

Further Reading

In the following chapters we examine ethical theories in order to find their strengths and weaknesses. We do this one position at a time, which is necessary but unfortunate because our best critical work comes when we are very familiar with many different, well-argued views. This chapter has attempted to give some sense of the different kinds of positions taken in moral theory. Other books, some quite brief, would be helpful in your evaluation of theories. Bernard Williams in *Ethics and the Limits of Philosophy*

(Cambridge: Harvard University Press, 1985) offers a solid, more advanced analysis of ways to do moral theory. Also, Gilbert Harman's *The Nature of Morality: An Introduction to Ethics* (New York: Oxford University Press, 1977) gives a helpful overview of basic approaches to moral theory. Many anthologies containing original writings by philosophers can be found in college libraries. Select one that contains a good mixture of classic and contemporary writings; use it to read some of the philosophers mentioned in the coming chapters.

3

Ethical Particularism

3.1 Making Moral Judgments without Principles

In this chapter, we will examine several forms of ethical *particularism*—the view that moral rules and principles should not be used to make moral judgments. In arguing against the usefulness of abstract principles and rules, particularists underscore the complexity of the circumstances involved in making actual judgments. They correctly claim that theories that do not take complexity seriously should be rejected. However, particularism itself has weaknesses, mainly stemming from its inability to provide adequate guidance for moral decision making. Nevertheless, we will claim that some moral judgments, even when made against accepted rules and principles, have a moral standing and may help us to interpret and apply principles and rules.

Moral judgments are often difficult to make. Suppose you promise, as a favor to a friend, that you'll go to a movie on Friday night, but then an opportunity opens for you to earn some badly needed overtime pay. What should you do? Breaking a promise appears to be wrong, yet the promise seems to be about a trivial matter, and you need the money. The claim that breaking a promise is wrong appeals to a *moral rule*. Moral rules relate specifically to a type of act—in this case, promising. But circumstances suggest that we have good reason to break the rule since the promise is about something we consider trivial, and the reason to break it is important. We may think that the moral rule against breaking promises is a good rule, but one that has proper exceptions. This means that in most cases we are to keep our promises, and that in unusual cases, those we claim to be exceptions, the rule need not be followed. If a rule does not always bind, we need to carefully consider whether an exception is appropriate so that the rule is not improperly followed. But this suggests that the rule is not a genuinely helpful guide to decision making because every situation needs to be carefully considered to determine whether we should act, in accordance with the rule or against it. That is, every situation needs to be considered on its own merits, without presuming that a rule gives us proper guidance.

Philosophers, in growing numbers, argue that moral rules and principles are *always* improperly applied; they should *never* be used to make a moral decision. The problem in the case of promising is that the circumstances of the case make the rule appear too rigid. Yet the circumstances in making any moral judgment are complex, so ethical *particularists* argue that real situations, the particular cases we face, make the application of moral rules myopic. A rule, in its rigidity, *always* misses relevant moral considerations. Consequently, rules should not be used in making moral decisions.

Real circumstances have depth. We gave an example about a promise. Perhaps you reacted by saying either that the promise should be kept or that it was OK to break the promise. But real circumstances are usually more complicated. Suppose the friend is socially insecure, or has been having difficulty dealing with a depressing situation, perhaps the death of a family member. What appeared to be a trivial promise now looks more serious. On the other hand, the need for extra money may be very pressing. Without it, you might not be able to pay a tuition bill, disrupting registration for your college courses. Real situations involve people with particular backgrounds, needs, desires, ambitions, problems, advantages, disadvantages, and much more. Unless all of these are taken into account, even in what appears to be a simple problem, the particularist believes that an adequate moral decision cannot be made. Simplistic rules, the particularist claims, lead to poor moral judgments. Recently, the British philosopher Jonathan Dancy presented an interesting argument against the use of moral rules and principles in ethical decision making.[1] He divides moral theories into three types, and in doing so combines moral rules and moral principles: (1) theories using one principle, (2) theories based on many principles, and (3) theories without principles. After arguing that (1) and (2) are not proper ways to guide behavior, he concludes that particularism, the theory that rejects principles, is the correct basis for ethical judgment. (The structure of his argument assumes only three ways to resolve moral problems, and he tries to show that two of them are improper, so the final way wins by default.)

Dancy first looks at theories with only one principle. For example, a theory may claim that we behave correctly provided we never harm anyone, including ourselves. This theory fails, like other single-principled theories, because by being overly abstract it misses too much that is morally important. In making moral decisions, we take seriously many things in addition to harm: freedom, rights, justice, integrity, and even promises. We might allow predictable harm in return for an increase in freedom. Who is harmed in the case of the promise, and how is that person harmed? How do we know how much harm is committed? Does a promise have any moral standing even if breaking it does not cause harm? Because it is abstract, a single principle will mask an overwhelming number of morally relevant features in any moral decision.

Dancy believes that one-principle theories are manifestly inadequate, so he does not believe that he needs to launch an argument against them. We suspect he has in mind reasons like those offered in the preceding paragraph: using an abstract principle leads to conflict and indeterminacy (or an inability to make a moral judgment). Instead he turns his argument against any theory that incorporates many moral principles or rules as a way to deal with the complexity of moral decision making. Now he argues that we face the problem of conflicting principles, one principle instructing us to do one thing while another tells us to do something else. For example, fairness might tell us to force a poor person to pay a debt to a richer person, while compassion may advise the opposite. With many principles, we increase the probability of conflict in moral deliberation; faced with conflicting principles, we must attempt to determine which principle takes precedence. Conflict forces us to make decisions that are not rule-guided because we have to decide which rule has greater moral force in each case. This judgment is particularistic because it is not guided by rules or principles. The dilemma is clear: the more principles we have, the more likely we will face conflict among them. Since the potential number of morally relevant features of a case is enormous, we need many principles. Because it has many principles, the most adequate principled theory is also the most likely, due to conflict among those principles, to force individual judgments in actual cases. (What about adding rules about how to resolve conflicts among other rules? Remember that cases can be complex, so rules for conflict resolution would also need to be numerous and complex.)

Thus the use of one principle and the use of many are rejected. This leaves, by default, a theory without principles. Dancy concludes: "So the progress is from **monism**, the view that there is only one moral principle, through **pluralism**, the view that there are many, to **particularism**, the view that there are none."[2]

Dancy's particularism may be called *extreme particularism* because it does not allow principles any role at all in moral decision making. We explore less extreme versions of particularism in the next few sections, so for now we only note that Dancy does make one concession: that some features in particular cases are more important than others. We may be uneasy about a theory that merely tells us that no general guidelines exist to help us make better moral judgments. So Dancy admits that some characteristics of cases are more likely than others to lead us to make a moral claim; these are the *salient* features of a case.

Dancy brings up the point about salience when he offers a positive case for particularism. So far his argument has been negatively oriented: he presents three choices and rejects two. This is risky argumentation because he may be missing another option. Also, we need to know that particularism is a workable theory because it might also be objectionable, leaving us a path from monism through pluralism and particularism to a rejection of morality. To show that particularism is workable, Dancy compares moral decision making with another branch of value inquiry, *aesthetics*. We do judge things to be good works of art, or we judge them to be beautiful. Dancy believes that this is successfully done without principles, which means, if correct, that particularism is successful in aesthetic evaluation. In his view, in judging something beautiful—say, a building—we take into account salient features. These are the features of a work of art that typically lead a person to form a judgment about its beauty. Salient features, unlike rules, are not cognitive. They are the features that stand out when we carefully consider a case, such that they evoke a decision. In some moral decisions, the display of great courage may stand out, leading people to the judgment that, in the context, an act is good. It is not because we have a rule that requires courage, but because *in this case* courage stands out, guides our attention, and evokes the contextual judgment. (How close does Dancy come to advocating salient features as rules?)

We make ethical judgments, Dancy argues, by giving special attention to morally salient features: interests involved, harm done, expectations, virtues, and so on. We don't use them in principles; instead we pay special attention to them, so that they are not overlooked and so that they may evoke a judgment. Even though the use of salient features is different from the use of rules, this avowal of salience does move him a step away from an extreme particularism.

Principles and rules are typically thought to help us to make moral decisions, but if the particularist is correct, how can an ethical decision be made without using principles or rules? One answer is that we use intuitions. *Intuitionism* is the doctrine that our best knowledge comes by direct awareness. We may not reason that a symphony is beautiful; instead we directly experience its beauty. After we are directed to listen to its salient sounds, we immediately know that it is beautiful, just as we know that the color of the wall is green after looking at it carefully and under the proper light. Particularism is typically a form of *moral intuitionism*. We don't need to reason that a brutal beating is morally wrong, or that taking unfair advantage of a child is morally wrong, or that ethnic cleansing is horribly immoral.

Particularists are often holists as well. *Holists* believe that the whole is more than the sum of its parts and that we can only adequately comprehend a situation when we see it as a whole. We cannot know whether a building is beautiful unless we view it in relation to all its surroundings. We cannot know whether an action is right or wrong unless we view it in relation to its time and place, to other actions before and after, to the individuals involved, etc. But a particularist does not need to be a holist; he or she may conclude that judgments may be made in relation to parts without attending to the whole. The particularist's unique claim is that principles are not validly used in making ethical decisions.

Study Questions 3.1

1. Explain why a particularist would object to use of moral rules like the following: Do not lie. Keep your promises. Do not steal.

2. In our example principle "Do not harm," "harm" is not a completely clear notion. To show how vagueness intrudes, suppose we consider doing some action with a *probability* of doing harm, but with a chance that no harm results—for example, driving drunk. Does the principle against harm result in the judgment that driving drunk is morally prohibited? Now consider some action with a probability of resulting harm that is lower than drunk driving—say, bungee jumping. Does the principle stand against this action as well?

3. (For class discussion.) Could rules be used to solve conflict among principles? For example, one principle may tell us not to harm while another instructs us to promote welfare. When these conflict, a rule might inform us that doing harm is a more serious moral consideration than promoting welfare. How would a particularist answer this question?

4. Must a particularist be an intuitionist? Can a particularist compare one case to another? Say two cases are much alike, but the first more clearly produces a firm moral judgment. The second, being like the first, will then be decided in the same way. Using comparisons would involve a rejection of intuitionism. But does the use of a prior case surreptitiously incorporate a rule? (This question helps us to prepare for an examination of casuistry and the case method in Section 3.4.)

5. (For class discussion.) Can a person be both a holist and an intuitionist? In answering this question, consider whether we can be holists without using reason. That is, can we really view the whole, or do we need to keep the whole situation in mind by a reasoning process? Remember, if the particularist is correct, any case will be quite complex. Because we need some way to manage that complexity, rules and principles are most helpful in determining which features of a case are salient and which need to be ignored.

6. Can an intuitionist properly make one decision today and a different one tomorrow in a case that is similar yet different? If so, is this a problem for the intuitionist? Can an intuitionist change his or her mind? Suppose a particularist judges that something is morally right,

and soon after that it is wrong. How could a particularist defend such a change? Is a change in opinion a problem for a particularist?

7. Does the particularist miss features in the moral domain or the moral range?

3.2 Evaluating Extreme Particularism

Extreme particularism has appeal. Part of the moral experience involves what we may call *revolutionary judgments* in ethics. These judgments stand against all accepted moral principles and rules. A short story by Shirley Jackson, "The Lottery," portrays a town run by custom. Each year in this town one person is selected to be sacrificed by stoning. Toward the end of the story one woman declares that the customary practice is wrong. She appeals to fairness: the act is unfair even though the lottery was conducted "fairly." Given the context of the story, her judgment is novel: it applies fairness in a way that was not previously considered. Historically some people stand against accepted practice by making new judgments, say by redefining past usage of words like "unfair," "unjust," or "harmful." (The same happens in science when a new, revolutionary theory redefines an old term, like "atom.") Because they amend or change principles, revolutionary judgments are not derived from principles. When widely accepted, revolutionary judgments lead others to see things differently, and then new considerations are incorporated into principles or new ways of defining the key terms used in principles come into common usage.

Moral judgments have a moral standing; they need to be allowed a reforming role, and sometimes a negating role. That is, judgments may indeed reform principles, or negate them in particular circumstances. When judgments have a reforming power, they may hold their own against old principles and rules by showing that a new interpretation of moral principles is more in keeping with overall moral experience than the old. Perhaps the new judgment points to salient features ignored in the past. Perhaps it shows a relationship between principles or rules that was not previously considered. Or perhaps it shows an imbalance in moral evaluations—say, that custom has been allowed undue control over ideals. The fact that some decisions are taken seriously by many people, yet cannot be accounted for by current rules and principles, is often enough to lead us to reconsider our basic moral beliefs. (Can you think of any once-revolutionary judgment that is now commonly accepted? Has this judgment changed the way we think of moral principles?)

While moral judgments have a moral standing as part of our moral experience, they are also problematic. The claim that we have an intuitionistic sense about right and wrong is suspect because moral judgments are influenced by individual background, cultural background, whim, and sympathy. We might not make judgments by a moral intuitive capacity but instead may be molded, even by some theory in ethics, to judge habitually in a way so natural that it seems intuitive. Furthermore, intuitions are inscrutable. Disagreements about conflicting intuitions cannot be argued; instead, each person simply "sees" things differently. Morality serves a social function. We want people to act responsibly, fairly, consistently, cooperatively, and so on. Moral judgments help us achieve such behavior. If we leave morality up to individual judgment, without even a consistency requirement demanding that people judge similar cases similarly, we negate the entire purpose of morality. Rules and principles help morality to stand as a publicly reliable system. (Think of how many moral rules have been followed by those around you today: telling the truth, not destroying your property or harming you personally, keeping appointments, refraining from insulting speech, taking one's turn in line. Without the guidance of rules and principles, implicit or explicit, it is unlikely we could get through the day.)

Complexity does not by itself negate the applicability of principles. Basic political decisions—say, over the moral value of universal health care—are very complex and cannot be made convincingly by direct moral insight. (Before proceeding, try to explain why.) We need to reason carefully about the possible impact of political decisions, taking into account harms caused, benefits gained, constitutionality, fairness, and similar factors. Nothing is directly perceived; political decisions are, or should be, principled decisions.

Extreme particularism fails to take into account the entire moral domain. Can it, for example, produce judgments about character? (Character involves a disposition to act, and so cannot be observed as a whole or in its actual complexity.) It also fails to account for, guide, or order judgments. Which judgments are morally proper? How can whim and self-interest be controlled? When are moral decisions unacceptably culturally dominated? Are moral intuitions simply conditioned responses?

Particularism is a challenge to the moral theorist. We cannot safely ignore particular moral judgments, especially revolutionary judgments, without falling into a narrow dogmatism. Yet we cannot order, direct, and explain moral judgments without appealing to general considerations like the presence of harm, the breaking of a promise, a violation of freedom. These features are morally relevant and do guide moral decision making.

Study Questions 3.2

1. Consider whether judgments made about actions of people from other countries, or adherents of other religions, are intuitions or are, more typically, culturally or theoretically conditioned.

2. Is it likely that we will believe a judgment proper that is out of line with widely respected principles? Suppose, for example, that a judgment is made that a physically harmful and degrading act should be done by a person who just lost his or her job because it appears correct in the circumstances. Are we likely to believe that this judgment is correct? How would the particularist answer this charge?

3. Does particularism deny the validity of general judgments? For example, does particularism reject the view that religious freedom should not be denied, that slavery is wrong, that promises should be kept? If so, is this a weakness or a strength?

4. Sometimes we are called upon to judge actions by those in other nations. Given the particularist's point of view, how would such judgments be made? Would a particularist believe that such judgments are proper? Defend your answer.

5. (For class discussion.) Can a particularist include political judgments as a proper part of the moral domain? If so, explain how.

6. Suppose (perhaps against your own conclusions) that a particularist is an effective judge of the actions of others. Would it follow that a particularist is an effective judge of his or her own actions? What special problems are involved in evaluating one's own actions as opposed to the actions of others?

3.3 Evaluating the Judgment Maker

Extreme particularism offers no way to decide which judgments are correct and which are not. It might evaluate self-interested judgments as no less valid than unbiased judgments. Extreme particularism is especially vulnerable to this charge because it seems to completely deny any reasonable deliberation on moral judgments. (The particularist would object, claiming that we could point to salient aspects of a case and try to persuade someone to have a similar insight as our own; yet this remains an unguided attempt to elicit agreement instead of a way to come to grips, reasonably, with an evaluation of moral judgments.) Can extreme particularism be amended in a way that would provide better moral guidance? In this section we explore one attempted amendment. This less extreme form of particularism centers on the judgment maker in order to determine *the qualities necessary in a good-decision maker*, or one most effective at responding in morally proper ways to concrete circumstances. The hope is that with standards to evaluate the decision maker, we can determine whether a moral decision is properly made. (Try to decide, as we proceed, whether this approach deviates so much from extreme particularism that we should no longer call it a form of particularism. In particular, does it present rules about judgment makers that suffer from the same critique as do moral rules?)

We often place requirements on judgment makers. We expect a teacher grading philosophy papers to be knowledgeable and trained in philosophy, and a ballet critic to be informed about ballet. Are there standards for a good ethical judge? In a seminal paper written in the 1950s the influential American philosopher John Rawls proposes standards that may be used to evaluate the moral judge and also to determine whether the judgment maker is making decisions under the appropriate conditions.[3] An acceptable judge, called a *competent judge,* is of at least normal intelligence; has adequate knowledge to be normally aware of the likely consequences of actions; is able to find reasons for and against a possible judgment; considers questions with an open mind; takes into account his or her prejudices; and has a sympathetic awareness of both sides of a case. We expect someone who makes sound judgments to have these traits, but we have increased confidence in a decision of a competent judge when the judge is immune from the consequences of the judgment, including personal gain or loss; the judgment results from careful inquiry into an actual case of conflict; the judge feels certain about the judgment; and other competent judges have made similar judgments in similar cases.

If all of these standards are met, Rawls maintains that we can have a high level of confidence that a judgment is good, and if any of these standards are violated, we have good reason to question a judgment. Rawls's standards are commonly applied in many areas of inquiry. For example, when a judgment maker in medicine is not immune from the consequences of his or her judgments, we have some reason to question the judgment.

Although Rawls's standards contain much wisdom, even when applied to areas outside ethics, we may certainly question each. We may wonder how one moral judge can really be sympathetic to all sides of an issue, and how such a judge is going to eliminate bias. Bias is often hidden from a person's full awareness. We tend to rationalize bias—that is, people try to find good reasons for even blatant biases. We need to have some form of control over bias so that determining whether a bias is present is not left in the hands of a particular judge. Traditionally, rules and principles have been used to limit the extent to which personal interest and bias enter into judgment making. Using a rule like "Don't lie" or a principle like "Treat people equally" limits the extent to which we can find biased reasons in favor of lying. (As you read this, be sure you take a broad view on bias, which can be quite subtle. We all know about bias against people with different backgrounds, but bias may also involve, in a subtle way, the respect we give to a well-dressed person. Even this relatively insignificant bias may lead us to improper moral judgments.)

Rawls's view is a form of particularism because it requires that no rules or principles be used in making a judgment, but he is not an extreme particularist because he advocates general requirements that function as higher-level rules—rules about the judgment maker—to regulate moral decision making. But Rawls goes one step further by requiring consistency across judgment makers. He says:

> It is required that the judgment be stable, that is, that there be evidence that at other times and at other places competent judges have rendered the same judgment on similar cases, understanding similar cases to be those in which the relevant facts and the competing interests are similar.[4]

This is Rawls's second abridgment of particularism. Not only does he put demands on the judgment maker, but he insists that judgments meet an important moral consideration: similar cases must be decided similarly, even when the judgment is made by other judges. Where similar cases are not decided similarly, we have reason to question those judgments. Moral experience includes the frequent demand for moral equality. If a teacher decides on a grade for one person, similar work should receive a similar grade when done by another person. If males and females, blacks and whites have grades established differently, we suspect that the teacher's judgment is faulty. The same holds for moral judgments. Rawls goes on to require that similar cases be decided similarly no matter who does the judging. This helps to limit bias and self-interest. One way to require that self-interest and bias are absent from a judgment is to demand that moral decisions be *universalizable*: when cases are similar, no matter who is involved, the cases should be similarly decided.

Rawls's position is developed in two main parts. In the first part, he proposes the development of a set of judgments meeting all the requirements already listed. The other part develops a set of general standards or rules that are induced from, or based on, the judgments of competent judges. Using these rules you and I can make proper judgments whether or not we are competent judges. Rawls says little about these general rules and instead concentrates, as we do in this section, on judgments formed without the use of rules or principles.

Rawls gives the judgments of competent judges a special status because they are used to generate moral principles. At least initially, we do not use principles to explain competently formed judgments. Under Rawls's view, once we have the principles (based on competent judgments), we check to see whether other judgments do fit the principles. Principles are derived from judgments, but once in place, contrary to extreme particularism, they may be used to make moral judgments. To view Rawls's position as a moderate form of particularism, we should keep in mind that the judgments of competent judges do not follow from principles, but are used to support principles. The judgments of competent judges are a sort of "moral fact" not reducible to any formula, or even to the known psychological disposition of the judges. We simply do not know how such judgments are made. What we do know, according to Rawls, is that the judgments of competent judges should command our respect.

The judgments of competent judges seem to play a role much like facts or observations in science. Of course, we don't respect all observation statements in science. Our scientific theories are well advanced, and observation claims must meet many tests before we accept them as scientifically interesting. Likewise, we expect that the judgments made by competent judges will be scrutinized carefully before they are given much status. Contrary to what Rawls claims, we are likely to use moral principles and rules in that scrutiny, just as a scientist uses theories and laws to judge whether to take an observation seriously. Rawls's reliance on a basic set of judgments fails to understand or take seriously enough the give and take of theory and judgment. But still, in science and in ethics, some judgments do seem to be unexplained by known theory and yet they are acceptable. We may determine that the judgment is better than our principles, and reform not the judgment but the principles. If a principle is basic, like the principle against harming, we are most unlikely to reject it out of hand; so in the face of a solid, reforming judgment, reinterpreting rather than rejecting the principle is more likely. (Try to think of a judgment that might make us reinterpret a principle rather than reject it, perhaps a judgment about abortion or about mercy killing.) The reforming role given to moral judgments is strengthened by Rawls's analysis because his standards help to determine how much status we should give particular judgments; for example, those that are self-interested, other things being equal, should be given less weight than those that are disinterested.

Rawls may be faulted for failing to note the role of principles in evaluating judgments because he does not use principles to evaluate the judgments of competent judges. But his position is an advance over extreme particularism because he spells out the need to test judgments at the particularistic level. Also, by seeking evidence that other similar cases have been similarly decided, Rawls moves us to a different, further qualified particularism: the *case method*, which will be considered in the next section.

Study Questions 3.3

1. Consider each of Rawls's standards. What is the purpose of the standard? Is it vague? Do you agree that each helps to identify a proper moral judgment maker?
2. How would we go about deciding whether a person meets Rawls's standards? If making this determination proves to be difficult, does this weaken Rawls's view?

3. If a judge meets all of Rawls's standards, would you accept the judgments made by that judge as morally proper? Why or why not?
4. Rawls believes that once we have a rich variety of considered judgments by competent judges we can use these judgments to create general rules and principles. He says very little about this, but he is clear that the value of identifying correct judgments rests in our ability to use these judgments to make general claims. In this way, even people who are not competent judges can make the correct moral judgments. We can now say that a particularistic methodology can be used to establish a basic group of correct judgments. These may then be used to institute and defend moral rules. How would Dancy react to Rawls's attempt to establish moral rules? Does Rawls's use of moral rules mean that he is not a particularist?

3.4 The Case Method and Casuistry

One of the hallmarks of contemporary ethical theory is its applied nature. More frequently than in the past, philosophers are not simply doing ethical theory; they are also actively engaged in applying it. This is particularly evident in *medical ethics,* where philosophers have been employed in hospitals and medical schools, and have written extensively about decision making in particular cases. Many philosophers doing bioethics have found that highly abstract principles fail to give adequate guidance. Nevertheless, without rules and principles we run the risk of leaving medical decision making about moral problems up to individuals. Thus we worry about leaving patients at the whim of the moral insights of medical care providers.

A middle ground may be sought: finding *paradigm cases.* A paradigm case is a model or "blueprint" case about which almost all can agree, a clear example of the right thing to do. With enough examples, almost all day-to-day ethical decisions can be made by showing that the case at hand is like some paradigm case. Thus, with an adequate supply of cases a physician can determine, for example, whether a patient is capable of making his or her own decision, or whether family members should decide for the patient. In similar circumstances, paradigm cases may show whose opinion should count when deciding whether to terminate life-supporting technology. (Think of other areas where paradigm cases may be helpful.)

Paradigm cases can help give clear guidance, make decision making more public, and increase our confidence that certain actions are permitted while other actions are not. By paying careful attention to paradigm cases, we can also determine whether given circumstances are so dissimilar that a unique judgment is required.

The case method is a type of *casuistry.* Casuistry involves the use of paradigm cases that exemplify a general ethical dictum. A *moral dictum* is a general moral judgment—for example, to tell a patient the truth. The paradigm case shows the circumstances under which the dictum clearly holds. Given the use of dicta and paradigm cases, casuistry is a clear movement away from extreme particularism, but the movement is small because the general judgment is closely linked to the set of circumstances exhibited in the paradigm case. Only when circumstances are just like those in the paradigm case do we have reason to believe that the dictum is properly applied. When the circumstances differ, the dicta may not apply. The casuist knows this, so many detailed cases are presented that differ from the paradigm case. Casuists then debate whether those differing cases should or should not be resolved in the same way as the paradigm case. The smaller the diverging circumstances the better, because a series of small changes show exactly how much difference is required in a case before a different judgment would be made. Hopefully, with enough cases and enough agreed-upon judgments, the judgment maker can have enough concrete guidance to make the right judgment.

Casuistry is a form of particularism because individual cases are decided according to how they differ from the paradigm case, without being dictated by general principles. Yet it is a method that recognizes, properly, that many cases are similar, and that similar judgments should be made in similar cases. However, the method fails to show how differences should be evaluated. Some differences between cases are very minor, yet even a minor difference may lead to a different moral judgment. Who decides when a case differs enough from a paradigm case to require a different decision? Furthermore, who decides about the paradigm case?

One problem with paradigm cases is that they may be biased or incorrect. The circumstances of a case have a broad context; hospitals, for example, work with given resources, a history of decision making, and a staff with special concerns, training, and background. Cases may be decided in the same way, or may seem to be paradigm cases, because of the way an institution is structured. The view of a physician may be weighted too heavily, as was suggested in the movie *Lorenzo's Oil*, because this is customary. The case method, by its failure to appeal to general principles—for example, to more democratic principles—may entrench morally improper ways of doing things. That is, the way things were done in the past may become ingrained in the paradigm case, even if that way is not proper. If doctors have routinely lied to help patients deal with pain and uncertainty, then paradigm cases may end up showing that such lies are proper.

The question of context is important. How can we decide on paradigm cases and central dicta? When all of us agree, the task is easy. But if the casuists involved are from one tradition in a pluralist community, they may agree with each other, but the agreement may be narrow. For example, in a Roman Catholic hospital, there may be general agreement that abortions should not be performed. But such agreement would not reflect any basic agreement in the society at large. Problems are multiplied when the paradigm case is altered. Even among those in one tradition, agreement may be difficult to reach.

Casuistry has been criticized as provincial, partly because it has been identified with religious traditions. For example, the medical ethicist Daniel Callahan claims: "Unfortunately, systems of that kind [religious casuistry] presuppose a whole variety of cultural conditions and shared world views which simply do not exist in society at large."[5] One problem is that casuistry rejects broad general principles from which opinions may be judged. General principles, like the principle against harm, tend to have appeal that bridges traditions and contexts, so more likelihood of agreement may exist about general principles than about specific judgments. Almost everyone is against harm, but people disagree seriously about whether withholding life-sustaining technology from a person in a coma is right or wrong. By ignoring general principles, casuists give up the opportunity to explain their judgments, and they give up the guidance needed for judgments about cases that differ from the paradigm cases. So while properly established paradigm cases are likely to help us make moral decisions, the key problem is the selection of proper cases.

Study Questions 3.4

1. Explain the relationship between (a) Rawls's belief that similar cases similarly decided support the decisions of competent judges, (b) the case method, and (c) casuistry.
2. Can the case method give adequate guidance in *typical* circumstances? Defend your answer.
3. Can paradigm cases be found that are not unduly influenced by bias or narrow traditions? How can they be discovered?
4. Is the case method a form of particularism?
5. Explain how the case method or casuistry might be thought of as a kind of moral mental calisthenics that does not make real moral judgments, but is merely a preparatory conditioning for becoming better at moral decision making.

3.5 Types of Judgments

In this section we classify moral judgments people commonly make. Hopefully, this classification can help us to decide how adequate particularistic judgments are. For example, if judgments that seem to be mere responses to circumstances actually involve implicit appeals to moral principles, we might decide that general principles play a more helpful role in moral judgment making than particularists admit.

By concentrating on contextual judgments about particular cases—which are sometimes quite complex—particularists conclude that moral rules and principles do not permit us to make proper judgments. People often make moral judgments and, contrary to the particularist view, give some basis for the judgment; this typically involves general claims. An extreme particularist would reject any reasons as proper in justifying a judgment. Faced with a situation, the particularist would claim, "This is wrong." The particularist should not say, "This case *of harm* is wrong" because that would suggest that the principle "Do no harm" operates apart from the web of facts in the given case.

Let us call a judgment that simply refers to an actual complex situation an *ostensive judgment*. "Ostensive" means that the judgment depends on directly observed facts of the situation being judged. An ostensive judgment is best communicated to those who know the case firsthand. Limiting justification in this way, making it dependent on firsthand knowledge of the case, weakens communication, restricts debate to those on hand, and retards moral education. (Can you explain why ostensive judgments restrict debate and retard moral education?) Moral education and moral debate are fundamental parts of morality; moral systems fulfill a vital social role. If we rely only on ostensive judgments, moral inquiry is thwarted and its social function cannot be served.

A *factually based moral judgment,* unlike an ostensive judgment, spells out the salient features of the case being judged. Instead of merely judging that "this is wrong," a factually based judgment might be made by the claim that "this case of *physically hitting* a *young child, without provocation,* and without an *intention to punish,* is morally wrong." By citing conspicuous facts, a judgment of this sort gives us some reason to understand why it was made. Such judgments come close to providing a plurality of principles. Yet the particularist may still claim that the facts presented are merely salient, indicating main concerns, and that we only have confidence that a decision is correct in light of our own experience with the case as a whole.

An *analogical judgment* appeals to similar cases. Two cases are *analogous* when they share similar key features, even though other features, including important ones, may differ. Suppose two people in the same company work at different jobs but have the same level of responsibility. An analogy can be drawn between the two jobs based on the claim that they have the same level of responsibility in the same company, even though in almost every other way the jobs are different. Analogies are tricky. Some analogies only point to one or a few similar features, and yet are strong because the features are crucial. Other analogies may point to more common features, yet these features may be rather incidental. When analogical similarities are clear and compelling, we expect similar moral judgments to be made about cases. An analogical judgment goes this way: **Since this case is analogous to one already decided, it must be judged, morally speaking, in the same way**.

So far the types of judgment distinguished are all arguably particularistic. No general rules are explicitly appealed to. (Do any appeal to rules implicitly?) Other kinds of judgments, however, do explicitly appeal to general rules or principles. A *rule-based judgment* contends that something is right or wrong, permissible or obligatory, on the basis of some rule. For example, "Since breaking a promise is wrong, this promise ought to be kept." Or, more concisely, "This promise is wrongly broken." A *principle-based judgment* similarly appeals to a principle: "Because harming a person is wrong, this punishment is wrong." People often make rule- or principle-based judgments implicitly, that is, without stating the rule or principle. When someone says, "This is wrong," that may simply be shorthand for saying, "Breaking this promise is wrong." Because people do not always make their principles explicit, the particularist might believe that the use of a particularistic methodology is more common than it actually is. If, for example, principle-based judgments are frequently made, even implicitly, then the claim that principles are not helpful looks weaker. The actual use of principles would suggest that principles can get to the heart of a case despite the complexity of actual circumstances.

Analogical judgments and rule- and principle-based judgments appear inconsistent with particularism. In each, something besides the case at hand is used to justify the judgment. With analogical judgments, no general rule is mentioned, which makes analogical judgments seem particularistic. But in such judgments an implicit appeal is made to the principle that *similar cases should be judged similarly*. Still it may be claimed that original judgments, the ones that set up a paradigm case, are not analogically made. Thus the base case would be decided on the method advocated by the particularist. Furthermore, we do not use the principle "similar cases should be judged similarly" to determine which cases are similar. Deciding similarity between cases is not as easy as it sounds. Two cases may have something similar about them even when the relevant facts about the cases are apparently different, and two apparently similar cases may be judged differently. For example, a teacher coming late to class and a student who fails to meet a friend for a movie may be considered similar cases; both involve failure to meet the valid expectations of others. On the other hand, two people may fail to keep the same promise, but in one case the promisor may be a child and in the other an adult; this difference may be enough to make the cases morally dissimilar. (Try to think of cases that appear to be very similar, yet should not be judged in the same way.)

If (as is *not* the case) all the particularist meant was that principles and rules are not conclusive when applied, the point would be quite correct. Many people incorrectly believe that a principle-based judgment adequately specifies what judgment should be made. Suppose we claim that forcing a person to have a blood transfusion against that person's religious beliefs is morally wrong. This conclusion can be stated as a principle-based judgment: Since violating religious freedom is wrong, forcing a person to have a blood transfusion against his or her religious beliefs is morally wrong. However, even with a fairly clear principle, a judgment is not automatic. In the case of religious freedom, we must first determine whether an action does violate freedom. Suppose a city requires members of a religion to pay tax on property used in religious services. Is this a violation of freedom of religion? Even if principles are used to make judgments, we must also make judgments about whether a case is covered by a principle. We must determine whether circumstances fit under a general rule or principle before the rule is applied. Suppose the person is an infant whose parents refuse the blood transfusion. Is an action done for a child in the name of religious freedom covered under the principle?

When we use principles and rules, implicitly or explicitly, we understand that they must be interpreted and the facts must be carefully examined to determine whether the principle is properly applied. Even though applying principles is not automatic and may require us to use our own judgment, this does not invalidate them or deny their usefulness. It means instead that they are sometimes difficult to apply. Dancy is right to claim that principles and rules may conflict. Here too we do not simply apply principles and rules; we also determine whether any rules or principles conflict. If conflict arises, we determine which rule or principle takes precedence, that is, which principle best allows us to make the correct judgment.

Particularism, as the extreme doctrine that rules and principles are invalidly used in moral decision making, stands or falls on whether we profitably group together cases under guiding concepts like "promise keeping," "equal opportunity," or "gratuitous harm." We do profitably group together cases in fields like physics and medicine, and we may reasonably believe that the presence of general features of cases will help us to make correct moral judgments. But if there are no good ways to decide that a particular case fits under a principle or rule, then the particularist may rightfully claim that rules and principles do not provide an acceptable account of moral judgments.

Study Questions 3.5

1. How do we usually make moral judgments? That is, which of the types of judgment listed above is most frequently used? In answering,

remember that the form of the judgment may be implicit. We might simply say, "This is wrong," when we mean, "This is wrong because it breaks the rule 'Do not lie.'"

2. Suppose several people are each judging the same circumstances and that they are restricted in the types of judgments used. First, they must all use ostensive judgments, then analogical judgments, etc. Which form of judgment would you expect to produce the greatest agreement? You might refer to a concrete case to make your speculation more realistic. You might also offer, as examples, the opinions of the two or three people in your hypothetical group.

3.6 Particularism, Act-Deontology, and Teleology

In this section we will show that particularism is best thought of as a form of act-deontology and as opposed to a teleology. Making this determination is helpful because it should suggest ways to clarify the nature of particularism, and it should assist us in determining its strengths and weaknesses. For example, if particularists reject teleology, then we might decide they are taking an overly limited view of the moral experience. We begin by explaining the basic difference between *act-deontology* and *teleology*.

Philosophers are divided about the purpose of morality. Some philosophers believe that morality establishes clear limits of proper behavior. Some actions are wrong, and other actions must be performed; these requirements hold no matter what the consequences. Other philosophers believe that morality is a way to help ensure a better life for all. The point of morality is to gain more of what people need or want, or perhaps more of what makes them happy. Under this view, in deciding what to do, we should carefully consider the likely outcomes of our actions: if our actions produce more of what people need, want, or makes them happy, then that action should be done. Whether an action is morally correct depends on its consequences.

These two positions form a basic division in ethical theory. Theories maintaining the importance of requirements that are independent of consequences are called *deontological*. Theories that give a strong role to consequences are *teleological*.

Those who believe that moral responsibility depends on the consequences of actions usually believe that the consequences that matter do not depend on moral evaluation. Some of the things we value, like telling the truth, are moral in nature. These are *moral values*. Other things we value, such as a good movie, good food, pleasure, a game, or reading a book, are *nonmoral values*. Anything valued may be considered a nonmoral good, and some things we may consider morally wrong—say, drinking liquor while driving—may be thought of as a good by some people because they might value acting in that way. In this sense drinking while driving is, to some, a nonmoral good, although those same people may believe it to be morally wrong. In short, anything may be considered a nonmoral good, even pain.

Teleologists often argue that nonmoral consequences determine moral obligations. That is, we are obliged to act in ways that produce the proper consequences, even though those consequences involve nonmoral values. Pleasure or happiness is a nonmoral good. Teleologists often think that it is the ultimate nonmoral good. If a person tries to make another happy, we may believe that person is doing a morally good thing. If a person always tries to make everyone as happy as possible, some think of the person as leading a morally fine life. Many teleologists believe that moral value is a function of nonmoral value. One teleological theory, utilitarianism, claims that we should always act to produce, for all people, the greatest amount of happiness possible. Those actions that produce the most happiness are morally correct. Once we decide which action produces the most happiness, then, according to this form of teleology, that action is morally required.

Teleologists are distinguished in three basic ways. (1) The first concerns the nature of the individual or group to be taken into consideration in determining whether consequences are proper. Teleologists require actions that produce good consequences, but consequences that are good for one person may be bad for another. A trade bill might be good for the United States but bad for Mexico. Some might claim that a United States Senator has a responsibility to protect members of his or her country, and only secondarily, if at all, to take into account the needs of people in other countries. Thus, when consequences are examined, the effects on some might be ignored. Some may argue that one should concentrate more on how an action affects oneself than on how it affects strangers. Others may give more weight to members of their own group or their country, or to the present generation. Different teleological theories select different sets of people as the people who count in determining whether the consequences of actions are good.

(2) The second distinction concerns the type of nonmoral good. Some teleologists claim, for example, that we should seek human perfection, while others contend that we should be concerned only about pleasure.

(3) Teleologists must also consider our standard in gaining the nonmoral good: do we seek the most possible, or the highest average amount, or merely an adequate amount? (Some teleologists attempt to gain some moral good, but this is an unusual form of teleology. However, the same three problems remain: selecting the good that counts, for whom, and how.)

Teleological theories do not simply claim that consequences determine moral obligations, but they also give direction on these three points. Different theories select different groups of people as those who count, different goods as the nonmoral goal, and different ways to weigh results. Teleological positions can be identified by how they respond to these three issues.

Sometimes public policies are presented using teleological language. For example, the International Labor Organization once called for worldwide action to ensure that each person's basic human needs were met. It called for action to provide adequate food, shelter, and education. This position may be read as a teleology centering on *basic human needs,* in relation to *all people,* and with the aim of acting to provide those goods to all *in an adequate amount.*

After this detour about teleological theories, we are able to state the point of this section. To a particularist, teleology is an objectionable doctrine. Teleologists give a rule, much like a mathematical function, from which we may calculate moral value. A complex situation is reduced to one value, or to a few values, sometimes by formula. We cannot judge a blues player or a symphony by a formula; we cannot determine how to take care of a patient by a formula. Likewise, the particularist claims we cannot judge the morality of an act by only considering a small list of nonmoral values. To the extent that we believe a moral theory should guide us in securing nonmoral value, we will view particularism as incorrect.

A particularist may believe that we should take into account salient nonmoral values and the way they are distributed to those involved in a situation. But more, indefinitely more, is always involved. Other values (only taken as salient)—fairness, justice, integrity—may be compelling features of a moral situation. For the teleologist, such moral values are dependent on nonmoral values, but the particularist does not draw such conclusions. It is in the particular situation that we find value; the particularist rejects explanations about how that value is determined. In fact, just listing considerations like fairness and nonmoral value appears to move us away from particularism.

The particularist's rejection of teleology leads us to question whether particularism is a type of *deontology.* A deontologist argues in favor of a uniquely moral component to moral value. Moral value, in part, is independent of nonmoral goodness. For an *extreme deontologist,* something may be morally right or wrong regardless of the nonmoral good involved. For a *moderate deontologist,* some nonmoral values must be considered in making moral judgments. *Act-deontologists,* as opposed to *rule-deontologists,* claim that we must not use general rules to weigh moral and nonmoral values in a given situation. We intuit or decide what is right or wrong by paying careful attention solely to the situation at hand, and not merely by considering consequences.

Some particularists are act-deontologists; they immediately judge an action without necessarily taking into account its consequences. Others are not. We may decide whether a particularist is an act-deontologist by considering whether the particularist is willing to consider other cases. Insofar as the case method rejects the use of rules and principles, it is a particularism, but it is not an act-deontology. An act-deontologist limits moral judgment to direct judgment, while a casuist or someone who appeals to similar cases goes beyond direct judgments.

When evaluating moral theories, classificatory devices, such as determining whether a theory is teleological or deontological, are not merely convenient ways to group theories or to talk about them. Although it is helpful to group theories together, this is not the main purpose behind classifying theories. If we consider a theory to be teleological, we are directed to the consequences of a situation as its important features. If this excludes too much of the moral domain, say moral rules, we call for an explanation. The burden of proof is on that theory to account for any missing aspect. Why isn't it needed? Can it be reduced to some other value? Is it a mistaken aspect of moral reasoning? When we know exactly what a theory takes to be central in the moral experience, we can better formulate a judgment about that theory. Likewise, a deontological theory may miss important aspects of moral thinking. Why aren't consequences taken seriously? How will a decision affect others? Thus, knowing whether and why theories are classified as teleological or deontological gives us a way to help to understand their strengths and weaknesses.

Study Questions 3.6

1. (For class discussion.) One teleologist may believe that moral judgment is dependent on happiness, while another may develop the view that morality entails trying to help us get more of the things we want. (Getting what we want is called *preference fulfillment*.) Use the ways to distinguish one teleological theory from another to explain the difference between these two views. Which is more reasonable? Defend your answer.
2. Act-deontology has been criticized because it can offer no reasons in support of moral judgments. Is this criticism valid?
3. Act-deontology has been criticized because it cannot aid moral instruction; for example, an act-deontologist cannot teach his or her children how to be moral. Is this criticism valid? Can this same criticism be made about forms of particularism?
4. Is an act-deontologist an extreme particularist?
5. (For class discussion.) Considering a particularist to be an act-deontologist, how would he or she respond to the following suggestion? We can evaluate a judgment maker, even morally. In making a moral judgment about a moral decision maker, the particularist should

include in the basis for judgment the salient feature that consequences of the moral decision have been ignored. Is this a salient feature the particularist can use to judge the moral judgment maker?

3.7 The Lessons of Particularism

The particularist points out that moral decision making is quite complex and rejects any simplistic approach as inapplicable. The particularist needs to be taken seriously; philosophers have often advocated single principles without adequately taking into account the difficulties in understanding, interpreting, and applying the principles. (We will examine principles in the coming chapters.) Given that circumstances are complex, the proponents of a single abstract principle ought to show how the principle can give proper guidance in real circumstances. This means that those who advocate a single principle are under obligation to explain how that principle can be fruitfully applied. As you judge theories presented in forthcoming chapters, you should carefully consider whether they adequately address the problems of moral complexity.

On the other hand, an extreme particularist also fails to give guidance in application. Without rules and principles, any decision seems as good as any other. Less extreme forms of particularism—the case method, casuistry, appeal to a competent judge—suggest ways to improve application. Although none of these may be fully effective without principles, each may help us to apply principles properly. The wisdom in particularism points to these as helpful ingredients in proper moral decision making.

The negative lesson in our examination of particularism concerns the need to control bias in ethical judgments. Extreme particularism almost encourages bias. Insofar as we do not need to compare cases, refer to competent judges, or to general principles and rules, prejudice, self-interest, or unevaluated custom may win out. Deciding in a biased way is the antithesis of moral decision making, just as it is the antithesis of scientific reasoning and judicial reasoning.

Particularism is a limited doctrine. It cannot adequately judge institutions, social practices, social conventions, moral rules, and moral ideals. These all require general reasoning because they involve so many abstract considerations, and much of the way we reason about them involves consequences. They do not simply involve individual concrete cases. Each organizes and directs many types of actions; each is in the moral domain, so the burden is on particularism to include them in its domain or find good reasons for excluding them.

Nevertheless, we must take seriously well-intentioned moral decisions, even those that appear to follow no rules. This is especially true in dealing with the moral revolutionary who sometimes stands alone with a judgment that later reforms moral thinking and even leads to new moral rules or a reinterpretation of old rules. An individual judgment may underscore something previously unnoticed, put facts together in an unusual way, or claim that old standards were prejudiced or unthinking. The change brought by the moral revolutionary may be like the change brought by a scientific revolutionary: although incomprehensible when claimed, it becomes over time part of standard practice. The person today who reacts with horror to the fact that we routinely eat cattle, pigs, sheep, chicken, and fish may tomorrow seem like the only sane member of our society. Such opinions should not be lightly rejected; they may be provisionally rejected, but they have a moral standing. Moral absolutism is a dangerous thing. The fact that serious people reject actions as immoral should suggest to us that they might be right—that we, not they, may be missing some "salient" fact.

Like other forms of decision making, morality is conservative. Many people have unusual views on everything from science to morality; we need not change our views simply because someone disagrees. We need to make the best decisions we can, given our principles, rules, practices, and institutions. That some people present opposing views, and that in the past opposing views have eventually been accepted as commonplace, gives us reason to carefully engage in continual reexamination of our moral beliefs, just as we should continually reexamine scientific knowledge. The history of science is the history of change in theory. Although scientists need compelling reasons to change their views, they do improve, modify, and even radically change basic beliefs. Moral theorists should show the same willingness to change views, with good reason. And these reasons may be found by exploring judgments apparently made without the use of rules and principles.

In this chapter we examined a basic position in moral theory, one that rejects rules and principles. It has its faults, but it challenges us to find effective, more general ways to make moral judgments. In the coming chapters we move away from particularism. Particularism is contextual: it stays near the case at hand in all its complexity. As soon as the particularist introduces a notion like "salience," we expect that some movement away from the case at hand, toward more general concerns, is taking place. Say that I don't agree that treatment of animals at the local zoo is inhumane. The particularist points out the small cages, with animals pacing back and forth, and claims that I am missing salient facts. If I question further, asking what's wrong with small enclosures, I may be told that they are harmful, as we can see from the restless pacing. Now the particularist has crossed the line (if it wasn't crossed sooner); he or she is no longer ineffably pointing out salient facts but appealing to common standards. In the next few chapters, we ask where standards, implicitly standing behind claims of salience, "come from" and how they may be used to make moral judgments. We especially wonder, in the next chapter, whether particular judgments are made in the light of customary behavior, and if so, what is the moral significance of local custom. So in the following chapters we move away from the case at hand, to cases decided by custom and, eventually, by principles and ideals.

Study Questions 3.7

1. Consider several disciplines, ranging from medicine to auto mechanics. Do people in these fields solve problems by the use, implicit or explicit, of rules and principles? Can the argument particularists use, that every situation is unique and complex, be applied to such fields?
2. Can particularism be used to answer basic questions about social and political structures? Answer in relation to specific social structures.
3. Who can better suggest ways to eliminate bias in ethical judgments, the particularist or the person who advocates the use of principles and rules? Explain your answer.
4. Give an example of someone from recent history you consider to be a moral revolutionary. Can a basis for that person's view be found in current moral thinking? Suppose a person presents a moral view that is entirely out of line with current moral thinking. Can we now argue that such a person is a moral revolutionary whose views will perhaps become commonplace in future years? Defend your answer with careful reasoning. (Your answer may be general, so that you give the generally appropriate responses to an unusual moral judgment, but you should also offer an example of an unusual judgment and determine whether it might become commonly accepted as morally correct.)
5. Some claim that animals should not be eaten. Support for this view may not depend on any moral rules or principles. But moral rules and principles are abstract, and therefore able to accommodate many interpretations. For example, when we say, "Do no harm," we are offering a principle often thought to include only human beings. With the judgment that we should not eat animals, the principle might be extended to include the rejection of unnecessary harm to animals. In this way, what looks like a decision made independent of principles might involve a reasonable extension of a principle. Thus, particular judgments, even those made by intuition, may help to give meaning to principles. Consider your answer to question 4. For the moral revolutionary you have in mind, is it possible to claim that what appears to be a rejection of current rules and principles is, instead, a reinterpretation of them?

Further Reading

Annette Baier's "Doing without Moral Theory?," in *Anti-Theory in Ethics and Mortal Conservatism* (Albany: State University of New York Press, 1989, pp. 29–48), offers a good analysis of reasons for rejecting moral theory. Thomas Nagel, in the chapter "The Fragmentation of Value," in *Moral Questions* (Cambridge: Cambridge University Press, 1979), argues that conflict among values forces particularistic judgments. In *Patterns of Moral Complexity* (Cambridge: Cambridge University Press, 1987, pp. 5–21), Charles E. Larmore explores the relationship between moral rules and moral judgments, with the conclusion that moral judgment is neither rule-governed nor arbitrary. W. D. Ross argues, in *The Right and the Good* (Oxford: Oxford University Press, 1930), that intuitions in individual cases form the basis for moral principles.

Endnotes

1. Jonathan Dancy, "Ethical Particularism and Morally Relevant Properties," *Mind* XCII (1983): 542.
2. Ibid., p. 542, emphasis added.
3. John Rawls, "Outline for a Decision Procedure in Ethics," *Philosophical Review*, 60 (1951): 177–197.
4. Ibid., p. 182.
5. Daniel Callahan, "Bioethics as a Discipline," *Hastings Center Studies*, 1 (1973).

4

Subjectivity, Moral Relativism, and Pluralism

4.1 Moral Objectivity and Subjectivity

Particularism can be construed as an extreme case of relativism in ethics. Suppose each of us follows the particularist moral methodology—the way the particularist proposes we judge moral right from wrong—and that we arrive at different judgments about the same problem. Many extreme particularists would believe this is fine; for them, any judgment is as good as any other because there are no objectively correct *standards* in moral judgment making. Other particularists may claim instead that at least one person is not adequately viewing the whole, is missing salient features, is mistaken about the facts of the case, or is not making a moral judgment but instead is making a self-interested claim and merely believes it to be a moral judgment. In short, to some particularists, the judgment of at least one, or perhaps all, is incorrect. This type of particularist maintains that moral judgments are *objective* in the sense that, when faced with the same circumstances, all people should make the same judgment because all judgments are relative to a similar human intuition or sensibility. We have already argued that this seems false; we do disagree in our moral judgments. Aside from the fact that we almost instinctively make moral judgments, we have little evidence supporting a common moral intuitive faculty. So the existence of a moral intuition or a moral sensibility that supports objectivity in particularism is in doubt.

In this chapter we explore the moral consequences of the fact that many people espouse different basic moral values even though they may agree about some other moral values. In general we may call such difference in moral perspective *moral pluralism*. When the differences stem from divergent cultural backgrounds, moral pluralism is more precisely called *cultural relativism*. Moral pluralism is especially evident among people in different cultures and different subcultures. Philosophically, we wonder whether moral standards are relative to different cultures, subcultures, or belief systems, or whether moral values are more objective, valid for people across different cultural and belief systems despite disagreements. This is a difficult issue. People seem to have legitimate differences in perspective, yet some values seem too crucial, such as respect for life, to be left up to the relative judgments of different groups and different individuals. The problems of moral or cultural relativism and moral pluralism are serious because moral experience suggests that there is truth in both viewpoints: both that values are objective and that they are relative.

People believe that many standards are relative to culture or to difference in individual commitment. A person who is fussy about the care of his or her front lawn adopts a personal standard that we do not view as either right or wrong, but that we allow to be a matter of taste. Some standards seem more objective because all or most people in a whole society regularly adhere to their demands. Almost everyone in Western societies, for instance, eats with a spoon or fork, and not with his or her fingers, at least at a formal dinner (assuming that eating a Big Mac doesn't count as a formal dinner). We do not believe etiquette standards are objectively correct in any ultimate sense, but instead believe them to be culturally relative. The standards we have been talking about, mowing a lawn or eating with a fork, are nonmoral standards. These standards are often taken seriously, even too seriously, but more importantly for our purposes, they suggest questions about moral standards. Are moral standards relative to individual perspective or cultural folkways, or are they more objective? Sometimes we find it difficult to determine whether a standard is moral or nonmoral, as when we call someone a good husband or wife. (Explain whether or why this is difficult.) Nonmoral standards and moral standards have no clear point of demarcation, so when we consider the best way to think of the binding force and origin of nonmoral standards, as we will in the coming sections, we also get some insight into the legitimacy and origin of moral standards.

Not all nonmoral standards appear relative. Standards, like those in mathematics and science, often appear to be more objective than moral standards. After all, people all around the world, from many different cultures, use the same standards in mathematics and science, while disagreements abound in ethics. Suppose we decide that the standards in mathematics or science are subjective. If science—which many would agree is more objective than ethics—is subjective, then it is easy to view morality as subjective. But if we believe that mathematics and science are objective in some sense, as most do, then we may be more hopeful that morality is also objective, and we may find that the ways other fields are objective helps us to understand or to support the objective status of moral standards. One question we pursue may be put this way: Are moral standards more like standards in etiquette or like standards in mathematics and science?

Since general philosophical questions about standards are often relevant to questions about moral standards, we will consider a basic question about standards in general and moral standards in particular: their *objectivity*. Are standards objective or are they subjective? You may be tempted to answer that it depends. Standards about what? Which food I like? What I do to relax? Whether my doctor is good? Whether a proof in mathematics is correct? The objectivity of standards partly depends on what is being judged. However, to decide whether a given standard is subjective or objective, we need to explore different views about the status of standards, moral and nonmoral. We will present a few basic positions on standards in general with the hope that these can offer good guidance about the objectivity of moral standards.

The difference between a standard as a guide, which tells us the most effective or right way to do something, and a standard as a way to define a human activity is sometimes crucial in moral inquiry. A standard defines an activity when we use the standard to determine whether a particular sort of activity is being performed. When a *constitutive standard*, a standard that defines the correct way to do something, is broken, someone might not be genuinely engaged in the practice governed by the standard. For example, if someone grossly violates the standards of guitar playing, that person is not considered to be playing a guitar. Or when someone makes a promise involving an activity that is impossible to do, that person is not really promising. A constitutive standard appears more objective because it helps define an activity and so it must be performed according to basic requirements by all people in order for them to count as engaging in that activity. In this way standards take on additional objectivity because they often determine whether an activity is being performed. Nevertheless, we still must decide whether such standards are subjective because activities can be defined in many ways, and whether one or another accepted way may be arbitrary.

In considering whether and how standards can be objective, we start with two extreme views: that standards are purely objective and that they are purely subjective. As we proceed, keep in mind that most of the positions we consider about standards in general may be applied to moral standards.

(1) Standards as Purely Objective

"Objectivity" has a several different meanings, all related to subjectivity. In general, a belief is *subjective* when it is based on an individual's personal perspective. My belief that LaPuma Bakery makes the best Italian bread in Cleveland may be entirely subjective, or personal. By contrast a belief is *objective* when it is based on a perspective that lies, at least partly, outside of an individual's belief system. This is a generic conception of objectivity. How can any belief "go beyond" an individual's point of view? In answering this question, a conception of *objectivity* is offered.

One of the most common views on objectivity claims that a view is objective when it is based on an existing thing that is external to humans. My belief that one person is heavier than another is based on an external comparison that appears independent from what I, or anyone else, believes. In this way, I can claim that my conclusion about the weight of an object is objective, its truth entirely dependent on the external facts. Also, claiming that a person is a fast runner seems to be an objective issue: we can use a stopwatch to settle the question. We may similarly believe that a moral or nonmoral standard is objective, based on observation. We can "see" that some things are wrong. For example, we do not need to be told that some of the violence we see on the nightly news is immoral. Denying its immorality seems as foolish as denying that an object is green.

This is one way standards may be objective: they may be based on facts, moral or physical. Thus, standards in general, including moral standards, may be completely independent of human belief. Under this view, human beings *discover* objectively correct standards; they do not invent them.

People often believe that many standards used to make judgments, even very serious judgments, do not have an objective existence in external, observable facts. Disputes about what makes a good guitar player seem to involve personal or social taste. Perhaps this is even true about standards for doing proofs in mathematics. Because we often view standards as involving taste, we sometimes find it difficult to believe that any standards are based on fact. Although it may seem to us to be a fact that violent acts are wrong, the same violence done to soldiers from one's own country appears wrong, yet to people in an opposing country, that violence looks commendable. It seems strange to claim that easily observable facts determine standards, moral and nonmoral, when people with differing perspectives look at the same thing and come to different conclusions. Disagreement thrives over value standards in a way it does not over, for example, weight or color. Furthermore, the fact that standards are often constitutive means that we can respond to guitar playing as poor *objectively speaking*, not simply as a matter of personal taste, without recourse to an *external fact*. We make the standard and then use it to judge an activity defined in and by human culture. (Could this be true of mathematical proofs?) The standard seems to be based in fact, but it is really a product of our heritage.

Some philosophers reject the claim that standards are based on facts because the claim seems to introduce an odd ontology. An *ontology* is a philosophical view about the basic kinds of things that exist or have being in our world. Moral facts are not obvious and are not required to make predictions or explanations, so an ontology that includes moral facts seems bloated, claiming the existence of unnecessary, confounding, and unhelpful entities. Basing standards, especially moral standards, on facts appears weak because it is difficult to determine what those facts are and how we can, even in principle, observe them. (What kinds of objective facts can support the standards of a good mathematical proof?)

We need to find a different way to claim that moral standards are not fully dependent on human thinking, a way that at once preserves objectivity while also explaining why so much disagreement exists over correct standards. Several plausible views have been offered. Some believe that God originates all standards. Anything that is good, morally or otherwise, is good because God has so determined; through God's wisdom, all things are properly evaluated. If human beings want to know what is good, they must discover God's plan, what God has in mind, even though knowing this may be quite difficult. While we might find it difficult to believe that some standards originate with God—say the standards of good jazz—many believe that God's will determines moral right from moral wrong. Moral standards are not up to us, but are, instead, dependent on God's will. This view preserves objectivity, yet also explains disagreement over moral standards because God's will is difficult to know.

The view about God has appealed more to religious people than to philosophers. The problem is that many people, with very different moral beliefs, all claim that they based their views and standards on God's will. Perhaps God's will is so obscure that we are really left to ourselves to determine correct from incorrect moral values. Furthermore, God is conceived of as all good, and we believe we could tell a good God from an infinitely powerful evil demon. This suggests that we have an independent standard by which we may judge that God is good and not evil. So even if we believe that God only wills the good and that God commands us to follow what is willed, we still understand that the standards of good and evil are, in some sense, independent of God's will.

Also, even if God demands that we act morally correctly, God may also put the burden on us to distinguish right from wrong behavior. This seems to be the case. We know of no way to determine, for example, whether God believes we are morally wrong to call a team "the Fighting Irish" or the "Cleveland Indians," but these are moral issues, to be resolved in a serious and thoughtful way. God may hold us responsible not for coming to the conclusion in God's mind, but for discovering the best conclusion we can given our human capabilities and limitations. So even if we do adopt a highly religious orientation, we are not done with the question of the objectivity of moral standards.

Some philosophers argue in favor of a different, yet also extreme, form of objectivity, one not in God's will or based in external facts, but one that we can discover but not influence. The claim is that standards, maybe all standards, exist in an independent *world of ideals*. This is a *Platonic* view. The ancient Greek philosopher Plato, whom many believe to be the greatest philosopher who ever lived, thought that correct standards, or ideals, are absolute, unchanging, eternal, and independent of human thought. So when we judge something as just or unjust, that judgment is correct if it complies with the absolute standard of justice in the ideal world. When we say that such standards are in an ideal "world," it should not be taken literally. When philosophers locate standards in an "ideal world" this sometimes means that the standards are not found in our ordinary world of sense perception and human thinking. These standards are considered real, and the use of "ideal world" is merely a code word for a more obscure form of reality.

Those of us who instinctively reject the reality of a Platonic ideal realm might think about where mathematical truths come from. Mathematical standards may be Platonic entities. Consider the standard for a circle, a set of points equidistant from some central point. This definition is a standard, telling us what counts as a circle even though an ideal circle doesn't exist in the factual world, nor does a mathematical "point" without dimension. It is not a thing, yet it certainly seems to have a powerful influence on us. Is that ideal standard of a circle objective? Does it depend on human thinking? Did we invent it, or discover it? We may believe that mathematical truths are ideal, that we discovered them, and that we still have truths to discover. They are objective, eternal, independent of human thought, and unchanging. But where are they? We may think that they are in the "world" of ideals, but that is just a way to say we don't really know where they come from, but that we do believe that they are absolute, unchanging, and independent of human thinking.

The view presented about mathematics is a instance of *Platonic realism* because mathematical ideals have a real existence. This plausible yet debatable view about mathematics is not our problem to resolve, but it may help us to understand the meaning of standards as existing in some Platonic world to be discovered, through study and insight, and not for us to invent or influence. Plato's position supports an extreme form of *moral realism,* the position that moral standards are discovered, not invented, by human beings. It is an extreme form because it assumes that standards are completely independent of human thinking, unchanging, and absolute.

Platonic realism is too mystical for many—including the mathematicians who view mathematical "truths" as human constructs. How can we know Platonic standards? Who is to say what they are? Can we really trust those who claim that they have discovered ethical standards based on knowledge about an ideal world? How can we test their beliefs? If you and I don't know anything about an obscure world of Platonic ideals, then our judgments don't count. Is that proper? Don't we have a right to our own moral opinions? Platonic idealism has been criticized as an *elitist* doctrine, granting moral wisdom only to those who have special insight into objective values. Platonic realism does little to help us determine which standards are correct, because the world it offers in defense of the objectivity of standards is more controversial than many standards it is supposed to support. The problem we face is to mediate between what many consider needed objectivity in morality and the existence of a plurality of different, sometimes hostile, standards. Platonic realism does not help because it rejects the value of moral pluralism without giving us much confidence that we can ever know anything about the world of moral standards, even whether such a world exists. (How would a Platonist answer these charges?)

So far relativism seems like the winner, if that means that no common basis for standards exists. We are skeptical about the existence of moral facts, and we have reason to doubt the helpfulness of standards in the mind of God or in some Platonic world. Now we consider whether we are best off considering standards, especially moral standards, to be subjective.

(2) Standards as Purely Subjective

Let's turn to the other extreme, *subjectivism*. Under this view, all standards are only properly decided by each individual. Every standard is relative to an individual; you and I have the same standards only by chance, or by a common conditioning factor that leads us both to accept the same views. A conditioning factor—say, the way we were raised—does not make a standard correct, and our agreement on standards gives them no additional objectivity. All standards are up to you and me, no matter how we make our decision. A similar background might explain why a standard is used, but a person may reject his or her upbringing and adopt a completely new set of standards. These new standards would, under subjectivism, be as good as the old, and perhaps more agreed-upon, standards.

The subjectivism of the previous paragraph is an *individualistic relativism*, applicable to all standards. If you like out-of-tune, random guitar playing, then that is the proper standard of guitar playing for you. If you and I approve eating raw, rotten chicken, then that is our standard even if we die; it is right for us. Even an odd sense of arithmetic is proper; $2 + 2 = 5$, if that accords with an individual's standard. Individualistic relativism applies as well to moral standards; they are up to the individual because any view is as good as any other view, even moral views that seem patently offensive to most.

Individualistic relativism denies that standards have a social function. It negates a purpose for having standards: to make our lives, collectively and individually, better. (Is this really a main purpose behind having standards? If not, what are the purposes, if any, for their existence?) Random musical sounds, the absence of any interpersonal standards in music, would deprive you and me of an enjoyable part of our lives. Joint conversation about the value of music, the sort that opens up new and satisfying experiences, depends on good standards, and not merely individually endorsed views. Think about going to a physician who believes that he or she can make up standards of good medicine, or to a lawyer who has his or her own code of law, both independently of their respective colleagues and peers. Many human activities depend for their existence on socially established standards. We could not have universities, football teams, symphony orchestras, movie theaters, or language without standards that go beyond individual valuation.

Individual relativism is close to, but should not be confused with, *moral nihilism*. An individual relativist takes standards seriously perhaps even by establishing a strict, burdensome moral code for himself or herself. In this way we view the code as binding only for that one person. A *nihilist*, on the other hand, believes that morality is an illusion. Nothing is really binding, even a code one establishes for oneself. Nihilism about any subject is difficult to overcome, if overcoming it means giving the nihilist reasons to believe that he or she is wrong, because the nihilist can continually reject the basis for our reasoning. We may claim that morality is needed for proper social function, to avoid harm, to do good, to preserve integrity. The nihilist keeps telling us that all of this is an illusion or that each involves an imposed standard (while he or she continues to enjoy the fruits of a social life). When we point out that values stand behind good reasoning and moral debate, and that many people do take morality seriously and attempt to make correct moral judgments, the nihilist can again keep rejecting what we say. We may try to move from standards in some other field, like medicine, to moral standards, in order to show that morality similarly needs good standards, but the nihilist may also claim that standards about good medicine, good mathematics, good reasoning, good physics are all illusionary, effectively ending the conversation.

We can leave the nihilist with the claim that people who take morality seriously need to find the best ways to make moral decisions and that those who reject morality, like those who reject the existence of the external world, are simply refusing to take social and moral experience seriously. Whether we confront the nihilist with moral experience, with well-supported judgments and the social need for moral constraint, the nihilist claims his or her theory survives. In ethics, as in science, we should be suspicious of a theory that refuses to enter into reasonable debate. The nihilist presents a challenge and then refuses to consider opposing good reasons, again effectively ending the conversation.

Extreme views are easy to fault. Even though some thinkers hold to extreme objectivism or extreme subjectivism, the truth seems to lie somewhere in between. In the following section, we consider a less extreme view about the nature of moral standards, the view that all moral and nonmoral standards are relative to social and cultural values.

Study Questions 4.1

1. List fields of inquiry where standards seem to be objective, like mathematics, and fields where they seem to be subjective, like taste in food. Does your list suggest that some standards are objective and some are subjective? Try to find subjectivism in the areas of more objective standards and objectivism in the subjective standards.
2. How do the following views differ and how are they similar: (a) that standards are based on God's will, and (b) that they are based on the existence of an ideal "world."
3. What standards do you use to evaluate music? Would you classify your standards as objective or subjective? Would you use similarly objective or subjective standards to evaluate your auto mechanic? Why or why not?
4. People often use standards to judge situations and things in their environment, for example, their families, friends, country, job, or education. Where do the standards people use "come from"? Do people typically use consistent standards? Do people evaluate their own use of standards? If so, what conditions seem to elicit such evaluation?
5. (For class discussion.) Can you think of any views about objectivity and subjectivity that are more extreme than the views presented in this section?

4.2 Evolutionary and Cultural Relativism

The extreme views we have presented both seem wrong. We need some objectivity in our standards, but we cannot expect that objectivity to come from a world no one really knows about. God's will is inscrutable, and a Platonic ideal world is an obscure and contrived device that seems to be projected in order to guarantee, even though we already may be convinced, that standards, such as the standards in mathematics, are objective. Perhaps a less extreme view can take the mystery out of standards, so that we can know where they come from and still have some objective confidence in them. A middle view should avoid the faults of Platonic realism and of individualistic relativism.

(1) Evolutionary Relativism

Evolutionary relativism is one way to find a middle course. Human beings have evolved in a way that gives them special needs, talents, capacities, weaknesses, strengths, desires, diseases, aggressions, and compatibilities. Our mathematics, music, medicine, sexual attraction, and philosophy all stem from our genetic endowment, gained and nurtured in the long process of evolutionary adaptation to an often hostile environment. Standards are proper when they are consistent with our genetic makeup and our evolutionary past; for example, standards of good food or good music do not properly include repulsive things.

An evolutionary relativist believes that standards are objective, not in the sense that they are completely independent of human beings, but that they can be judged correct or incorrect by a measure independent of human thinking and choice. Good standards are based on objective genetic makeup and on evolutionary survival value. Ignoring genetics and evolution invites idle, foolish, and dangerous speculation. We developed standards through a long evolutionary past, adapting as we went, so that given our genetic endowment, we can better survive the rigors of social life.

The evolutionist may not believe that there is a single best set of standards. Instead, our genetic nature and evolutionary past may be consistent with many standards. The way we respond to sound may mean that some standards in music are improper, while others are better. But it might also mean that several standards, though quite different, are equally consistent with our genetic structure. The linguist believes that many languages are equally good, but still insists that languages must have some essential ingredients, for example, that all languages draw from the same basic set of sounds human beings can make. In some languages, meaning varies by tone, but all languages must have some regularity in meaning. Evolutionary development of languages provides a basic list of standards, but each language has its peculiar standards, all consistent with the universal standards and all responding to different evolutionary scenarios.

Evolution does not produce eternal or absolute standards. All standards are relative to a particular time and place in the evolutionary flow of human life. Presumably, sometime in the long distant future, human standards may be considerably different. That depends on our future evolutionary path. In this view, evolution supports or directs all standards, whether in science and mathematics, or in ethics. If this is true, it explains why so many have different standards and why standards also have commonality. We have different languages, yet each language serves common needs and meets common requirements. Similarly, a moral standard is inadequate if it is out of line with genetic makeup or with our common evolutionary past, but our past differs from group to group, perhaps even from person to person. This evolutionary view respects differences, but recognizes the importance of genetic and evolutionary commonality.

Evolutionary ethics finds little support among philosophers. Although our evolutionary endowment may have a significant influence on moral and nonmoral standards, we are able to select standards that conflict with, or are independent from, our evolution. Some music is harmful to listen to because it impairs hearing, yet as it is played it is considered good music and it is only properly played when played loud. This seems to be a matter of personal preference, even though it has harmful consequences. Whether listening to very loud music is morally proper cannot be answered by an appeal to an evolutionary past.

People have adopted standards that require almost inhuman self-discipline—for example, the standards of sainthood. Those standards are not judged in terms of evolution, except to say that without the genetic makeup we have, they would not be considered. This criticism claims that genetic endowment forms a *very* loose set of requirements for any standard and that human thinking and creativity are capable of developing an enormous range of standards that cannot be adequately evaluated by, and may be inconsistent with, an appeal to evolutionary background.

Philosophers typically reject the view that the existence of a widely accepted standard is evidence that the standard is good for human beings, as an evolutionary view suggests. While an evolutionist might believe that all aspects of a human organism do have some survival value for the species, a moral theorist understands that too many different and conflicting standards exist for us to claim that they all have survival value. Some moral standards even appear to be designed to negate species survival value: for example, the Shakers are a religious group whose numbers were depleted partly because they refused to allow sexual relations.

As we grow up in a society, we learn that society's standards and values. We do have needs based on an evolutionary past, and these should be respected, or at least considered. Although our evolutionary past plays a role, we find it difficult to use only our past to determine which standards are correct and which are faulty. Evolution might give us insights into standards, but it cannot resolve the tension between needed, universally endorsed values and value pluralism. We turn therefore to a weaker form of objectivity in moral thinking, *cultural relativism*. Cultural relativism is, in many ways, similar to an evolutionary view, but it is quiet on the origin of values within a social group.

(2) Cultural Relativism

One criticism of evolutionary relativism appeals to the fact that human beings are more than their genetic makeup or evolutionary background because a cultural environment influences the behavior of people as much, and maybe much more, than evolution. Although many standards stem from an evolutionary past, from a slow "natural" development, this is not necessary, because values could have been developed quickly, perhaps even based on the whims of some ruler. Whatever the cause, people in different cultures have different standards, even dramatically different standards, about things ranging from dress codes to proper treatment of the dead. Some groups have practiced infanticide, while in other societies everything possible is done to save the lives of newborn infants; some societies practice polygamy while in others polygamy is thought immoral. A genetic thread, making such actions possible, may run through these cultural standards, but the thread seems slim. The survival value of values can be questioned, partly because humans can use a creative capacity to quickly modify social standards and partly because changing circumstances often make old values obsolete.

When people appeal to cultural standards as the proper basis for evaluation, they are appealing to something objective because culture is not dependent on what you or I think. Cultural standards, which include evolutionary standards (can you explain why?), often involve many people over thousands of years. The fact that a culture accepts a standard is an objective fact, and it is also a fact that different cultures have accepted different standards. What is often unclear is how those standards were developed.

Though different cultures have different standards, with mass communications and quick transportation diverse cultures are coming closer together. Although we know that differences exist, and that due to communications differences are becoming less extreme, the fact of difference or confluence does not tell us which standards are proper. We know that many people have unusual beliefs about medicine, but that does not tell us whether those beliefs are correct or incorrect. When we examine differing standards, we might claim that difference is not relevant to correct standards and correct moral values, but we can also claim that differences are fundamental and that cultural difference means that different people properly follow different moral codes. The fact of culturally different standards does not entail the view that standards are *properly* based in cultural difference, which is a philosophical position requiring adequate defense.

Cultural relativism, as a philosophical doctrine, informs us that proper moral standards are relative to a culture. Taken a short step further, it informs us that all proper standards are derived from culture. We are not, individually, the keepers of our own standards; cultural relativism denies that sort of subjectivity. We are obliged to use the standards of our culture, and these standards are objective because they are a matter of fact.

Cultural relativism does gain some support from the fact that so many people around the world have different moral standards. Support also runs deeper. Three claims can be made about these differences, each attempting to support the legitimacy of cultural relativism as a philosophical doctrine:

1. If correct standards, like those in ethics, are independent of culture, one would think that after millions of years of human existence we would find more agreement among people around the world, the sort of agreement we find in science.

2. In ethics, the nature of objective truth is contentious; no single theory in Western tradition has convinced philosophers about the correct nature of objective moral evidence independent of cultural commitment. In some fields, like science, most agree that factual observation plays a key role. In ethics we find little agreement about values and about the basis for values. We do know that people are committed to the values of their cultures, and we have little reason to believe that any more objective basis actually exists. In this way, moral standards are much like the standards of etiquette.

3. Those who study the values of people in other countries often find that those other value commitments make sense given different attitudes and beliefs. It is only when judged in relation to foreign values and beliefs that the standards of others look strange. There is, in short, no good reason to reject other peoples' values; the basis for rejection is typically merely another set of cultural values, which itself can claim no objectivity in addition to its cultural base.

For these three reasons—the lack of agreement about moral values, the absence of a clear standard for objective truth in ethics, and the invalidity of cultural chauvinism—cultural relativism should stand as a serious doctrine in moral theory. Cultural relativism makes sense. Think of those occasions where people you associate with violate basic cultural standards. These violations may involve personal hygiene, or improper standards about behavior in a group, say in a classroom, or failure to pay proper respect to friends or relatives. We believe that many standards involved in these areas are culturally relative and not based on values independent of cultural life. When a person violates basic cultural standards, everyone becomes uncomfortable; we don't know what to expect from such people, and we often judge them as immoral. At those moments when basic cultural standards are violated, we come to place increased value on them. The same may be true even for life-and-death issues. Although we feel uneasy with people who eat their dead, they may feel just as uneasy about burying the dead. That shared feeling of discomfort over the values of those in other cultures, and comfort with the values in our own, seems to support the notion that values are culturally relative.

Philosophers often argue that the existence of cultural differences does not prove that cultural relativism is a correct doctrine. This is correct, yet the defense of cultural relativism does not merely rest with differences, the first point mentioned above. The other two points are as important. Nevertheless, some philosophers claim that cultural differences have been exaggerated; groups do have different values, but these differences might stem from conflicting factual beliefs and from differing circumstances. For example, a group facing economic hardship might believe that the humane treatment requires infanticide, or religious beliefs, thought to be factual, might dictate the way the dead are treated. Both groups may equally value respect for human life, but they may apply that value under different circumstances, so that the factual and not the value difference would produce different judgments. (Explain the difference between the *factual* and the *value* differences in conflicting judgments.) It is not that values conflict, but that the facts of the cases are different.

This analysis seems correct. Given divergence in circumstance and belief, a similar principle will produce different conclusions. How we try to avoid harm depends on the circumstances we face. Differing beliefs and differing circumstances may take away much of the strength of the first reason in favor of cultural relativism, but even if exaggerated, it still remains the case that significant differences in value commitment exist. Even faced with hardship, people in many cultures would typically refuse to kill a newborn infant. (Can you think of good reasons for thinking that the last claim, that values conflict, is not conclusive? If so, can you think of an example that would conclusively show that some values are independent of different factual beliefs?)

Philosophers not only object that too much is made of the moral differences between groups, but they also claim that cultural relativism contains the seeds of its own destruction. When we are in foreign circumstances and notice that people behave differently, we are reminded that these actions are consistent with their values and culture. Judging foreigners by the values of our culture is chauvinistic. Who are we to say that our way is better? Here is the problem: Cultural relativism is thought to teach tolerance on the one hand yet intolerance on the other. We are advised to be tolerant of cultural differences, yet we are not advised to be tolerant of those outside or within a culture who violate the basic way things are done.

Following cultural values is sometimes a good thing, but like most good things, it can be taken too far. The cultural relativist refuses to be tolerant when someone violates a cultural standard. Most believe this commitment to a culture's values is a mistake because many cultural standards are arbitrary, personally harmful, confusing, or even ridiculous. Those who know about other cultures may find some of their own cultural standards, formerly accepted, to be unacceptable. Perhaps tolerance should be shown for such people, even by those committed to preserving their own cultural standards.

Another issue intrudes. Tolerance is taught by the cultural relativist, who says that we should not reject the standards, moral and nonmoral, of any culture. But suppose our own culture or subculture is chauvinistic. Are we then obliged to be intolerant? In general, should we be tolerant of the intolerant? Should we tolerate destructive, harmful, hateful, or offensive action done in the name of a cultural commitment?

Cultural relativism is incorrect; we typically do evaluate cultural standards, and look at this as one of the functions of ethical theory. We live in a rapidly changing world that is making many cultural standards into relics of the past, better off rejected or superseded. Also, in some cultures we find many types of moral standards. People believe in principles, rules, customs, and practices. These are often in conflict. As a member of a profession we may come to respect aggressive behavior, but as a member of a religious group, we may consider such behavior immoral. Cultural relativism incorrectly suggests that people in a culture have one set of standards. When one person is faced with a variety of perspectives, cultural relativism is unable to offer guidance because it apparently claims that all those standards are proper and should be followed, even when they conflict. People in one culture may believe it is proper to avoid harm, but may also approve practices that cause great harm. For example, prize fighting is supported by many who also claim to respect the principle against doing harm.

Standards and moral values conflict within cultures, and, furthermore, people are capable of using standards that are largely independent of their own cultures. (Are any standards independent of all cultures?) If we know about standards in other cultures, these may be used to check the value of our own standards. We can independently use principles and ideals that human beings have fashioned through creative use of their reasoning skills, sometimes apparently independent of a cultural past. Principles and ideals can show us that some cultural artifacts are not good; for example, the ideal of equality rejects social discrimination on the basis of race or sex even when discrimination is culturally supported. Because human beings are resourceful, we can distance ourselves from our cultures and subcultures to a significant degree. Since some cultural practices may be outdated, or even immoral, being able to judge a culture is sometimes advantageous. Even when a blanket condemnation of a culture is ill-advised, because it may leave us aimless or without secure ways to act, efforts to make cultural life better may be proper. The cultural relativist cannot offer beneficial judgments on a cultural environment but claims instead that all judgments are bound by that environment.

Problems raised above suggesting that moral standards are relative—that standards are not objective in the way similar to scientific standards and that we have no basis for rejecting the actions of others in different cultures—can be answered. First of all, it took human beings millions of years of develop the current sense of scientific objectivity. Though disputes, even basic disputes, still exist in physics, the level of agreement does surpass that in ethics, but this doesn't mean that objective standards do not exist in moral inquiry, and it doesn't preclude the movement toward greater agreement, even over the basis of moral inquiry, in the future. Furthermore, some practical disciplines, like medicine, that are thought to be more objective than morality rest on moral presuppositions involving, for example, the value of good health. In medicine much disagreement exists over the proper balance of risk versus benefit, a moral question. People often exaggerate moral differences between cultures even though most cultures reject lies, murder, and gratuitous harm. This exaggeration is unhelpful. In short, points (1), (2), and (3), raised earlier in support of cultural relativism, overstate the case.

The judgments that all proper standards come from cultural endowment is mistaken, yet cultural standards are part of the moral experience. They help to determine who has what moral responsibility in given circumstances. They also help to establish expectations about the behavior of others that when violated can cause great disruption, and when obeyed can facilitate social life. Ignoring cultural standards is often morally risky, but pinning all of morality on them is improper.

Cultural relativism can explain value differences among groups or cultures, and it can explain why those within a culture share values. It has a great difficulty explaining why members within a culture have different standards and why agreement over basic values—nonharm, freedom, respect, and justice—is widespread even though not universal. Though cultural relativism is informative, it is not a full answer to the problem of objectivity in moral reasoning.

Study Questions 4.2

1. Which is closer to extreme objectivism: evolutionary relativism or cultural relativism?
2. Suppose human beings are aggressive and individualistic by genetic endowment. Would an evolutionary relativist be forced to reject standards that are peaceful and cooperative? Answer this same question as a cultural relativist but assume an aggressive and individualistic culture.
3. Which of the following types of standards are more likely and which are less likely to be based on evolutionary endowment: scientific standards, political standards, standards of etiquette, moral standards? Answer the same question in relation to cultural relativism.
4. Think about your cultural background. We all are influenced by many

different subgroups within the larger culture. For example, some in North America might claim that their basic cultural identity is European, or European-American, or perhaps Anglo-American, African-American, Hispanic-American, Native American, or Canadian. Does such cultural diversity strengthen or weaken cultural relativism? (The problem is that the overlap of cultures, and the ability to move from one culture to another, may undermine the existence of clear cultural standards.)

4.3 Pluralism

Most people in advanced industrial societies today do not have the strict cultural ties of previous generations. Mass media, migration, decline in religion, spread of public education, weakening of traditional gender roles, increased level of education, and job and professional mobility have weakened traditional cultural affiliations. Political and large-scale economic institutional structures, with their own "cultures," play a greater role in contemporary life than previously. All of this weakens the claims that without closely following cultural standards social life is not possible or desirable. People often have difficulty in identifying their cultural affiliation, while identifying with one's profession, political affiliation, or religious association is relatively easy. Today we often choose key structures that influence, sometimes basically, the way we live our lives. We select our neighborhood, occupation, city, and religion to a greater degree than people did in the past. People today, even those from similar backgrounds, live by different moral codes. The fact of moral difference is more pervasive than the differences represented by the diversity of cultures. All the reasons listed above that support cultural relativism also support its rejection given the existence of a broader moral pluralism today. (As an exercise, you should explain why increased moral diversity stands against cultural relativism as a moral doctrine.)

Much of our lives are led in conformity with the standards of practices we have adopted and with the moral code, within those practices, that we explicitly or implicitly endorse. *Pluralism* refers to a variety of basic lifestyles within a society and to the absence of any comprehensive set of general standards. Each lifestyle has its special standards. Some are less demanding than others, leaving the individual to follow his or her own moral and nonmoral standards, while others involve practices or institutions that dictate almost every move.

Pluralism presents problems. In an advanced industrial society pluralism exists side by side with a high level of social integration. That is, people of diverse beliefs, ideals, standards, backgrounds, and religions regularly act in concert on the job, at play, in school, vacationing in the same places, taking the same means of transportation, and living in the same neighborhoods. As strict common values and common ideals have receded, people have become more interdependent. Specialization, government, unions, large corporations, common media, transportation, health care, and education make all of us interdependent. One challenge for moral theory is to face the demands of pluralism, a multiplicity of standards existing side by side, coupled with increasing interdependency.

The ways to deal with different standards that we have examined so far in this chapter are not adequate solutions to the problem of value pluralism and interdependence. We will examine several other suggestions offered by philosophers, each relevant to the concerns of this chapter, dealing with the objectivity and subjectivity of moral and nonmoral standards. Each involves looking for some generally valid standards while accepting the fact that, aside from these standards, each person has significant freedom to adopt, or to live by, different standards.

(1) Liberalism

The word *liberalism* has to do with liberty or freedom. Liberalism is a political and moral doctrine opting for the greatest political, religious, social, and moral freedom possible for each person, consistent with a like freedom for others. Routine interaction among people means that we need to have some form of control over that interaction, but because each person should be free to make many personal choices about his or her moral and nonmoral standards, social control over people should be as limited as possible. This is the liberal doctrine: moral and social dominance should be as limited as feasible. The problem is to identify the required forms of control.

Traditional liberals consider people to be basically independent or self-reliant. However, since people do interact, general standards are needed to keep people from interacting in harmful ways and to facilitate the interaction that is socially required. Since people are basically independent, only a few generally valid moral standards are directly relevant to human interaction, like the prohibition against harming another. Other standards, such as those required in the performance of a legally binding contract, or paying taxes to support public transportation, are needed to facilitate economic commerce. Traditional liberalism rejects as overly intrusive the idea that society should enforce personal standards, leaving them instead up to each individual. Pluralism is not a problem for a traditional liberal; because people are basically independent, different lifestyles need not be mutually destructive. A few basic common rules are enough to allow people to go their own ways.

Traditional liberalism fails to realize the actual extent of mutual interaction. A strike of subway workers in New York City or the signing of a trade agreement with Mexico can affect millions of people. Failure to take proper care of a house may cause the value of a neighbor's house to fall. The availability of handguns and cigarettes costs those who do not use them billions of dollars in the United States alone. The list could go on and on, but we say, in short, that interdependency seems pervasive. The trouble with traditional liberalism is that it is outdated. Whether people ever were basically independent, they are not today. This is not to say that traditional liberalism is incorrect in its conclusion, that the enforcement of common restrictions should be limited, but that the basis of its argument, that people are largely independent, is incorrect. In effect, traditional liberalism is left without support.

Modern liberals view the faith in our nearly thorough independence as a mistake. Social structures, social power, and economic power influence our life prospects at birth. If we lose a job, we face significant harm because we cannot fully care for ourselves in a world where so much of what we need depends on having money. In days of greater independence many people could raise their own food, make their own shelter, etc. Health care was primitive, and most people did not have a formal education. These things are not true today. One way or another, social influence is pervasive, even in a pluralistic society.

Modern liberals desire to overcome the harmful aspects of social life through local and national governmental action. Modern liberals believe we should all be committed to basic rights, basic economic livelihood, basic education and health care, equal justice, and equal opportunity. These, for the liberal, are the main generally acceptable values; all else—religious, sexual, and personal lifestyle standards—are up to the individual.

Liberals reject aggressive behavior toward other people; the criminal law, however, must only regulate harmful activities. If drug use is not harmful, or is less harmful than the cost of its regulation, it should be left alone, and speech, religion, and thought should not be regulated or controlled, unless these prove to be directly and clearly socially harmful. The modern liberal hopes to establish a safe zone for pluralistic styles. One need not respect the style of another, but all need to support the right for people to have the basic goods needed to successfully pursue any reasonable lifestyle. The modern liberal's answer to pluralism is to establish the support needed to bring about basic effectiveness in relation to the demands of social life, and then let people go their own way. For the liberal, evaluating the standards of others means little; what we need instead is to provide a rich common, safe, and secure environment so that people can be genuinely free to do what they want within the environment (even if we find that repulsive).

Liberalism answers pluralism by refusing to interfere with private values, and it insists that private values can only thrive under socially supportive conditions establishing high standards of welfare, health care, education, and safety.

(2) Conservatism

Conservatives see things the other way around. Basic economic organization is best left up to the market because the more people do for themselves, in a capitalistic framework, the better. If people want good health care, they should work hard to get it. The same is true for all other goods, except those people cannot reasonably get for themselves, like police and fire protection. Conservatives believe that the state does more harm than good by providing long-term basic welfare, environmental regulation, business regulation, etc., even when all is done out of the best motivations (which is often not the case). Furthermore, the governmental structures required to do what liberals want is unresponsive, bureaucratically organized, and power-prone; it serves selected interests, from big business to big labor, better than it serves the needs of the individual. Because it has much power, government stands as a constant real and potential threat to the interests and well-being of all individuals.

Government should only supply what individuals cannot get for themselves or through private market structures: transportation networks, the regulation of some monopolies, and police and military protection. A legal structure is needed to regulate harmful actions, ensure that contracts will be kept, and see to it that disputes can be settled by an impartial legal system.

So far conservatism sounds like traditional liberalism. It is not. Contemporary conservatives do recognize that people are increasingly interdependent, and do accept wide-ranging social programs, such as the social security system in the United States, as somehow essential. But another dimension of contemporary conservative thinking addresses the issue of pluralism. The conservative believes that some standards, even those that appear to be private, cannot be left up to the individual. For example, conservatives consider sexual morality a fundamental part of social life. The public has an interest in careful regulation of marriage, suggestive public sexuality, homosexuality, and sexually provocative language. Furthermore, U.S. conservatives encourage the adoption of common values: a traditional family structure, and respect for God and for the flag.

Unlike liberals, conservatives are not tolerant of a plurality of private values. They believe instead that some apparently private values are crucial to a common social structure. Once certain basic values are protected, a plurality of values is not offensive; indeed, conservatives believe that their approach will support a greater variety of lifestyles by relieving people of the repressive weight of big government, which, they believe, hampers private enterprise. They also believe they can reduce the repressive weight of socially harmful moral values through, for example, government censorship.

After examining liberalism and conservatism, albeit briefly, we begin to bring into focus a real problem for moral theory: the need for governmental control over the lives of private individuals. Both liberals and conservatives see the need for control and intervention; they refuse to leave all moral issues up to individuals. But in each view the need for control, whether through moral values or through state intervention, is often directed to a different aspect of life. Each sees social impact from a different perspective, and each view has some plausibility. We have not resolved the debate, perhaps because each view is presented as a political view and we have not considered the full range of moral questions that might affect our reasoned endorsement of a political view. In coming chapters, we do consider moral values from different and more comprehensive perspectives, which may help you to return to the political issues in the debate between the liberal and the conservative. The debate between the ways government should try to control behavior grows more complex. New perspectives, stemming from contemporary liberalism, seem to negate the motivation behind both liberalism and conservatism. New views opt for additional controls, not envisioned by either conservatives or liberals, that are not meant merely to avoid harmful interaction and to support effective participation in social life, but also to promote the integral value of group identity.

(3) Diversity and Multiculturalism

Besides general structures needed to safeguard common needs, those favoring *multiculturalism* believe that traditionally disadvantaged groups need special protection or special emphasis; new standards need to be developed to ensure that old forms of disadvantage and exploitation are eliminated. Multiculturalism is partly a response to the failures of the past. Multiculturalists believe that any attempt to ensure a full range of social opportunities for all runs into problems because the social system has been organized and controlled by Eurocentric white males, who have the best opportunities. The system has given power to white males, and along with power has gone the basis for self-respect. In order to adequately meet the demands of social life, people must all have an adequate basis for self-respect, based on a social respect for who they are. According to many multiculturalists, since minorities and women have been denied this, at least to a degree, governmental and social resources should be used to strengthen respect for those disadvantaged groups. This involves new standards, which must be imposed and instilled by education, law, morality, and social practice until they are adequately internalized and institutionalized in social life.

New multicultural standards involve considerations that contemporary liberals claim ought to be left up to the individual. According to a multicultural perspective, speech, whom one associates with, values, and university curricula should be guided by moral values and institutional control, often against the contemporary liberal's support for individual freedom. Offensive vocabulary is thought to be a serious part of the exploiting behavior and so needs to be eliminated. Sensitivity to the reactions of those in traditionally oppressed or disadvantaged groups should be required, both in private and in public. Members of those groups know best what sort of behavior has caused them disadvantage, and so they best express the limitations needed. Behavior others believe to be harmless may foster an environment of unequal opportunity and exploitation. Positive images need to be secured by ensuring that the contributions to society of those in all groups are taught and learned.

Those supporting diversity insist that each group has its unique and valuable heritage, but in order for such diverse values to flourish, common standards need to promote individual growth within disadvantaged groups. The proper response to plural cultural perspectives is to ensure, through social policy, that each group receives adequate attention, and that all become especially aware and supportive of the needs of women and minorities.

Multiculturalism is not a full pluralism but a selective one. Values supported by those in some groups are given preference over other values, such as the value placed by liberals on free speech. This conflict is interesting because contemporary liberals, long supporters of welfare and civil rights, now have intellectual sympathy for those supporting special advantage and special concern for some over others, based on the categories once thought to be morally irrelevant. The liberal's previous answer to pluralism—providing a strong social environment and tolerating all private action—is challenged as failing to provide the sense of individual worth and effectiveness needed to bring about a genuine expression of equally valid cultural and sexual backgrounds.

Multiculturalism underscores the need to carefully examine such basic values as nonharm, freedom, welfare, and equality. Under multiculturalism each is redefined. Questions about the extent to which old values are improperly violated or whether multiculturalism properly amends those values require serious, open consideration.

(4) Josiah Royce's Philosophy of Loyalty

In advanced industrial countries today, the reactions to pluralism are often heated. We need good debate and reasoning to determine how best to react to a plurality of values, to subcultural and sexual identities. We now turn to a philosopher, Josiah Royce, who explicitly confronted the problems of a plurality of values in a way that shows toleration and support for many values and argues for the need to support the development of the basis for expression and commitment to those values.

Royce, a classic American pragmatic philosopher writing around the turn of the twentieth century, decided that values are basically the property of social groups. As a member of a group, we can share the standards of that group: its sense of excellence, of moral right and wrong, of the relative value of goods. Royce rejected the idea that an individual could adequately, or consistently, formulate his or her values because as an individual each can only base values on desires, yet desires are fickle, changing with mood. If we base value on our desires, we lose stability in our lives and become, in effect, the servants of our own emotions.

Royce argues that a person is defined by his or her pursuits—we are what we consistently and seriously do—but for pursuits to have stability, they must go beyond individual desire. Stable standards and a stable sense of personal worth come when a person loyally pursues some cohesive group activity. Royce insists so strongly that values and standards come from group identification that he calls his moral theory the *philosophy of loyalty.* Once we are loyal and dedicated to the goals of a stable social enterprise, we can adopt an objective and more or less permanent set of standards: the standards of the group.

Royce makes sense. We know that people do get values from the religions they join or from professions they adopt. Students and teachers accept the standards of their pursuits, as do police officers and accountants. We also are members of a nation, of a culture and a subculture, and we may adopt values consistent with loyalty to those groups.

Being loyal gives security and definition to a life, provides ready-made standards, and ways to influence those standards. But Royce faces a problem. Often different loyalties cause conflict and set people in hostile and sometimes warring camps, as we see around us every day. Since loyalty is a value for Royce, acting in a way that is destructive of someone else's loyalty is a disvalue. Royce answers this problem with his notion of *loyalty to loyalty.* We should act, he believes, so as to preserve, enhance, and defend the right of everyone to adopt his or her sense of loyalty. Socially speaking, we should adopt laws, and political and social structures, that defend and enhance the mutual adoption of individual loyalties.

W. E. B. DuBois, one of America's greatest African-American intellectual and social leaders, a founder of the National Association for the Advancement of Colored People (NAACP), the founding editor of *The Crisis*, and author of many books, including *The Souls of Black Folk* and *Dusk of Dawn*, was a student of Royce at Harvard. Before Royce published his philosophy of loyalty, DuBois published a call to racial loyalty in a pamphlet, "The Conservation of Races." He argues that each race has a unique cultural mission; through the contribution of each, human ability and achievement is enhanced. His position, written a century ago, was an attempt to support unique cultural standards for the enhancement of all. Since DuBois believed that racism stemmed from ignorance, he thought that it would be diminished by knowledge of the achievements of others.

DuBois and Royce are examples of people who believe that values are bound up with social group identity. Nevertheless, both thought that some common values were needed to ensure against mutual hostility, and to secure social support for effective group membership. Royce found that support in loyalty to loyalty, while DuBois found it in mutual knowledge. DuBois eventually rejected his early confidence in knowledge and turned to social activism and to attempts at economic development because he came to believe that knowledge was not as powerful as political and economic organization. He eventually believed that social power and social laws are required to ensure against mutually conflicting loyalties.

DuBois, Royce, and multiculturalists face a similar problem: in a pluralistic society, we are influenced by members of many groups simultaneously. If group identity gives us consistency and purpose, then the membership in many groups, with different standards, will throw us back to our own sense of value and culture. A common sense of loyalty to loyalty is not enough to keep us from being set adrift in competing standards: family versus profession, group versus nation, nation versus world community. A sense of common values within plural commitments needs to be more firm, more structured, than either DuBois, Royce, or the multiculturalists suggest. The question is, how do we get those shared values?

The rest of this book may be read as an examination of attempts, many showing significant wisdom, to find an adequate set of common values that may bind people together in a pluralistic society.

Study Questions 4.3

1. Interdependency in society is largely a function of specialization, with people doing jobs that have different educational and even social requirements. Does specialization lead to a plurality of values?
2. Explain what, if anything, traditional and contemporary liberals have in common.
3. Explain what, if anything, contemporary liberals and conservatives have in common.
4. Explain what, if anything, multiculturalists have in common with contemporary liberals and with conservatives.
5. Explain the relationship between Royce's philosophy of loyalty and DuBois's view on racial contributions. Was DuBois correct to give up the idea that knowledge could overcome racism?

4.4 The Lessons of Relativism and Pluralism

Pluralists and relativists rightly point out that many sets of standards and values are equally valid and that the attempt to find one correct set is illusory. At different times and different places, given different backgrounds and a different history of decisions, different codes, standards, and moral values have been adopted. This plurality of values can be healthy or harmful. Relativists have attempted to come to terms with the differences among standards, but have not adequately addressed harmful effects of conflicting systems. Many moral theories can be thought of as providing an envelope of security within which people with different values can flourish and provide mutual support. The general ethical principles supported by a moral theory can serve to mark off universal obligations and goals in moral experience, but this need not negate, and may actually secure, local values.

Cultural relativists focus on local values common to many people. This is a way, different from adopting universal principles, to hold a society together. But common cultural values, enforced through social suasion or legal coercion, may diminish the freedom of an individual to reject cultural restraints and to adopt moral standards different from the larger group. While commonality is needed in an interacting society, individual freedom is also valued. The balance between the need for common values, the need for group values and group identity, and the need for individual freedom is difficult to strike, yet striking that balance is most important in a pluralistic society. Morality is about mutual respect and mutual support; a common sense of freedom, opportunity, welfare, and harm-avoidance is crucial if different moral and cultural systems are to flourish together. These are some of the issues we examine in the following chapters.

Further Reading

M. Hollis and S. Lukes put together a helpful collection of essays on relativism and objectivity: *Rationality and Relativism* (Oxford: Blackwell, 1982). John Ladd's edited collection is a good source for speculation on the relativism of moral value: *Ethical Relativism* (Belmont, Calif.: Wadsworth, 1973). Also helpful is Chapter 9, "Relativism and Reflection," in Bernard Williams, *Ethics and the Limits of Philosophy* (Cambridge: Harvard University Press, 1985). In Chapters 1–6 of *Ethical Theory* (Englewood Cliffs, N.J.: Prentice-Hall, 1959), Richard B. Brandt explores relativism and objectivity from different perspectives. Paul Taylor offers a solid philosophical discussion of ethical relativism in *Principles of Ethics: An Introduction* (Belmont, Calif.: Dickenson Publishing Company, 1975).

5

Virtue Ethics and Feminist Ethics

5.1 Introduction

In this chapter we examine two forms of ethical theory, *virtue theory* and *feminist ethics*, each particularistic in tone. Both help us gain added insight into particularism, and both give particularism greater content and specificity. However, neither is a pure form of particularism, because both may permit the use of rules, at least in typical cases.

Virtue ethics and feminist ethics are considered together because they have many similarities; in fact, the *ethics of care*, a crowning feature of feminist ethics, is a type of virtue theory. Although care is presented as a feminist view, it is not exclusive to any gender. We should all, male and female, attempt to learn from and evaluate the morally crucial, yet too often ignored, concept of care. Because care is one of the virtues, examining virtue and feminist ethics together helps us to better understand each. We note, however, that in general, these points of view are independent. Many feminists do not subscribe to virtue theory, and acceptance of virtue theory is consistent with a rejection of a feminist perspective. Furthermore, many of the issues discussed in feminist ethics involve not virtues but the needs, role, and treatment of women in society. In our study we will explore the common rejection, in virtue theory and in much of feminist ethics, of a rule morality; both theories rely on character traits, or on virtues, rather than on abstract, constraining principles.

5.2 Virtue Ethics

Virtue ethics is as old as the ancient Greek philosopher Aristotle, but until recently, nineteenth and twentieth century philosophers mainly ignored the virtues, concentrating instead on developing moral principles, moral rules, and theories about the origin and significance of moral statements.

Many philosophers are unhappy with the constraining nature of moral rules and principles. Many who believe that real situations are too complex to be neatly classified under a rule have turned to evaluating character traits. Good choices and good moral judgments depend on good character. People of good character display practical wisdom that flows from the virtues they possess, virtues like truthfulness, justice, sympathy, love, kindness, care, reverence, discretion, fortitude, gentleness, and patience. They know what is right in the context of real circumstances, though they may have difficulty explaining their views because explanations depend on generalizations and simplified assumptions.

Elizabeth Anscombe's 1958 article "Modern Moral Philosophy"[1] signals the beginning of the contemporary examination of virtue, as opposed to rules, as a better way of doing moral theory. Anscombe argues that the whole idea of basing morality on obligations is a mistake; we cannot be obligated to follow a set of moral rules without a moral lawmaker, for example, God. Yet modern moral philosophy pretends to develop moral rules and principles without a moral rulemaker. She suggests that we are better off to avoid calling actions "morally wrong," that instead we should call them "unjust," "unkind," or "unfair." A just person does not do unjust things, but injustice depends on circumstances, not on consequences, as the utilitarian would have us believe, or on universal laws, as Kantians think. A third way, relying on virtues, is signaled by the failure of the first two ways, consequentialism and deontology.[2] Under a virtue view, excellence of character is fundamental in morality; actions are judged by whether they flow from desirable motives and character traits, and not by how well they conform to rules and principles.

Michael Stocker recently offered an example intended to support virtue theory by showing the inadequacy of a rule approach.[3] Imagine being visited by a friend several times during a hospital stay. After a visit you thank your friend for coming, feeling gratitude and a sense of your friend's moral goodness; your friend then informs you that he or she came simply out of a sense of moral obligation, not out of kindness or affection for you. Now your sense of your friend's moral rightness fades, and you start thinking that you prefer not to be visited by a supposed friend who acts merely from disinterested obligation. While the actions, the visits, are the same, the motivation is different, and you now look upon the actions negatively because they are not done from a loving or caring disposition, but more formally out of respect for the moral law. This example shows the moral need for more than mere formal deontological or consequential thinking: morality includes personal involvement—personal commitment following from a good character.

Stocker's example shows that character and motivation are involved in acts involving personal relationships: we want parents to act out of love, not simply out of responsibility. But virtue ethics is meant to extend beyond close relationships to all moral decisions. When we decide whether and how much to give to charity, how much time to allot to our job, how to divide responsibilities in an organization, or whether to tell a lie to a patient, we cannot simply consult rules or consequences. More is required. We need a kind of *practical wisdom,* free from constraining rules, to make good decisions. (Think of what is involved in the difference between rule following and wisdom.) Rules are too aloof, too independent from concrete circumstances and consequences to take into account all the demands of a situation. Practical wisdom is not simply a matter of personal commitment; it allows us to make a thoughtful, informed, proper decision that is not merely intuitive and is not based on emotions. It comes instead from a wise *disposition.*

Virtue theorists have difficulty explaining what practical wisdom is. We can get a better feel for it if we think according to a craft analogy. We know what it is like to do something like playing a musical instrument, giving a medical or scientific opinion, or criticizing a movie. All of these activities are guided by some rules, but at some point the rules are not adequate. More is needed to do the job. That extra ingredient that allows a person to do excellent work in a craft is practical wisdom. Some people have more of it; some have less. If we are interested in getting a good legal opinion, we go to an excellent lawyer. The lawyer may work on hunches or on intricate schemes, even subconscious schemes, that may only make sense to him or her. We may have confidence in the lawyer based on a past record of success, but we may be unable to explain exactly what makes that lawyer so good. Think of the best teacher you have had. Does that teacher teach by the rules? Can another person follow those same procedures and be as good? How does that teacher respond to a difficult question? Does he or she follow some rule about answering questions, or does he or she react out of his or her disposition? A good teacher is attentive, considerate, clear, and thorough; responds to the students' needs and abilities, etc. None of these dispositions can be defined by rules. To claim that a teacher is excellent or virtuous does not mean that he or she teaches by the rules. Instead it describes a disposition, a tendency to act effectively under appropriate circumstances.

N. J. H. Dent, in *The Moral Psychology of the Virtues,*[4] argues that the virtue of generosity, a morally praiseworthy disposition, cannot be specified by rules. First of all, the circumstances under which generosity is appropriate are so unpredictable that even the most complex rule could not offer adequate guidance about what generosity entails. Instead generosity is a disposition involving "a steady and consistent direction of concern and intent, willing and desiring another's well-being. . . ."[5] A person is not generous because he or she does acts labeled "generous," but because that person has a "generous heart." "It is because someone has a generous heart that we can specify such acts as generous, since they are just such as would be typical of (though not necessary to) one possessed of a generous heart."[6]

Dent's claims are typical of a basic virtue perspective. He denies that the virtues can be encapsulated in moral rules. He rejects the notion that moral theory can proceed without incorporating the third way, based on virtues, and he claims that a virtuous disposition makes an act generous or just, rather than that people should develop habits of acting justly or generously according to some prior conception of justice or generosity based on rules or principles. According to the radical virtue perspective, virtuous dispositions are basic in ethical theory. The best way to know right from wrong is to elicit the judgment of a morally virtuous person. Rules and principles may be used; after all, even the virtuous physician typically follows rules, or, rather, follows rules in easy cases. But rules and principles, even when used, are secondary. Their validity is based on the past actions or the habits of the virtuous. When the case is difficult, or when the virtuous person chooses not to follow the rules, then rules are not proper.

On the other hand, some virtue theorists reject rules altogether. As we will see when we explore feminism as a type of virtue ethics, rules are thought of as restricting. All that is needed is a virtuous disposition because rules hide the true complexity and real concerns in individual cases. A parent's love, a disposition, is not shown by following rules but only by acting from loving concern. When rules play no role in a version of virtue ethics, then that version is a form of particularism, but one based on character or dispositions rather than on intuition or emotion.

If rules and principles are permissible, then to be a virtue theory, the rules and principles must be supported by, or derivable from, virtues. For example, virtuous people might support a rule, say that those in the middle class or above should give ten percent of their income to charity. But since virtue is the foundation, virtue theorists would consider any rule to be, at best, *prima facie,* meaning that the rule holds if the virtuous person believes that the rule doesn't hold in a particular case. More likely, the rule is a *rule of thumb* that summarizes how virtuous people have behaved, or have made decisions, in similar cases in the past.

Rules may help those who are not virtuous to imitate the virtuous. I may watch a great chef prepare food and try to copy his or her technique, carefully formulating rules of behavior to aid me. Following such rules may make me a better cook, but it will not give me the same results because the virtuous chef is constantly adjusting to ingredients and cooking conditions, like relative humidity. The virtuous chef can judge by taste that too much basil has been added, perhaps because the basil used is especially strong, whereas I would merely approximate the correct amount by following a rigid rule that fails to respond to flexible circumstances.

Virtue ethics centers on *dispositions* as primary. This is partly in reaction against contemporary theoretical concentration on *actions*, on the right thing to do. Basic moral judgments should not be about the right action, but about the proper character. Virtue ethics provides an example of a call for a change in the moral domain. If only acts are judged, then it is a mistake to claim that it is good to be courageous in a setting that requires little or no courage. In virtue ethics, it is good for a person to be courageous even if the opportunity to act courageously never arises. Having a virtuous character is thought to be a good in itself, indicative of human flourishing—that is, of what it means to be an excellent human being. (Consider whether you agree that having an unused virtue is good in itself.) On the other side of the coin, a person may act courageously, say under the influence of a drug, and not be a courageous person. That courageous act has no moral status; it is not a morally good act, although it may be a good thing that the person was courageous.

Even when they do not follow rules, people with the appropriate moral virtues do the morally correct thing. This leads us back to Anscombe's point about the lack of moral motivation to follow moral rules, which began our discussion. Moral rules provide little motivation, but a virtuous disposition inclines a person to act; it supplies the motivation to do the right thing. Even if we consider ourselves as making moral laws for ourselves, it is not clear why or what motivation we have to follow moral rules. We have all made rules for ourselves, like studying more or eating better, and find that without motivation we routinely break the rules. The virtue theorist argues that the person of virtue is motivated to do the right thing, just like the person with great drive to succeed will study more or work harder. The disposition is not only valuable in itself, but it also motivates a person to act in a morally proper way. Philippa Foot, in a foundational book in the movement toward reliance on virtues, *Virtues and Vices*,[7] claims that although we may legitimately *apply* moral standards to an agent, moral standards do not motivate that person to do the right thing because it does not give a *reason* to act, except perhaps for external reasons of punishment. (Consider carefully whether you agree with Foot's view.)

Despite the apparent need for virtues in various fields, from accounting to zoology, philosophers have not generally supported a radical or pure virtue theory. Part of this failure to attract a large following has to do with the difficulty in describing a "virtue." Much of the work in virtue theory has been negative in tone, indicating what is wrong with contemporary approaches to moral theory. Not enough has been done to explain what a virtuous disposition is, how it develops, how it can be located, and how moral judgments are made based on moral dispositions. Even one of the strengths of a virtue theory, its claim that virtues motivate, is obscure. How do virtues motivate? We know how to motivate externally, using praise, blame, and other rewards and penalties. We know that habits develop in response to such external factors, but we know little about internal motivation, even though it appears to be a very significant part of being a good human being.

Furthermore, the person of virtue is not easy to identify. We all know of cult leaders and political leaders who are revered and followed by many, yet thought to be charlatans by most others. Are these people of virtue, but with virtues that are unrecognized by most, or are these evil people who immorally use their charisma for power over others? The identification of people of virtue is a central problem in virtue ethics, to which we turn in the next section.

Study Questions 5.2

1. Consider experts in fields like medicine, law, physics, sports, and dance. Can their evaluations be summarized in rules? Can their evaluations be deduced from rules? Is it possible that such people follow very complex rules, perhaps like a large computer program, that tell them all the right moves to make in difficult circumstances? If this is so, could "virtue" be a term we use when we are ignorant about the actual rules followed?

2. If we know that a person is virtuous, say a great lawyer, are we more willing to permit that person to break established rules? For example, suppose a person is charged with a serious crime and his or her lawyer, known to be excellent at what he or she does, proposes a defense that seems to violate the established "rules." Is it more likely that we would recommend following the advice of this lawyer than that of a lawyer who is less "virtuous"? How do we identify a virtuous lawyer?

3. How would you go about determining whether a person has a moral virtue—for instance, kindness? (When you read the next section, compare your answer to some of the techniques suggested by theorists.)

4. Kindness, truthfulness, fidelity, courage, and honor are often considered moral virtues. List other moral virtues and explain why you consider each a virtue.

5. Can a person have one virtue, e.g., honor, and not another, e.g., truthfulness? Is this likely?

6. (For class discussion.) Is it possible to be *motivated* by a self-imposed rule? Think of people you know who have strong "willpower." Are these people who are motivated by self-imposed rules? Do such people offer a counterexample to Foot's claim that moral rules do not motivate? In answering, consider if and how these people with

willpower are motivated. Do they have a disposition, describable as a virtue, that stands behind their willpower? If such a virtue exists, does this help or hinder the claim that virtues, such as justice or truthfulness, are more basic than rules?

5.3 Identifying the Person of Virtue

In this section we examine four basic ways to identify a person as virtuous: by *acts*, by character *traits*, by *personality*, and by *practices*. Each has weaknesses, but used together they may allow us to identify a true person of virtue.

The first way to identify a person of virtue, by actions, is the clearest. We simply notice that a person does good things. Mother Teresa is a person of virtue because she does good. Similarly, a good philosopher produces good arguments, a good lawyer wins cases, a truthful person tells the truth, and a courageous person acts courageously. Although this seems a most reliable method, it suffers from the problems we mentioned in the previous section; the same action may display a virtue or a vice, or it may be morally neutral. Acting courageously out of greed is different from acting courageously out of a virtuous disposition. Furthermore, in a pure ethic of virtue, acts are secondary to virtues—that is, we know that acts are good because they are done by virtuous people. To know a virtuous person by his or her actions is to subvert the intentions of virtue ethics by putting actions in a primary position.

Furthermore, the complexity of circumstances makes it impossible for all but the virtuous to determine the right thing in the right circumstances. The problem we face is to identify the virtuous, and so we beg the question by relying on the virtuous to identify virtuous actions. (*Begging the question* is a fallacy in which we assume what we attempt to prove.)

Another problem arises: a good person may act in ways that seem out of character. He or she may have a bad day, or may have experienced some personal tragedy. So a vicious act, even one clearly done out of malice, does not entail the claim that the person doing the act is not virtuous. It might mean that the person is not perfectly virtuous, but we expect that nobody ever was or is. (Do you agree that there are no fully virtuous people? What would it mean to be perfectly virtuous?) The upshot is that observing only some of a person's acts does not conclusively tell us whether that person is or is not virtuous.

Instead of identifying the person of virtue by correct action, we may try to identify the virtuous person by the existence of *character traits*, by realizing that a person is disposed to act an appropriate way. Concluding that a good character trait exists is not only related to the acts done. The general demeanor of the person, whom the person associates with, statements made, refusal to accept rewards, the level of sacrifice involved, and the kinds of people who praise the individual all go beyond a simple evaluation of a person by individual acts. We might not rely merely on the number of faithful acts done to determine that a person has the virtue of fidelity. Instead we may turn to personal and social characteristics. These may mislead us, but even the best scientific tests are sometimes wrong, so this is not a devastating criticism.

The use of traits to identify the virtuous person leads to another crucial consideration. Particular traits are different from personality in general. A person with some virtuous traits may lack others. A courageous person may be cruel. Suppose a person is courageous, yet immoral in most other ways. Are we still willing to call that person morally virtuous? Some would say that virtuous traits are only virtuous in relation to a virtuous personality. In other words, unless a trait belongs to a virtuous person, that trait is not a virtue.

Plato believed that a person is virtuous if that person has some special insight into goodness. The presence of such an insight means that a person will not have vices, will be courageous, kind, and generous based on a general knowledge of goodness. If a virtue and a vice coexist, that person who has them is not genuinely virtuous but merely appears to be so. Platonic knowledge of the good is very difficult for a person to attain, but once it is, that person has a basic virtue, the virtue of wisdom, that guides all of his or her actions. The person of wisdom is also courageous and self-controlled. We might say that Mother Teresa is considerate due to a special religious perspective, her relationship to God; we expect that her orientation, perhaps the source of her virtue, means that she does not have any significant vices. If we found that she were not truthful, we would begin to doubt that she was genuinely considerate.

Determining whether a person has a particular trait is one thing; a generally virtuous personality is even more difficult to detect. The conclusion that a cult leader is a generally virtuous person is going to get us in more trouble than the determination that he or she has virtuous traits, like courage or loyalty. Many conclude that by ignoring overall character, we may mistakenly believe that a person is virtuous in a particular way. But the other side of the problem is equally serious. If we assume a virtuous character and ignore some traits, we may be led to believe that cruelty is a virtue because a charismatic person, apparently a person with a virtuous character, is cruel. The history of the world is filled with cases where actions and traits are ignored because of obsession with personality, like the personality of a political or cult leader.

Discovering true virtue is difficult. Relying on publicly observable actions is not adequate, and knowing a person's character, including intentions, beliefs, and desires, takes us into the unobservable. Another standard for determining the presence of virtue, one that may help to draw a better conclusion, involves *social practices*. Practices, with their standards, rules, and notions of success, establish who is virtuous from the perspective of those in the practice. Actions or characteristics defined independently of the practice do not indicate virtue, but success in the practice, however that is determined, is the measure of virtue. In medicine, physics, baseball, and ballet, people can, more or less, determine who is successful and who isn't. Standards can be quite rigorous in some disciplines, like classical music, yet genuine success tends to surpass the standards. It may involve intangibles like charisma, or perhaps even luck or proper relationship to others in the practice, like having the "right" teacher. If you become part of that discipline, virtue is determined by whether or not you *flourish*, or do well, within it. The people who flourish have the virtue defined by their practice. It is not successful acts but *general*, or typical, success, or perhaps general esteem, that determines the presence of virtue. This involves the conclusions of other virtuous people within the practice, even though those conclusions may not be based on specific actions, or on an analysis of character.

We may consider morality itself to be a practice. Each epoch or society has its way of defining the morally important virtues. Bravery, intelligence, or kindness may be virtues in one time and place but not in another. The meaning of bravery may vary from practice to practice. But the practice determines how to figure out who is virtuous. In short, the person who flourishes in a practice is the virtuous person.

We may feel uneasy about leaving it up to some vague notion of a practice to determine who is virtuous. This appears to assume that the practice itself is virtuous. Many are not. Part of the moral experience involves the evaluation of practices, and we can partly evaluate our own practices by determining whether they produce virtuous people. On the other hand, our practices do help identify virtuous traits. The moral experience involves give and take. Practices help to define virtues, and virtuous people judge practices.

We cannot use simple criteria to determine who is virtuous. Yet we do have a good idea that some people are more virtuous than others, and that some people are paradigms of virtue. Perhaps we use, and should use, all the techniques explored above.

Study Questions 5.3

1. In exercise 5.2 you were asked to state how you recognized a person of virtue. Does your answer rely on techniques like those presented in section 5.3?

2. Evaluate each of the methods presented above. Which is the strongest? Which is the clearest?
3. Can a person realistically use all of the standards to determine virtue? Do these standards conflict?
4. Suppose a person passes all the best tests used to determine virtue. Can such a person act in a vicious way or display vice?
5. (For class discussion.) The clearest standard used to judge virtue involves actions. Relying on character and practices seems to involve intangible items. Some may claim that this is not true. We know a person's character or that a person is successful in a practice by the *actions* that person performs. The difference is that many actions may need to be taken into account before we make conclusions about character, and we might need to rely on the observations of others. If we know character by actions, then is it correct to say that only actions count in the evaluation of virtue? To what extent does the evaluation of character and of success within a practice rely on actions?

5.4 Aristotle and Alasdair MacIntyre on Virtue

Many virtue theorists believe that Aristotle best presents the basics of virtue theory. Aristotle believes that a person of virtue can determine the morally correct action without recourse to previously established rules. For Aristotle, a person of virtue is happy and personally successful. He defines *virtue* as "a disposition of the soul in which, when it has to choose among actions and feelings, it observes the mean relative to us, this being determined by such a rule or principle as would take shape in the mind of a man of sense or practical wisdom. We call it a mean condition as lying between two forms of badness, one being excess and the other deficiency. . . ."[8]

Practical wisdom is a key term in Aristotle's definition. A person does not simply follow a previous rule by exercising careful judgment. To know the good, a wise person balances many ingredients, just as the good chef balances the ingredients of a recipe; the "rule" for this case takes shape in the judgment about the case. After much experience, a virtuous person is able to give a unique judgment, which may be misunderstood by a person lacking virtue. The important point is that the moral judgments of a person of virtue determine what is good; only a virtuous person understands what courage or truthfulness involves in particular situations. In this sense, goodness is not established by rules and principles. Goodness flows from practical reason; a wise person, a virtuous person of solid experience, knows what is good.

Aristotle uses the "Golden Mean," the "mean relative to use," or the middle ground between extremes; this middle path toward practical goodness begins to suggest his reliance on the wisdom of the virtuous. A truly generous person does not give too little. That is obvious. But for generosity to be a virtue, a person must not give too much. Imagine a parent who gives away so much money that his or her children become deprived. In this case we are not willing to say that genuine generosity, a real virtue, exists. Instead, the supposed generosity seems like a vice.

Because true generosity occupies the mean between the extremes, we must carefully determine what giving too much or too little means under given circumstances. We cannot determine in advance, or by a rule, just how much too much is. Only a person of practical wisdom can determine, in particular cases, where the mean lies.

Aristotle thought in terms of goals. The object of a virtue is to function well. A virtuous musician plays music well. Excellent functioning as a human being distinguishes a person who is virtuous from one who is not. The point of morality is to allow us to function well as human beings, to become excellent at being human. Aristotle believed that the proper function of a person, the thing that indicates human excellence, is to reason well—for example, to know the principles of philosophy and logic. In order to live a life of reason, an excellent life, a person must lead a moderate life. A life of practical excess destroys the ability to reason effectively. So the Golden Mean is a requirement to function well as a person, or, in other words, a condition for being a virtuous person.

Aristotle's view does not coincide with an ordinary view of virtue today. People like Albert Schweitzer and Mother Teresa are not thought of as avoiding extremes. Yet they do typify a virtuous person. Furthermore, Aristotle's notion that reasoning is the characteristic of a human being seems too specific. Many paths lead to a good or excellent life, and most have little to do with highly refined intellectual virtues.

The contemporary philosopher Alasdair MacIntyre follows Aristotle in believing that excellent achievement marks the person of virtue. But for MacIntyre the conception of excellence is not closely tied to intellectual virtue or to the Golden Mean; instead, virtue is a social product, the product of a practice. For MacIntyre, every practice, like playing classical music or being a college student, is a socially established way to direct actions in a complex organization of cooperating persons. The main point of a practice is to create the "goods" defined by the practice. In this way, standards of excellence are set by the practice. By engaging in a practice, a person accepts the standards of that practice and often internalizes its standards. A virtuous person acquires the ability to achieve the goods of the practice, to live its standards in an exemplary way. A practice is cooperative, so people must also be just and truthful in order to enrich it. Without justice and truthfulness, the social cooperation enriching the practice would be thwarted.

Practices exist in social networks; we do not make our own practices, but become part of an already defined practice, albeit one that we may change. Once we enter a practice, the roles and structures of that practice determine what we should do and then how well it is done. Almost all of our actions, to one degree or another, are guided and defined by some practice. Given the ubiquitous presence of practices, it makes sense to claim that all virtues, even the virtues thought to be characteristic of human beings as such, are socially defined and identified within practices. One step further: humans flourish as human beings by finding some role in some practice, and by using this role to realize its internalized goals.

The point is that "the practice" forms the opinion about the existence of virtue, and this opinion is not easily reducible to actions and characteristics. The decision about the presence of virtue is based on a form of life in which many people participate. In the case of Martin Luther King, Jr. and Albert Schweitzer, that form of life involves basic humanitarian concern for others. You and I participate in this "practice" to a degree, as well as in many others, some of which may be in conflict with contemporary moral concerns. Those engaged in humanitarian concerns form a community, broadly speaking, that passes judgments through a social consensus in ways nobody fully understands. This social consensus informs our views about who has which virtue.

MacIntyre is the leading proponent of a practice view. His analysis suffers from the general problems of this approach. Practices are vaguely defined, and may even promote contradictory conclusions. We may find the consensus shifting within a practice, perhaps on a daily basis, or we may be convinced that consensus is deluded. Indeed, a practice may propose evil ends, so we may be more inclined to say that someone who flourishes within certain practices—those involving criminality, abusive treatment, or aggression—may actually be people of vice and not of virtue. The verdict of a good practice is crucial, but we need to evaluate actions and characteristics to determine which practices produce judgments about virtue that we should respect. Although a practice may help to define virtue, morally virtuous people are able to critique the practices in which they are engaged.

Study Questions 5.4

1. Do you agree with Aristotle that practical virtue typically involves finding some Golden Mean in actions? You probably can think of people you regard as virtuous who are not engaged in finding a mean. Even if this is so, do you agree that, in general, virtuous people do follow the Golden Mean?
2. To what extent do practices today define success? Before you give a general answer, consider some practice with which you are familiar,

like higher education.
3. (For class discussion.) Suppose practices conflict, with one practice defining as a virtue an action the other defines as a vice. Can you think of such conflicting practices? If practices do conflict in this way, can it be true that virtues are defined in practices? Is it possible, or likely, that gradations of practices exist so that virtues in some practice take precedence over virtues in another practice? In this way, a higher-level practice could determine which conflicting practice has the correct view. For example, someone may belong to a religion that can determine which among conflicting practices takes precedence. Can you think of a larger practice that is not religious in orientation but that still may play some role in determining which conflicting practice takes precedence?
4. (For class discussion.) Can rules, principles, and ideals be used to evaluate practices and apparent virtues? If so, can we derive virtue in a practice from rules and principles?

5.5 The Lessons of Virtue Ethics

People like Philippa Foot and Elizabeth Anscombe were right to point to the failure of modern philosophers to take virtues seriously. In effect, the range of moral experience is broadened in virtue ethics. We not only claim that an action is right or wrong, but also that it is just, kind, or courageous. Philosophers have tended to use terms like "justice" as a way to make a claim about whether an action is right or wrong. They may say, "X is wrong because it is unjust." And then they make justice into a convenient rule. Those doing virtue ethics make a different claim. The conclusion is "X is just," but this is known through the judgment of a virtuous person. Furthermore, a virtuous person is motivated to do the just thing, the kind thing, or the courageous thing, not because this is the morally right thing to do, but because these are admired, valued actions. Virtue motivates. This is perhaps the most important conclusion in virtue ethics.

Virtue ethics changes the moral range, and, more obviously, it broadens the moral domain. We do not judge merely actions but also persons and character traits. Virtue ethics centers on this part of the domain, often to the exclusion of the rest. Although virtue ethics helps us to broaden our domain, a pure virtue position imposes its own limitations. It does not take seriously the whole of the moral experience. Rules and principles are a part of the moral experience, perhaps even the dominant part. Morality is social; we need ways to distinguish correct from incorrect behavior. The turn to the person of virtue for advice, while sometimes crucial, cannot be the whole of moral inquiry. We need ways to regulate everyday behavior so that all can respond properly in typical circumstances.

One of the problems with virtue ethics is the extent to which human personality is unique. We look for a person of practical wisdom, as did Aristotle, or a person of philosophical wisdom, as did Plato, but we know that people are not socially isolated. MacIntyre understands that people together create a virtuous life. We begin to identify with others in a practice, grow, and become virtuous within the practice.

The practice view of MacIntyre shares something with the views of Derek Parfit, a contemporary British philosopher. Virtues may exist in you or me individually, but this would require a personal identity that separates one person from another. Instead, Parfit believes that people are continuous with those who influence them. That influence brings continuity with the other's beliefs, knowledge, and experiences. We are what we are to a large degree because of our environment. But this means that our virtues come from social life as well as from our characters. We do not determine what is right or wrong individually; our sense of right and wrong is largely socially shared. A person of virtue is partly a social product, but a product that can critique the producer. The best critique comes from a rich base in the moral experience.

5.6 Feminist Ethics

In our survey of ethical theories we find that many views are restricted to a limited part of the moral domain. We have examined, or will examine, theories concentrating on moral ideals, principles, rules, virtues, and practices, as well as theories geared to unique moral judgments and culturally based judgments. We also consider the impact of different cultures and different practices on ethical beliefs. Even conventions play a role in moral theory. All of these have engaged the attention of moral theorists, usually from a limited perspective. We have found, or will find, faults and strengths in each position. By now you should clearly realize the difficulties involved in deriving all of morality from any limited view because the strengths of one type of theory are typically overlooked by other theories. Viewing moral experience from many perspectives is helpful; each perspective provides a thorough account of a limited part of moral experience. Even when limited, the account may be helpful in guiding our own judgments and may also aid us in developing a more satisfactory, and broader, moral theory. In exploring feminist ethics we attempt again to broaden our refined knowledge of the moral domain through a modern theory with its own unique account.

Over the last few decades feminists have claimed that in the history of ethics, and in contemporary ethics, a crucial, perhaps dominant, part of the moral experience has been excluded. That part is associated with the biological status and cultural roles of women. The American philosopher Mary Ellen Waithe demonstrates, in her four-volume examination of women in the history of philosophy,[9] that women have been a significant and fruitful force in the history of philosophy generally. Yet most of the dominant theories today and much of the work done in philosophical ethics have been developed by men. This fact alone raises the prospect that any special feminine perspective on moral experience may have been excluded. Added to this, many philosophers have portrayed women as subordinate. These facts led to an examination by feminists of the history of philosophy in general and of ethics in particular. In ethics, their results, till now, may be summarized under three headings: gender bias, women's issues, and a feminist ethics.

The feminist movement in philosophy is diverse. Some feminists have rejected ethics altogether, and others call for amendments or extensions to dominant theories. Some believe that a special ethical theory, *lesbian ethics,* can be developed around sexual orientation as a pervasive aspect of human life.[10] Others have claimed that women have a unique view that is capable of supporting a different ethical theory, centering on the notion of *care.* In the remaining pages of this chapter we examine gender bias, women's issues, and feminist ethics, with special emphasis on the ethic of care.

Study Questions 5.6

1. Do any of the approaches we have examined so far display a gender bias? Explain your answer.
2. Do you believe that whether you are a man or woman will influence the way you answer question 1? If so, does this difference in perspective have moral and philosophical implications?
3. Do the biological differences of women, especially their childbearing ability, suggest any different or unique ethical perspective? Or is it more likely that social and cultural differences suggest differences in a moral perspective? List and evaluate the differences, if any, in terms of their possible influences on ethical theory.
3. List issues that are considered uniquely women's issues. Explain why they are women's issues. How do these issues affect men?

5.7 Gender Bias

Many ethical theories are presented in an apparently gender-neutral way. For example, John Rawls's theory of justice stipulates that principles must be established without any consideration of gender. He wants us to consider what principles hypothetical people would select given that these people would not know, among other things, their sexual identity. Feminists have claimed that such gender-neutral perspective may mask gender bias. For example, a theory of justice that excludes the importance of family life, as does much of ethical theory, including that of Rawls, may involve gender bias. This is because traditionally women have been oriented toward home and family. Philosophers have ignored issues about the ethical status of family arrangements, the social impact of such issues, and their differential impact on men and women. Since many of these issues affect women differently, a bias may be present that favors issues that dominate male attention.

Without paying special attention to gender, we may have difficulty establishing whether boys and girls are raised differently, counseled differently, treated differently in school, and assigned different career paths regardless of skill. An ethic that insists without exceptions on following rules may ignore previous differential treatment. Moral rules that disregard gender differences may be insensitive to the use of offensive language, or to the need for special career guidance or laws relating to discrimination.

Feminists can easily point to explicit statements from the history of philosophy that downplay or denigrate women, but finding subtle bias is more difficult. Complaints are made that women have been ignored in the history of ethics, or that their concerns have not been aired. Bias is often difficult to detect. Bias may be found where it does not exist, and the finding of bias may be biased. Although bias can be subtle and difficult to detect, we know that it does often exist. The way male and female children are called upon in classrooms, even by women, appears to be biased in a subtle way. Rules that ignore special categories, perhaps based on past discrimination, may be criticized when they are applied in ways that refuse to make exceptions or in ways that compound past difficulties.

Feminists are united on one thing: that bias against women is wrong. The contemporary philosopher Alison M. Jaggar claims: "The feminist commitment is incompatible with any form of moral relativism that condones the subordination of women or the devaluation of their moral experience."[11] Though many feminists have supported a new ethical code that does not rely on rules but is contextual and caring, this statement sounds much like a rule. Similar statements relating to minorities—or, indeed, to anyone— should receive support. Avoiding rules is difficult. They do have a moral status, and when they are violated people rightly respond with moral indignation.

Feminists frequently point out that a society biased against one gender also harms the other gender; a society without gender bias would be better for almost everyone. Thus, the concern with bias should be the concern of all, and certainly of all moral theories. Traditional theory can be applied to questions of bias. Moral ideals such as freedom, equality, and justice are readily applicable to issues of race, gender, and age bias. Rule theories and consequentialist theories can be as well. Although bias should be the concern of all, the victim of bias is often better situated to understand exactly what it involves and is often more motivated to expend time and energy exploring its causes and consequences.

Study Questions 5.7

1. Can claims similar to those made above about bias in philosophical ethics also be made about psychology, sociology, or physics?
2. Is a man or a woman more likely to be biased in examining bias against women? Explain your answer.
3. Is it proper to label a moral examination of bias against women as a "feminist concern"? Can traditional moral theories handle this question just as effectively?
4. Are there circumstances in which males may be better situated to understand bias against women?
5. Annette C. Baier, a contemporary American philosopher, writes: "Males are those accused of tyranny over women in many societies, but the confederacy that supports the tyranny that needs to be broken may not be an exclusively male one, indeed has not been an exclusively male one."[12] This claim broadens the responsibility for sexism. Can women really be responsible for discrimination against women? Can we rightly claim that all men have some responsibility for sexism?

5.8 Feminist Issues

When the roles of men and women are different, their moral experience is also likely to be different. In traditional relationships, women have raised children and have had less impact on politics, business, and higher education. Military leaders, police officers, firefighters, construction workers, medical doctors, and lawyers were mainly men. These jobs—involving social power— tend to have their own sense of morality, their own moral regulations, and their own responsibilities. But such jobs are usually impersonal. The goals involved are often objectively defined, and personal involvement is limited by rules, procedures, and regulations. Many believe that male experience has been more associated with such environments, while women have been traditionally more associated with the personal commitments involved in family life. These differences may lead to unlike perspectives on ethical responsibility and to divergent attitudes about the importance of social problems and social responsibilities.

Many women's issues may be defined around women's special roles as mothers, as the traditional focus of family life. The following concerns all have been considered to be of special interest to women, or to address the special needs and circumstances of women: justice within a family, women's responsibility to the family, the need for adequate health care, the need for adequate day care, protection in divorce, children's rights, and education. Other concerns deal with the treatment of women in the workplace, in education, or in daily interaction: just opportunity, fair advancement, sexual harassment, rape and assault prevention, maternal leave, on-the-job day care, equal treatment in counseling, equal sports opportunity, the representation of women in education, and the use of sexist language. These interests, feminists claim, have been overlooked or shortchanged by traditional and contemporary male-centered ethical inquiry. Each presents an occasion for exploitation and discrimination, and so any theory or point of view that fails to address any of these is considered incomplete or immoral.

Women's moral experience is different from men's in relation to bearing and raising children, to sexuality, to education, and to the workplace. On these issues feminists have rejected the idea that a male-dominated investigation can adequately represent their point of view. But women do not all agree on conclusions and evaluations relating to women's issues, and some women reject the notion of a feminist perspective. Feminists often do not, and should not, talk for all women on any point. Nevertheless, a woman's experience, especially when supported by many other women, has moral weight. Moral experience is properly "ours"; it should be as inclusive as possible. To have some views, whether ultimately accepted or rejected, underrepresented, or not represented at all, diminishes the value of moral theory and precludes taking moral experience as seriously as it should be.

In the abortion debate we should take seriously the claim of many women that the prohibition of abortion puts them at special risk, takes their bodies out of their control, and gives them a less significant moral status than the fetus. This experience, the experience of unfairness, is part of our moral experience. Other women experience an attachment to the fetus as their child.[13] They support it as a unique moral entity. The experiential closeness to the fetus is not one that many men easily appreciate. This experience is also part of our moral data. Without taking into account all aspects of moral experience, proper decisions on the morality and legality of abortion are unlikely. To take into account all aspects of moral experience is not to insist on an extreme relativism; it is instead to insist that the debate be full. In a full debate sometimes one side or the other wins, but often partial compromise and mutually supportive alternatives appear to be viable and may be supported by both sides. In the case of abortion these may involve increased sex education, availability of contraceptives, widely supported adoption alternatives, and financial support. This is consistent with the legality of abortion on demand, but may reduce its occurrence.

The debate over abortion is not likely to be solved soon. When the point of view of those who have most at stake is not given full consideration, the conclusions reached are suspect.

Study Questions 5.8

1. Consider the position of the particularist. Can this ethical view successfully address women's issues? In your answer, explain what a feminist who is a particularist might say to someone who rejects the moral status of the moral experience of women.
2. Suppose someone genuinely believes that abortion is murder. Can this person support a compromise position on abortion, one that makes abortion legal? Explain your answer.
3. Do women have a unique role in the debate about on-the-job discrimination, including sexual harassment? What is that role?
4. Many particularists argue against giving rules any role in making moral judgments yet claim that special qualities are needed to make proper moral judgments. Suppose one of those qualities is a sympathetic understanding of the issues of all concerned. Could a feminist accept this form of particularism? Given this view, could particularism uphold Jaggar's rejection of any view that subordinates women?

5.9 The Ethics of Care

(1) Carol Gilligan's Different Voice

A main theoretical contribution in feminist ethics centers on the notion of *care*. The attempt is to build an ethical theory that moves away from individual rights as central, away from strict rules and principles, to a concern for establishing and preserving good relationships, helping others, and promoting mutual well-being. All of this is summarized under "care."

We may wonder why this emphasis on care is considered a contribution of feminist ethics. The answer takes shape with the influential work of the psychologist Carol Gilligan. In 1982 she published the results of her studies of moral development of women and men: *In a Different Voice: Psychological Theory and Women's Development*.[14] Gilligan takes to task influential psychologists, including Freud, Piaget, and Kohlberg, who ignore the moral development of women or else relegate women's moral sense to a lower level than that of men. The contemporary psychologist Lawrence Kohlberg presents six stages of moral development. He locates most women at stage 3, related to interpersonal helping and pleasing, while men frequently reach "higher" levels, involving moral rules and the principles of justice.[15]

Gilligan rejects the notion that the movement toward the so-called higher stages indicates a superior moral aptitude. For her, women exemplify the important moral characteristic of care. Theirs is a more inclusive morality, one that strengthens relationships and solves problems without resorting to the binding authority of rules and principles. (Is this similar to the point made by Foot about rules and principles in relation to a lawgiver?)

The difference between Kohlberg's and Gilligan's points of view is exemplified by the answers, analyzed by Gilligan, to a question posed to two preteens, Jake and Amy. The question involves Heinz's hypothetical dilemma: Heinz cannot afford a drug needed to save his wife's life. He considers stealing the drug. Amy and Jake are asked whether stealing the drug is morally proper. Jake responds that it is morally proper because people are uniquely valuable, worth more than the loss of income to the druggist. Furthermore, if Heinz were caught, Jake believes a judge would probably understand why Heinz stole the drug.

Amy, on the other hand, believes that the dilemma is not genuine. Stealing the drug doesn't solve the problem because the wife may get sick again and Heinz may have to go to jail. She is convinced that the couple can find another way to get the money needed or else come to some agreement with the druggist.

Gilligan concludes that Amy attempts to preserve relationships, and to solve problems by mediation. Jake sees the world more in terms of doing the right thing, and using rules to solve—as one solves an equation—the problem he confronts. Additional questions posed to Amy and Jake reveal that Amy considers her personal worth bound up with relationships involving care for others, while Jake judges himself against his own ideal of personal perfection.

Gilligan argues that women's statements exhibit a desire not to hurt others, the belief that morality calls for resolution of conflicts, and the judgment of themselves in relation to their ability to care for others. With the women's rights movement, and the problem of abortion that puts into focus women's needs, Gilligan sees an expansion of care for others to care for self.[16]

Whether or not Gilligan's study is an empirically accurate portrayal of how most women react to moral problems, her work suggests that a morality of care is an often-neglected although enlightening approach to moral problem solving. The different voice she points to is a call to a new moral perspective, a call that is answered, as we will see, by Nel Noddings.

Study Questions 5.9 (1)

1. Suppose that Carol Gilligan's empirical studies are correct. Does care show a higher or lower level of morality than a rule- or justice-oriented morality? Does talking about one sort of moral view as superior to another make sense? In answering this second question, be sure to refer back to some of the positions on moral theory we have already examined. For example, would an objectivist or relativist be more likely to make such a claim?
2. Gilligan suggests that the role of women as mothers fosters a sense of care. Is this an accurate statement? Could the same be said about fathers? Doctors? Police officers?
3. Can rules be applied in a caring way, or are rules usually hostile to care?
4. (For class discussion.) What does an empirical study have to do with the development of a moral theory? Can psychological studies inform us about the best moral theory?

(2) Nel Noddings's Care

In *Caring: A Feminine Approach to Ethics and Moral Education*,[17] Nel Noddings presents an approach to ethics that she considers to be feminine, meaning not that it is only for women but that it represents characteristically feminine virtues: receptivity, responsiveness, and relatedness. Women often define themselves in terms of caring, and they use caring relationships as a way to analyze moral problems. According to this view, a feminine approach rejects the universality of high-level principles and centers on feelings, personal joy, impressions, personal ideals, and needs, while principles and rules separate and devalue people, often making them self-righteous.

Noddings characterizes what it means to care. She identifies both *natural caring* and *ethical caring*. Natural caring happens when someone is engrossed in another and feels joy when helping the other, even if the help involves self-sacrifice. The paradigm case is of that a mother caring for a child. Natural care is accepting; it does not evaluate the other person but allows the one cared for to pursue his or her own projects. Natural caring is not judgmental; instead, it involves sensitized perceptions and awareness of the needs and the nature of the other. "Ethical care," a technical term as Noddings uses it, does not involve such natural attachment, but is a extension of natural care. Moments of joyous caring are remembered, and can be used to direct concern for others, to display ethical care, when the strong feelings of engrossment and concern are not present. This ethical caring must be practiced and involves effort. Nevertheless, it is based in, and is informed by, natural caring.

Noddings emphasizes that caring of either type is a relationship because it involves response to another. When the response by the cared-for is confirming, as it is in the infant's expressions, caring is a fulfilling act. The cared-for is vital in the caring relationship because without some appropriate response—a recognition of care or development under that care—the caring relationship is broken. Furthermore, when a caring person receives care back, then that person learns to care for himself or herself. Implicit in Noddings's account is the ethical demand not only to be caring, but to respond to care. Proper response establishes the proper conditions for caring.

Care is a local phenomenon; it responds to the demands of a situation. An ethics of care does not admit proper control of actions by rules or universal principles. Yet care itself is universal. Natural caring is the same in all places and all times, and becomes the base of universal concern in ethical caring. However, care always occurs in a context or a situation, and as such it seems to be forged anew in each occurrence.

Although Noddings explicitly rejects the binding force of universal prescriptions, she insists that caring relationships respect the freedom of the other. This is a universal demand that leads to difficult problems, often faced in the history of ethics, about the nature of freedom. We all know about suffocating "care," a care that is not in the interest of the free development of the cared-for. That care may feel the same, by everyone involved, as genuine care. So the resort to a universal prescription about the freedom of the cared-for is in order, but it suggests the limitations of the notion of care as the sole foundation of moral outlook.

Since caring occurs locally, although from a universal sentiment, we may question how caring can deal with relationships that are distant, perhaps institutional. In contemporary life we frequently influence the lives of others we do not know, and we often do not know about the consequences of our actions. (Explain why this is true.) Noddings deals with such relationships, distant relationships, with the notion that we are engaged in *concentric circles of caring*, ever more distantly located. The natural feelings of caring are attenuated at the more impersonal levels.

At the impersonal level, Noddings admits a legitimate value to the use of rules. The rules of the game, institutional and social rules and moral rules, allow us to comfortably participate in impersonal circumstances. She believes that custom and rules can guide us to meet the minimum requirements of care. To her, these rules are most appropriate in unproblematic circumstances. Once conflicts occur, she believes we should resort to our heightened ethical sense of caring. In the final analysis, rules and customs represent "someone's sense of relatedness institutionalized in our culture."[18] So Noddings calls for rules that reflect a truly caring attitude.

Our culture is filled, she states, with customs that distort caring.[19] Rules and customs need to enhance rather than detract from caring. A caring person does not steal, does not kill, betray, etc. But all such rules are simply aids to moral behavior. Moral rules, like the rule against lying, may be broken without the need for explanation or justification.

We may read Noddings with a sense of joy and a sense of apprehension. We respond in a joyous sense, understanding that she is correct about the value of a nonjudgmental care. We remember the care others have extended to us and our own caring actions. A world built around care is a world we naturally endorse. But we may experience apprehension. Folk wisdom abounds: the path to hell is paved with good intentions. We are rightly uneasy about being the distinct object of the careful attitude of another who feels free to violate moral rules and principles without explanation. We understand the need to regulate even a caring attitude.

We know that the moral domain involves circumstances and institutions on the outer level of Noddings's concentric circles of care. At the outer level, we are most unsure about the meaning of care. We need the wisdom of proper moral rules and moral principles, adequate customs and traditions, and consensus on parameters and responsibilities of social roles. Care cannot sustain a full moral view. Yet Noddings's feminist view shows that we should approach the evaluation of rules and customs through an extension of natural sense of caring.

Study Questions 5.9 (2)

1. Why does Nel Noddings contend that principles separate and devalue people?
2. Is it possible to commit great harm in the name of caring? If so, how does this affect a moral view based on care?
3. Can we use the natural caring relationship to determine, in concrete situations, whether a person should break a promise, tell a lie, steal, etc.? Give examples of how this might be done.
4. Is an ethics of care, as Noddings presents it, a particularism? How does it differ from Dancy's particularism?
5. (For class discussion.) How effective is care as a guiding notion in the criticism of institutions and practices? Provide examples.

5.10 The Lessons of Feminist Ethics

Feminists rightly insist that without explicitly addressing women's concerns, bias and exploitation will not be adequately addressed. All exploitation is wrong, whether it is the exploitation of men or women, blacks or whites, or of the people in one country by the people in another country. Feminist ethics is not an attempt to say that one sort of exploitation is worse than another, but that a particular form of exploitation is difficult to locate because most of the writers traditionally charged with identifying exploitation may have biased views.

Locating bias is difficult. Under the conditions of general equality, basic and genuine freedom, and a high level of universal welfare, bias will be easier to detect. (You should evaluate this claim.) As things are now, we search out bias from one unequal perspective or another. As long as we lose track of the general movement toward equality, freedom, and welfare, we will likely remain under conditions of exploitation. These are general concerns, but somehow the moral perspective must attain universality while addressing special forms of discrimination and bias. This means that as we move toward basic universal reforms, we must also eliminate particular forms of bias. Both movements are required.

Insofar as feminist ethics uncovers moral concerns and ignores aspects of the moral domain, it increases the universality of the moral perspective. Care, while not always ignored in the past, has been undervalued. Rules and principles have dominated. When these are uncaring, or harmful, we rightly object to their control. We should also keep in mind that proper rules and principles may protect us from well-intentioned but harmful care, and may make the notion of proper care more precise.

Annette C. Baier[20] claims that "women theorists will need to connect their ethics of love with what has been the men theorists' preoccupation, namely obligation." This belief tends to sum up the point of this chapter. The entire moral experience needs to be taken into account. Care is a point of view from which we may judge and act, but care itself is part of the moral domain. It may be evaluated. A balanced moral perspective does not ignore any part of the moral range or the moral domain. The instruction from feminist ethics is that part of the domain has not been given adequate attention.

Further Reading

Gilbert C. Meilaender examines the renewed interest in virtues in *The Theory and Practice of Virtue* (Notre Dame, Ind.: University of Notre Dame Press, 1984). He focuses on the virtue of gratitude. Christina Hoff Sommers, in *Vice and Virtue in Everyday Life: Introductory Readings in Ethics* (San Diego: Harcourt Brace, 1985), put together a collection of essays by both classic and contemporary writers on courage, compassion, wisdom, generosity, honor, and respect. Volume 13 of the *Midwest Studies in Philosophy, Ethical Theory: Character and Virtue*, edited by Peter A. French, Theodore E. Uehling, Jr., and Howard K. Wettstein, is an excellent collection of contemporary writings on virtue and character. James Wallace's *Virtues and Vices* (Ithaca, N.Y.: Cornell University Press, 1978) explores ways to identify the presence of a virtuous disposition.

The collection of essays *Explorations in Feminist Ethics* (Bloomington: Indiana University Press, 1992), edited by Eve Browning Cole and Susan Coultrap-McQuin, surveys a wide range of views on the feminist perspective in ethics. Mary Jeanne Larrabee's edited collection, *An Ethic of Care: Feminist and Interdisciplinary Perspectives* (New York: Routledge, 1993), centers around the debate over care versus justice and includes African-American perspectives. *Ethics: A Feminist Reader* (Cambridge: Blackwell, 1992), edited by Elizabeth Frazer, Jennifer Hornsby, and Sabina Lovibond, provides a thorough collection of readings on the relation between gender and ethical theory.

Endnotes

1. Elizabeth Anscombe, "Modern Moral Philosophy, " *Philosophy* 33 (1958): 1-19
2. N. J. H. Dent, *The Moral Psychology of the Virtues* (1984), pp. 32–33.
3. Michael Stocker, "The Schizophrenia of Modern Ethical Theories," *Journal of Philosophy* 73 (1976): 453–466.
4. N. J. H. Dent, *The Moral Psychology of the Virtues* (Cambridge: Cambridge University Press, 1984).
5. Ibid., p. 30.
6. Ibid., p. 30.
7. Philippa Foot, *Virtues and Vices* (Berkeley: University of California Press, 1978).
8. Aristotle, *The Nicomachean Ethics*, trans. J. A. K. Thomson (Baltimore: Penguin Books, 1955), p. 66 (1107a).
9. Mary Ellen Waithe, ed., *A History of Women Philosophers* (Dordrecht: Kluwer Academic Publishers, 1991).
10. Sarah Lucia Hoagland, *Lesbian Ethics: Toward New Value* (Palo Alto, Calif.: Institute of Lesbian Studies, 1988).
11. Alison M. Jaggar, "Feminist Ethics: Projects, Problems, Prospects," in *Feminist Ethics*, ed. Claudia Card (Lawrence: University Press of Kansas, 1991), p. 95.
12. Annette C. Baier, "Whom Can Women Trust?" in *Feminist Ethics*, ed. Claudia Card (Lawrence: University Press of Kansas, 1991), p. 233.
13. See, for example, Nel Noddings, *Caring: A Feminine Approach to Ethics and Moral Education* (Berkeley: University of California Press, 1984), p. 88.
14. Carol Gilligan, *In a Different Voice: Psychological Theory and Women's Development* (Cambridge: Harvard University Press, 1982).
15. Ibid., p. 18.
16. Ibid., p. 149.

17. Nel Noddings, *Caring: A Feminine Approach to Ethics and Moral Education* (Berkeley: University of California Press, 1984).
18. Ibid., p. 46.
19. Ibid., pp. 117–18.
20. Annette C. Baier, "What Do Women Want in a Moral Theory," *Nous* 19 (1985): 56.

6

Moral Rules

6.1 The Status of Moral Rules

In the preceding chapters we have investigated theories that rejected or assigned to a secondary status moral rules and moral principles. Those positions support widely held aspects of moral experience, and indeed try to make these into the whole of morality. The particularist focuses on unaided, intuitive judgments, while relativists reject the universality of rules and principles, opting for local judgments based on conventions and folkways. Other theories claim that a refined view of human character, supporting those who are able to make proper moral judgments, is the base for moral inquiry. Philosophers have found faults as well as strengths in these views. In this chapter we begin to turn our attention toward those who claim that the weaknesses of the viewpoints we have previously explored can be corrected by use of moral rules and principles. Furthermore, many of these theorists believe that moral experience, insofar as it is valid, can be completely expressed by rules and principles, and that these can be learned and applied by almost everyone. We will evaluate these theories, attempting to find their strengths and weaknesses. We will find both, which suggests that a moral theory based solely on rules or principles is inadequate but that theories that ignore rules and principles miss a crucial ingredient in moral decision making.

Particularists object to the abstract nature of moral rules and principles, claiming that concrete situations are enormously complex. Relativists are willing to accept rules and principles, or any other type of moral requirement, provided they are based in a local way of doing things. Many philosophers have rejected both paths by claiming that particularists fail to understand the value and the influence of universal moral rules. We do use moral rules to make moral decisions, and, as we have seen, we often use moral rules, albeit implicitly, to defend our moral judgments. (Do you agree with this

119

claim?) In short, moral rules are used by most of us, much of the time, to solve moral problems. Almost all the moral problems we face have a central core, some main ingredient, that is the object of some moral rule. For example, if Jones promises to Smith to do some action A, then whether to do A should become part of Jones's moral decision making. This claim can be universalized: no matter who makes the promise to whom, doing the promised act ought to be accounted for in moral decision making. The fact that promising in general leads to moral obligations, and is thus a moral consideration, makes a moral rule about promising generally applicable.

Rules may be precise enough to be applicable and may address the moral core of a situation succinctly and compellingly. The rule theorist may agree that real situations are complex, even enormously complex, but even so a few features can direct moral judgment. We look for general features in historical situations to explain why a war began or why a recession ended, even though such circumstances are more complex than the background environment of most personal moral problems. Rule theorists believe that we can, with the succinct use of rules, adequately cover the ground of moral decision making, but in doing this, they limit the moral domain to the features of life actually covered by rules, a limitation many philosophers find extreme.

Moral rule theorists stand opposed to relativists because some rules are applicable across societies and cultures. For example, a society in which harm and deceit are widespread and accepted is a morally bad society. Rule theorists think the universally binding nature of moral rules is a strength, an essential part of moral experience, and not a weakness. They agree that morality is social, but argue that moral rules are the common, necessary cement in all social life.

Rule theorists argue that relativists cannot adequately defend against the charge of bias. A caste system, no matter how well ingrained, is morally improper and biased, even if supported by local custom. We can have more confidence in something when it is more widely accepted than local practices; moral rules have side support in many different places and at many different times. When many people from different places accept the same thing, we believe that *local* bias is not a factor. Moral rules that are widely accepted express basic moral demands, and in this way diverse people find significant commonality.

Although the statements made above about moral rules apply equally well, perhaps better, to moral principles, rule theorists believe that principles are not properly used in moral deliberations. First of all, basic principles are vague. They believe that a principle like "Do no harm" gives inadequate instruction, but a moral rule like "Do not steal" is much more precise and clear enough to be readily applied in most circumstances. If we apply the principle against harm, we may believe that stealing in some circumstances does no harm or that it does real good. By allowing us to speculate on what causes harm, how to determine harm, what kinds of harms are more hurtful (is physical harm more harmful than offensive behavior?), we find ourselves without adequate moral guidance.

Rule theorists want to limit speculation about morally proper behavior. Morality is social; we need some social guarantees so that people will generally avoid undesirable kinds of behavior. If we invite a guest into our house, we do not want that guest to steal our goods, even if we don't realize something is gone (so that the guest might think no harm is done), or even if our guest is poorer than we are (so that perhaps some good is done). We want the secure enjoyment of our goods, so we have laws and moral prohibitions against stealing. Moral prohibition, like the moral rule against stealing, is a needed complement to the law against stealing. Often the moral prohibition is more compelling than the law because laws are sometimes difficult to enforce and moral prohibitions are often generally followed. (Consider whether this claim is true. Give examples from current news events to test it.)

Those who believe in the value of moral rules often believe that they are the only valid part of our moral experience—that all of moral experience is properly derivable from moral rules. For most rule theorists, morality provides the basic glue of social life. It is intended to prohibit the things that are typically destructive of social interaction while leaving us free to do whatever else we care to do. These prohibitions, expressed in moral rules, give the negative bounds of actions, describing the types of things we may not do. This limits the moral domain. Such theorists believe that moral rules are *negative* in orientation because they simply tell us what not to do, not what to do. A negative approach is thought to have the virtue of giving universal and clear guidance. A positive rule, like "Give to charity," is indefinite; it presents an *imperfect duty*. It does not tell us how much to give, what charities to give to, or when to give. "Do not steal," by contrast, is a precise duty that always applies to all. All people can obey negatively oriented rules. But many people cannot obey positive commands; for example, a poor person may not be able to give to charity. For these reasons, rule theories tend to state rules negatively, making prohibitions rather than general positive requirements.

For the rule theorist, a negative morality provides the best basis on which we can get along, no matter where we live or where we were raised. It tells us what we may not do but otherwise leaves us free to pursue any positive action we see as fit. When morality is extended beyond a small domain of actions, these theorists insist, it robs people of their moral freedom, imposes the will of some on others, and cannot be rationally defended. We can defend negative moral rules because without them life would be very difficult for all, but, they argue, the use of positive responsibilities makes life easier for some at the cost of others. (Can you explain why positive responsibilities can be thought to have this effect?)

Study Questions 6.1

1. We already mentioned moral rules like "Do not steal." Make a fuller list of moral rules (perhaps ten). Do you think these rules are morally binding on all? Are they reasonable? Do they have exceptions? Are your rules negatively oriented? Are they widely accepted?
2. Suppose someone believed that society doesn't need a moral rule against stealing. Give the best argument you can think of in favor of that position. (Perhaps your argument centers on the use of a moral principle, or virtue, or cultural relativism.) Does the argument work? Can it be refuted? Explain what you take to be the best refutation of the original argument against the prohibition of stealing.
3. Suppose the rule considered in question 2 deals with murder. Could the same argument be used against this rule?
4. Consider these rules:
   a. Do not commit adultery.
   b. Do not break promises.
   c. Do not steal.
   Which rule is the most difficult to defend? Which is the easiest to defend? Are any of these rules positively oriented?
5. Do virtue theorists and feminists reject the foundational status of moral rules? If so, how would they answer the charge of rule theorists that without moral rules social life would be difficult? Do virtue theorists and feminists impose positive responsibilities that go beyond the negative orientation of most rule theorists?
6. Suppose "Do not break a promise" and "Do not steal" are both proper moral rules, and also suppose that someone promises to steal money for a needy friend. An *extreme rule theorist* believes that all valid moral judgments can be expressed in moral rules. Does this conflict of rules go counter to that belief, or can a rule theorist answer such conflict at the level of rules, say by making one rule more important than another? Does this conflict show that negative moral rules cannot always be followed? If your answer is "yes," could this be explained by the contention that "Do not break a promise" implicitly introduces positive obligations that cannot always be kept? If this is so, should "Do not break a promise" be considered a negative rule?

6.2 Bernard Gert's System of Moral Rules

Bernard Gert, a contemporary philosopher, is a rule theorist who contends that morality is basically summed up in a list of moral rules.[1] He claims that moral rules are definite, negatively stated, and universal. Each rule in his list is *rationally* acceptable to everyone. This does not mean that all people actually accept all moral rules, but that if people are rational then they would accept his list of moral rules. (As soon as a claim like this is made, we must pay special attention to its defense. Think of how you might argue that all rational people would accept basic moral rules.) According to Gert, rational people want others to follow these rules because without them life would be intolerable.

For Gert, the American philosopher Kurt Baier has presented the best general way to defend a moral system in *From the Moral Point of View.*[2] Baier asks us to imagine a world in which moral prohibitions are not generally obeyed. Would we want to live in such a world? All of us, Baier claims, want to live in a world where people do behave morally. Rational people want a morally good world, because without it none of us could realize our life goals.

According to this view, rational people need and want moral rules. But what kind of rules should be accepted? Gert proposes a deceptively simple answer: all rules that all rational people would accept. This leads us to wonder what rational people would accept—indeed, what it means to be rational. In other words, Gert needs to offer an account of *rationality.* Gert rejects the standard account, that a rational person seeks to satisfy as many personal *preferences* (the things people rate more highly than other things) as possible. This standard definition is typically coupled with the denial of any reasonable way to critique personal preferences. In the standard account, as long as preferences are consistent, it is rational to satisfy as many preferences as we can. Gert rejects this view by arguing that rational persons might not attempt to gain all they can. Even if I prefer more, I might decide to settle for less, without giving a reason. Gert's point is that, contrary to the standard notion of rationality, such a rejection is not irrational.

In Gert's own account, rationality is a negative concept (like his conception of rules). A rational person does not do *irrational* things; a person is not irrational for failing to act to gain desired ends. That is, a failure to optimize the satisfaction of personal preferences is not irrational. Some things are plainly irrational: without adequate reason, a rational person does not desire to die, to suffer pain, or to be a slave. To do so is irrational. To be rational, under Gert's negatively oriented conception, is to avoid doing such irrational things. He uses this definition to defend his list of moral rules. A moral rule is acceptable if it is irrational not to accept it.

(Consider carefully what this means.)

Based on Gert's notion of rationality and on the claim that all moral rules must be rational, Gert is bound to present a negatively oriented list of moral rules. The desire not to be a saint is not irrational, so any moral rule or principle requiring saintly actions could be rejected. Similarly, it is rational not to give to charity or not to care for others, so it is not irrational to reject a rule demanding that we give to charity. Rules demanding special actions go beyond the requirements that Baier's general test—about a possible world without such a morality—would endorse. Rationality demands rules against killing and against stealing; only an irrational person would accept a world where these acts are commonplace.

Gert presents the following rules as the core of morality:
1. Don't kill.
2. Don't cause pain.
3. Don't disable.
4. Don't deprive people of freedom.
5. Don't deprive people of pleasure.
6. Don't deceive.
7. Keep your promises.
8. Don't cheat.
9. Obey the law.
10. Do your duty.

Many of these rules seem to fit well with Gert's conception of a negative morality, rules it would be irrational to reject. But are all these rules acceptable on the grounds that they would be irrational to reject? We may be least comfortable with rule 10, the only one that seems at first sight to involve open-ended positive requirements, because we expect rules to present negative bounds, prohibitions rather than positive responsibilities. Doing your duty is indefinite: what is your duty? But other rules also seem to demand too much, given his restrictions concerning irrationality, because they are overly general. How do we deprive people of pleasure? Does a boring college professor deprive people of pleasure? If so, does a boring teacher violate moral rules? When a friend does not want to go with you to a show, he or she may deprive you of pleasure. Does your friend violate a moral rule?

Moral rules are meant to be specific and definite, not principles in disguise. Gert does not intend to use his list of rules to make difficult positive moral requirements, but perhaps a list of negative rules fulfilling this intention leaves out too much of the moral domain. This may be why Gert includes indefinite rules like rules 4, 5, and 10, which may be implicit appeals to a very demanding morality. Aggressively interpreted, these rules go beyond Gert's aim to present a limited moral code that sets social constraints on the actions we should perform and allows, after that, all we want to do.

Gert's rule 9 is controversial. Do we have a moral responsibility to obey the law? Good reasons can be given one way or the other. Law may be a public expression of the basic demands of citizenship; it is a basic way to fix expectations about how other people will behave in a society. As such, it has moral standing. But it may be dictatorial, as it is in many places, or imposed without regard to the general good, as is true in even more places. Deciding whether laws are morally proper is a complex matter, so a simple rule to obey the law, presented as a basic obligation, does not do the job.

The criticism of the rule to obey the law indicates a basic fault in Gert's approach: it is unable to respond to the complexity of the moral experience. Instead of giving a careful analysis of rules and the justifications for them, he starts by listing what he takes to be irrational desires. He is often right about their irrationality, but he does not give a good indication about how something makes the list as irrational. When we object to a moral rule, the apparent appeal is to what all people may rationally endorse. This is as controversial as his notion of rationality, defined by a list of irrational items. Rationality is a contentious concept. The link between morality and rationality is not clear. One way to think about morality is that it puts limits on the rational pursuit of personal interests. Morality is social in nature; social constraints cannot be derived from individual rationality, no matter how it is defined. (We examine the relationship between social constraints and individual rationality more fully in Chapter 7.)

Study Questions 6.2

1. (For class discussion.) Gert's use of "irrationality" claims that apparently irrational acts may be justified by giving good reasons. Does this notion of giving good reasons appear circular? That is, is a good reason defined by some notion of a standard that rational people would accept?
2. Compare to Gert's list the list of moral rules you selected in answering study question 6.1.1. Evaluate each list. Which seems more adequate?
3. Is Gert's list of rules meant to be the minimal constraints rational people would want? Would you rather have a world in which rules 1–10 are supported or one in which they are violated? Perhaps you would prefer a world where a different list of moral rules holds. Can we know whether we have the "best" list of rules?
4. (For class discussion.) Gert does not consider the social dimension of human personality. We are all brought up in society, and we are interdependent to a degree. Are negative rules adequate to solve

moral problems given that harm is often done through social systems and through lack of opportunity stemming from a person's position in a social system? Are demands for positive actions morally justified by Gert's moral rules if those actions are required to avoid harm? To do one's duty?

5. Suppose someone claims that rule 7, "Keep your promises," is not a moral rule. How can Gert defend its inclusion in the list? Can you give good reasons for believing that it should not be considered a moral rule?

6. Compare the Ten Commandments to Gert's list of 10 rules. How similar are they? Which list is more specific? Is either list more negatively oriented? (A negative list of rules tells us what *not* to do, while a positive list instructs us to perform specified actions.)

6.3 Defending Moral Rules

A rule morality is distinguished from a moral system based on principles by the specificity of rules; moral rules are fairly well-defined, like keeping promises, while principles cover broad basic concerns, like "Avoid harm." A morality based on principles reduces all moral obligations and evaluations to a small number of basic ingredients, usually one or two. These basic ingredients, such as attaining happiness or promoting freedom, are independent in that no one of them can be reduced to, or derived from, the others. A rule morality proposes a longer list of basic obligations and standards. Ten or more rules may be listed, and the rule theorist may believe that the list does not include all the moral rules, but merely gives examples of the types of rules to be included. Regardless of the length of the list, none of the rules should be reducible to the rest. For example, Gert has a rule, "Don't deceive." If lying is a form of deceit, we can derive "Do not lie" from this rule. Thus, we would not want to add "Do not lie" to Gert's list because it is not an independent rule. Gert also has the rule "Keep your promises," which some may believe to be derivable from the rule about deceit. But this is not the case: we may make a sincere promise, then find that some other activity—say, helping a parent—is more important than keeping our promise. The promisor may even inform the promisee that the promise will not be kept at the time the decision to help the parent is made. This behavior does not violate the rule against deceit, but it does violate the rule against promising, so we conclude that the two rules are independent. (Do you agree that the failure to keep a promise in this case does not deceive? Can you argue that it does involve *some* deceit? If so, is the rule about promising derivable from the rule about deceit?) So we do have one good standard about what should *not* be on a basic list of rules: rules reducible to other rules.

But how do we know which rules should be on the list? Those who advocate rules as the basic ingredient of the moral experience propose several theories about where rules come from and how they get their legitimacy.

(1) Some people argue that the moral rules come from God, and that we know the rules through revelation. This defense provides a religious, not philosophical, view of the origin of moral rules. Philosophically, the view is problematic for those outside a particular faith. Many religions exist and have different concepts of revelation, appeal to different sets of rules, and interpret rules differently. Philosophical problems stem from the fact that many religions claim support for different rules by appeal to the same source: God's will. The ultimate appeal is often to faith, although faith may be backed by philosophical argumentation. But philosophy, by its nature, is willing to question faith.

Because of the variety of different and conflicting beliefs about what God wills, some believers must be wrong even though they have faith in what they believe. This does not mean that faith is always mistaken. But philosophers also argue that if God wills specific moral rules, we would still be under obligation to question whether those rules were proper. Suppose God is evil and wills evil rules. How can the sole fact that God wills them make them the proper rules? A religious orientation would reject such reasoning; because God is all-wise and all-good, anyone who believes God's commands are evil would be wrong. Our wisdom and our goodness pale in comparison to God's. Again, this view, which may be correct, appeals to faith, and not to philosophical argumentation.

(2) Cultural relativists believe that rules come from social practice. From a global perspective, this would make moral rules arbitrary; different people in different places would have different rules based on some accidental past circumstances, perhaps including the will of a dictator. But as we discussed in Chapter 4, people have also insisted that rules serve basic functions. So although rules may diverge from society to society, they may be judged within a society by the extent to which they coordinate social activity, or by the extent to which they are stable and supported and genuinely express the character of a people. Under this view, we know what the moral rules are by examining a society's practices. Cultural relativism, as we already observed, does not adequately deal with cultural conflict. And moral rules are usually considered to be universally binding, so a defense based on local culture seems to miss the point.

(3) The third view about the origin and support of moral rules is supported by Gert: moral rules are best supported by human rationality. If we have a solid conception of what is rational, we may be able to use that view to

formulate a set of moral rules. For example, suppose all people are rational according to the "received view." This view, which Gert rejects, holds that people act rationally when, and only when, they seek to get the most of what they desire or prefer. Each person has constraints—limited time, limited money, limited talent. Given those constraints, rational people try to get as much as possible of the things they prefer. This definition of rationality may preclude the existence of an acceptable set of moral rules. Why should people support rules that limit the extent to which they can get what they want? Why not steal, or even kill, to get what we want? Nothing in the standard definition of rationality says that we should not do those things. David Gauthier[3] argues that this perception is mistaken. We do need each other's help. We do need to cooperate. If moral rules help us to cooperate, and thereby help us to get more of what we want, then rational people would be willing to be bound by rules. This is so even if, on a special occasion, more could be gained by breaking the rules. However, we all know that the other may gain by breaking rules, so we may all rationally decide to bind ourselves, in advance, to rules, because in the long run this may be the way to get more.

Many thinkers object to this line of defense for moral rules. It runs into the problem of the *free-rider,* a person who gains by the cooperation of others while failing to cooperate himself or herself. A skillful free-rider may support rules in public, condemn others who do not obey the rules, and yet, for his or her own advantage, break the rules in secret. If this person is good at deceit, he or she may rationally deny the moral force of any list of rules. Furthermore, other thinkers object to the notion that morality is bound up with this artificial received view on rationality. The received view depends on the existence of an isolated self; it rejects a social self, with basic social ties and extended, often amorphous sympathy with others. People do not have individually defined, stable preferences but instead respond to social fads, social customs, and social evaluations. (If these facts are true, how can they be used to deny the moral base given to the received view of rationality?) Finally, some thinkers object to basing morality on the received view of rationality because it is the antithesis of morality. Morality is a social constraint on self-regarding action. At its best, the defense of morality on the basis of a self-centered notion of rationality is amoral. At its worst, it supports immoral action.

As we mentioned, Kurt Baier challenges us to consider whether we would prefer a world with moral rules to one without. Most would agree that moral rules are generally beneficial. Gauthier and those who support a moral system on the basis of the received view of rationality attempt to generalize this benefit by making it a requirement of morality. Although general benefit may partially validate the use of moral rules, that defense cannot adequately address the problem of the free-rider, or the social identity of human beings. Moral experience is compelling in its rejection of the general, exclusive pursuit of self-interest.

(4) The last defense we examine claims that no adequate reasons can be given in favor of the moral rules. We simply know, perhaps by intuition or even by social conditioning, that a rule is proper. That promises should not be broken is self-evident. If someone argues that keeping promises is not rational or that better consequences follow without the duty to keep promises, we may respond by saying that we have a self-evident duty to keep promises. By careful reflection on what we believe, we will understand that we are more convinced of this duty than we are of the reasons offered against it, or, indeed, offered in its favor.

As you might expect, many philosophers reject self-evident or intuitive support for moral rules. Intuitions differ from person to person and, if they exist, may be socially caused. Yet we do have strong beliefs that we cannot adequately defend. Often we find ourselves responding emotionally when we encounter behavior that breaks moral rules. This emotional or intuitive response is tapped by literature and movies. We know that the treatment the "Elephant Man" received was wrong; we may have more confidence in the belief that it was wrong than in any reasons we may offer for why it was wrong. We may be amazed by or shocked at someone who can view such inhumane treatment and believe it morally proper. Regardless of where such apparent intuitions come from, some reactions against immorality are widely shared and are a significant part of our moral experience. In the end perhaps the best defense of a list of moral rules is the fact that many people, at different times and places, have accepted such rules as a basic part of moral experience.

We have examined some basic ways of defending moral rules. Each of these defenses assumes that moral rules are primary in one way or another. They may be founded on rationality, God's will, the demands of social life, or intuitions. But we cannot deduce the moral rules from these considerations because we do not know what rules people intuitively support, or what rules God wills, or what rules all rational people accept.

Another defense of the moral rules may come from the use of principles, but this defense would undermine the autonomy of the moral rules. In this section we have been examining a rule approach to morality, one that rejects the use of basic principles. A rule-oriented approach accepts rules as the foundation of moral experience. However, some approaches combine the use of rules and principles; such views will be explored below.

Study Questions 6.3

1. Many people do accept moral rules like the rules presented by Gert. Why are they accepted? Are the reasons people accept moral laws the same as those offered by philosophers? Which explanation of the origin and status of moral rules, presented in this section, is the strongest? Does this defense help you to select the best list of rules?
2. Can the defenses for a list of moral rules be combined into one strengthened position? For example, can we start with moral rules presented by religious faith, and then modify the list by an appeal to human rationality (or vice versa)?
3. (For class discussion.) Suppose one of the defenses is correct? Does this mean that the moral rules are not basic in moral experience? For example, if all the rules can be derived from rationality, then rationality, not the rules, may be the basis of moral reasoning. Furthermore, we may derive principles and individual judgments from rationality. So if rationality is an adequate basis, we may not need moral rules at all. Critique the following: if moral rules are adequately supported, they are not needed.
4. Considering the ingredients in the moral domain, which position on the best defense of moral rules is the most inclusive?
5. Can you propose a defense of moral rules not presented in this section?

6.4 *Prima Facie* Duties

Rule morality is not monolithic; different philosophers have proposed different sets of rules. That the lists are different should lead us to take more seriously the ways such lists are defended because knowing the proper defense may help us choose the proper list. We already presented Gert's list, and you likely know about the Ten Commandments. Now we add one more list not only because it is interesting and morally instructive, but also because it aggressively introduces vague positive requirements. A theorist who lists positive requirements is forced to openly face the eventuality that rules will conflict.

The following list is taken from Sir William David Ross,[4] the Oxford philosopher who died in 1971. Ross believes that rules are not absolutely binding; they couldn't be because they often conflict. Instead, they are binding unless rules conflict or unless good reasons can be found to act against them. They are, in short, binding *prima facie*. This means they are binding at first sight, without taking into consideration conflicting circumstances, but when the time comes to follow the rules, we need to be aware of the ways our obligations are mitigated or overruled.

Ross proposes six basic, or independent, types of *prima facie* duties. (1) Duties to behave according to our agreements or in reaction to our previous wrongdoing. These rules state obligations that we create by our past actions: we are morally required to keep promises and make proper reparations. (2) When others help us, we are sometimes morally required to do something for them in return, to reciprocate in order to show proper gratitude. (3) We must be just. For example, people should be rewarded according to their merits. (4) We are also duty bound to help others in need. This is the moral requirement to act with beneficence. (5) We are all under the moral obligation to perfect ourselves, intellectually and morally. (6) Finally, we should not harm another person.

These types of rules are less precise, or cover more types of actions, than Gert's rules; for that reason they better account for more of the moral experience. But in their vagueness they are more difficult to evaluate. Do we really have a duty to improve ourselves intellectually? Why not make it a duty to improve our social graces, or our looks, our musical ability, or our ability to ride horseback? Ross and his colleagues at Oxford spent considerable time and energy improving themselves intellectually, but is that a *prima facie* moral requirement? Aren't we morally free to decide how to improve ourselves, or whether to improve ourselves? That freedom is as much a part of moral experience as the way we morally praise those who do try to improve themselves.

Ross has little to say about what we should do when moral rules conflict. An adequate moral theory should instruct us on the resolution of moral conflicts. This means that we should have a sense of a priority order among rules, of which rules tend to be followed when conflict arises. Perhaps we would have priorities dictated by circumstances, claiming that certain rules make better sense in certain circumstances. For example, deceit may be worse among friends than among strangers. We might say that a medical practitioner has more obligation to give proper care to a patient than to keep a promise. (Do you agree with these last two claims?)

Better yet, we may also decide that when conflict arises, we should attempt to find ways to mediate it. This is a *mutuality principle:* seek ways to fulfill as many obligations as possible, or seek to avoid conflict among duties. Socially, we should, for example, try to find ways to help others while avoiding conflicting duties. Proper day care may help a parent to fill the role of a teacher and to raise a child properly. A health care practitioner has an obligation to seek ways to meet obligations, to keep promises, and to care for patients. This mutuality principle may seem like part of a list of moral rules because rules implicitly demand that we attempt to obey all of them. But this is mistaken. Conflicts are often socially caused, based on social structures, or individually caused, based on prior choices. The mutuality principle insists that before particular conflicts arise, we try to find ways that tend to reduce conflict in general as much as possible. This sort of action, designing social structures and choosing in advance to avoid moral conflict, is not typically presented as an aspect of rule morality.

Moral rules, by themselves, cannot tell us which takes priority over the others. (Explain why.) Once we take seriously the need to order moral rules, we must rely on other aspects of the moral experience to help us set up priorities. These other aspects, principles, social roles, ideals, and the like will then stand on at least an equal footing with moral rules. In this way, in order to set priorities, a fuller morality is required. If this claim about setting priorities among rules is correct, then a rule morality, by itself, is inadequate, and so the use of moral rules needs to be supplemented. Rule-utilitarianism, which we examine in the next section, indicates one way to do this.

Study Questions 6.4

1. How would a particularist or a virtue theorist respond to the claim that moral rules are binding in a *prima facie* way? Would the particularist accept that the *prima facie* status allows the complexity of particular cases to play an adequate role in moral decision making?
2. (For class discussion.) Ross claims that we can identify moral rules intuitively, but that the intuitions involved are the intuitions of the "best" people. If an intuition belongs to a very good person, does this give the intuition a stronger moral standing? Is the reference to the "best" people circular? That is, do we identify the best people by the extent to which they follow moral rules? If so, how can the intuitions of the best people be used to identify the moral rules? Can we identify the best people without going beyond a rule-based morality?
3. If a duty is only *prima facie*, does this mean that it is not really a duty? This question hinges on what it means to have a "duty." Does it mean to try diligently to do something, or does it mean something should be done if possible? Explain your answer.
4. Suppose an action is supported by two rules but conflicts with one. Describe a real or imaginary circumstance where this is so. In the rule-centered position, should the fact that an action is supported by two separate rules give it a stronger moral weight?

6.5 Rule-Utilitarianism

Utilitarianism is thought of as a one-principle theory: that we should always act to produce the most good. As such it stands at the antithesis of both particularism and rule theory. That one principle is intended to guide all human action and to be used to make all moral evaluations. The dominant form of utilitarianism states that we are morally obligated to choose the action that will contribute the greatest happiness to the greatest number of people.

Suppose we have only two choices: to lie or not to lie. The utilitarian would then instruct us to lie if that action contributes, on balance, more happiness, and not to lie if avoiding the lie contributes, on balance, more happiness. In theory, every act should be directly evaluated to determine how much happiness is produced, and we should do the action that, out of all our alternatives, produces the most happiness. And happiness is the only consideration that matters. If any instance of lying, breaking promises, killing, or any other apparently reprehensible action causes more happiness, on balance, it should be done.

This doctrine is called *act-utilitarianism* because every action is to be individually evaluated. Philosophers have frequently pointed out that act-utilitarianism has many serious weaknesses. For example, we may have difficulty in determining how much happiness an action will produce, and the burden of calculating happiness for each action would be enormous. Perhaps more importantly, act-utilitarianism is placed in the paradoxical position of recommending, as *morally required*, actions that almost all people would recognize as *immoral*, such as murder, when this produces more happiness.

As a result of such problems, some utilitarians, chief among them the Oxford moral philosopher R. M. Hare, turn to a two-tiered theory called *rule-utilitarianism*. Although the balance of happiness is the ultimate moral value, the way to go after it may be *indirect*. A two-tiered theory would evaluate types of actions generally—such as murder, telling the truth, breaking promises, remaining faithful in a marriage, caring for children, respecting parents, punishing the innocent—to determine whether doing these *types* of actions produces the greatest happiness. Since types of actions are evaluated, rather than individual actions, many people need to be considered in such calculations: should all in a society be allowed to cheat? If a moral prohibition against cheating produces more happiness, then rule-utilitarians would support the moral rule "Don't cheat." If not, the rule would be rejected.

Rule-utilitarianism is a *quasi-rule-oriented* system: rules play a crucial role, but the system is based on a principle. The basic utilitarian principle is used, with facts about social interaction, to derive rules. (Be sure you understand how this is done.) Once the rules are in place, no direct calculation of utility is needed. The rule must be followed even if the individual actions produce more pain than pleasure.

In his recent work, the contemporary American philosopher Richard Brandt added a new twist to rule-utilitarianism.[5] Rule-utilitarians hold that rules should be evaluated to determine whether they produce more happiness or more pain for the greatest number of people. But making such evaluations is a difficult thing to do, especially since judgments have to be made about the future: will this rule, as it is applied in the future, create more happiness or pain? Evaluations are about the future of a rule, but we need to look to the past to determine which types of actions will produce happiness. Assuming the future is like the past, which is always to some degree incorrect, we may with confidence predict that the same types of actions will produce similar results. Since in many ways the present is unlike the past, the reliability of the past as a proper guide to action may be questioned.

Brandt hopes to solve problems involved in selecting the proper rules by accepting current moral rules as a starting point. The current system of moral rules has, after all, survived many decades of social evaluation. And the way things are now done has a moral standing because people rely on such behavior. Brandt calls the current system of rules an *optimal moral system*. We are obliged to obey that system, but he adds that this system, though it is the best system we now have, may be reformed. Utilitarian goals are already achieved to some degree because the current moral system, to survive through social evolution, must be producing a good deal of human happiness. But with the evaluation of the current system, the utilitarian principle comes into direct play. Reform comes from a direct application of the utilitarian standard to the current moral system. When the system is reformed, the new optimal moral system should be followed.

It is unclear how the system gets reformed and by whom, but we may presume that however social rules are selected, the process may be speeded along by direct appeal to the utilitarian principle. When the principle is used successfully, the new moral code, now slightly changed, must be followed. As the system is increasingly modified, and taught to children and others, the moral code becomes progressively better; it should approach a list of rules that will actually produce the greatest happiness.

Rule-utilitarians believe that they can avoid the basic problems in act-utilitarianism. Individual calculations of each act are no longer needed; by following rules one is relieved of the burden of constant evaluation. Also counterexamples are avoided. We no longer need to decide whether an individual murder will produce more unhappiness; the rule against murdering is firm because murder, generally speaking, produces much unhappiness. Some rules that we now accept, like old-fashioned views on sexual morality, may be rejected by the utilitarian calculation. But most rules we inherit are not likely to lead to counterexamples. (If you agree, explain why.) So the rule-utilitarian believes that if a two-tiered theory is followed, a set of rules could be developed that avoids key utilitarian problems and produces, in the long run, the greatest happiness for the greatest number.

Rule-utilitarianism is often thought of as a compromise. We would prefer to have each action produce as much happiness as possible, but that is not feasible because it involves herculean knowledge and effort. So we settle for the evaluation of a system of imposed rules. A rule cannot be broken for the sake of more happiness because the only acceptable utilitarian calculations are about rules.

In *Moral Thinking*,[6] R. M. Hare argues in favor of a two-tiered system that does not impose a set of moral rules because in any application a rule might not be followed. He recognizes that because of lack of time, ignorance of circumstances, or inability to make proper moral calculations, people may need to follow proper rules, rules that do tend to produce more happiness than pain. But ideally one would make all moral choices by putting oneself in the place of all concerned, and then making moral decisions in a way that optimizes everyone's satisfaction by taking into account the strength of each person's preferences. Putting oneself into everyone's place is required, Hare believes, by the logic of moral statements; if something is obligatory, it is obligatory for everyone in similar circumstances. If we do not take all into account, we are not using moral terms correctly; we are engaged not in moral thinking, but perhaps in prudential or self-interested thinking. Hare believes that by appreciating the perspective of each person involved, he meets the universality required in moral theory, and by optimizing the satisfaction of preferences by taking into account the weight of each, he meets utilitarian demands.

At this level where no rule is followed but direct calculations are made, people engage in a "higher" form of moral reasoning that is especially appropriate when rules conflict. For example, I may find that I have good reasons not to keep a promise made to my children—say, to take them to the zoo. To keep my promise may mean that I cannot keep another moral commitment—for instance, visiting a sick relative. To decide what to do, I place myself in the position of each person involved and decide to do what optimally satisfies preferences. Normally, without conflict, I simply keep the promise, staying on the lower level of moral reasoning, even though, ideally, I would calculate the satisfaction involved in all moral decisions.

Hare's position is a compromise; he recognizes that we cannot always make proper moral calculations. But he does not attempt to impose a system of rules, allowing that rules may sometimes be violated. Hare's position, allowing for the possibility of direct calculation of happiness in each act, may simply leave us with many of the problems of act-utilitarianism. He does insist that we take all into account, but the decision depends on the strength of preferences, and so some people may be used for the gain of others in unusual circumstances, and this may lead to counterexamples. In effect, Hare's position might not allow rules a firm enough standing.

A stronger role for rules is more of a compromise. Compromises often seem unsatisfactory from every point of view. Many utilitarians find a strict rule perspective to be basically flawed and present the following dilemma to show why. Suppose we know that a lie would produce more pleasure than pain. We cannot argue that making an exception does not produce more happiness. The rule-utilitarian must claim that by generally following rules, without exceptions, more happiness is produced, on balance. But by hypothesis, we now are asking what we should do when we know that, all things considered, an action that goes against a rule will produce more happiness. The act-utilitarian cannot understand how a rule-utilitarian can insist on following the rule in such a case. After all, both act- and rule-utilitarians want more happiness for all. Allowing clear exceptions, against the rule-utilitarian's view, seems to permit increased happiness.

In effect, this criticism makes the claim that an exceptionless system is plainly too rigid. Exceptional cases do occur, and morally speaking, we should be allowed to use discretion in dealing with them. On the other side, rule theorists, like Gert and Ross, reject the evaluation of moral rules on the basis of happiness. Moral rules do not serve the interests of the sum of happiness; they are partly meant to control how we act in the name of happiness. Even if breaking promises produces the greatest happiness, we should not break our promises.

Study Questions 6.5

1. Evaluate Gert's moral rules by determining whether they produce more happiness or more pain. Do the same with Ross's list of *prima facie* moral duties.
2. (For class discussion.) Richard Brandt contends that the current way of doing things, pruned of egregious exceptions, has survived the test of social scrutiny, and is thus a good approximation of the optimal moral code. Evaluate Brandt's claim.
3. R. M. Hare argues that a two-tiered moral theory is required because of human ignorance. That is, we do not have enough knowledge about the future to decide each case individually. If we knew all the results of any current action, we would be like gods, always able to make the right choice. But our human condition means that we do not know what will follow from any individual decision. But we are better at determining what *types* of actions lead to happiness, so we are often better off following general rules. Evaluate this view.
4. Can rules contain clauses indicating when they are not to be followed? For example, we might decide to allow exceptions when reasonable, obviously and clearly required, or even agreed upon by all involved as morally supportable. Would this be acceptable to rule-utilitarians?

Would such rules deflate the argument that rules are too rigid? Or would it bring us back to the problems we found in act-utilitarianism?
5. (For class discussion.) Should rules be evaluated by the utilitarian principle based on the assumption that all will follow the rule, or should rules be evaluated assuming that some people may violate the rule? In answering, consider current debates about giving condoms to teenagers or making drug sales legal.

6.6 Two Concepts of Rules

So far rules seem to be external commands: do this or don't do that. Rules always seem to have exceptions, and we can always inquire about whether they should be followed. Rules are constraints on our actions and seem to have little to do with the nature of what we do. We always have the option to choose to violate a rule.

John Rawls argued, in 1955, that rules are not always external constraints on actions. Instead, actions are sometimes defined by rules. He presents two types of rules: summary rules and practice rules. A *summary rule* is a rule of thumb that tells us that good or bad results follow from certain types of actions. For example, drinking too much alcohol typically leads to physical problems. A summary rule tells not to do certain things because they lead to bad results and to do certain things because they produce good results; these facts are known through past experience. If we want one result rather than another, a summary rule gives us advice about how to proceed. A good logic teacher notices that certain ways of explaining a technique are effective and other ways confusing. Such knowledge can be stated as a summary rule, and the rule can be followed to gain the desired result. But if circumstances are exceptional, then the rule might not be helpful. If a rule-utilitarian is talking about summary rules, he or she is mistaken in holding that rules should not be broken. When an exception arises, exceptional action may be required.

A *practice rule* is different. This sort of rule defines a type of action; if the rule is not followed, then we are not engaged in the defined activity. Consider playing chess. Suppose a mother is playing chess with her young daughter. She may decide to let the child win, or to allow taking moves over again, or even to permit exceptions for the child by letting some pieces move in unusual ways. Now the parent is no longer playing chess. She is instead teaching her daughter how to play, or perhaps just having some fun with a chess set. To play *chess*, we must obey the rules. Making exceptions to the rules is not possible. Once we do, we are no longer playing that game.

Suppose we are at a college basketball game. The home team is losing badly, so the referees, noticing the unhappiness of the spectators, decide to count all the home team's baskets at three points. This, they argue, will make the game more interesting, help motivate each team, and make the home crowd happier. They make an exception to the rules of basketball. But we all know that such exceptions, for whatever good they do, are not acceptable. When this happens, the game of basketball is given up; something else is being played.

Over the years the rules of basketball do change. Official bodies preside over the rules and sometimes change them to make the fans happier. Different rules exist in different leagues and in different levels of play. High school–level rules are different from college-level rules. This is acceptable. Practices, like basketball, may be defined in different ways in different places. And the rules may be changed, perhaps by applying principles like the utilitarian principle. What cannot happen without destroying the game as we know it is for exceptions to be made ad hoc on individual occasions. (Is this always the case? Consider games that do have flexible rules. Perhaps even basketball sometimes involves flexible rules.)

Rawls's reference to games is well taken. Games often have rigid rules, with well-defined structures for changing those rules. The rules may define the practice. And the rules may be evaluated at a higher level, thus changing the practice by producing a new set of rules that cannot be broken while the practice is pursued. But Rawls extends his notion to the moral realm. Promising, for example, is considered a practice by Rawls. Once we make a promise, it must be kept, under Rawls's view, because exceptions negate what it is to make a promise. But promises are not like chess. Promises are routinely broken, without guilt, when unexpected circumstances intrude. We have no clear rules about when a promise may be broken and when it should be kept. Because we have no clear rules about promising, we may doubt that promising is a practice. In cases where a promise is not kept, we do not say, as with games, that a type of action is no longer being engaged in. This is true even when a promise is broken, and we believe that breaking the promise is consistent with the original promise. (Explain how.)

The idea of having an exceptionless rule would be more compelling, and would bolster the case of the rule-utilitarian, if moral rules were like practice rules. But they are not. Even large-scale practices, like being a student or a parent, are filled with unexpected exceptions. Promising, like the activities involved in many other moral rules, is not a practice like being a lawyer or an elementary school teacher; promising is even more amorphous. In better-defined practices, like being a lawyer, the rules are not as well-stated as the rules of chess or other games. The analogy with games is suggestive, but ultimately the problem is to show that moral behavior is like behavior in a game. In many ways it is not, so the analogy breaks down and the attempt to support rule-utilitarianism with practice rules is unsuccessful.

Study Questions 6.6

1. In raising children, parents often act as though rules do not have exceptions: "Never talk to strangers," "Always tell the truth," and so on. Are parents wise to present moral rules to children as though they do not have exceptions?
2. Do you agree with Rawls that promising is a practice governed by rules? Explain your position.
3. Suppose the rules that rule-utilitarians support are practice rules. Does this overcome the objection that rules should have exceptions?
4. Are exceptions ever made in games like chess? Do exceptions need to be spelled out in advance, or can they be made in the middle of the game? If you argue that exceptions can be made in games, is this a rejection of Rawls's argument?

6.7 The Lessons from Rule Theorists

Rules are commonly employed in activities ranging from mathematical calculation to driving an automobile. The use of rules does make life easier. Rule theorists in ethics argue that precise formulation of moral rules can better help us guide our own behavior and can help make the behavior of others more reliable. Moral rules have been incorporated into criminal and civil codes, and without such laws we would all be in trouble. These observations suggest that particularists are wrong; moral rules do have a place in moral reasoning.

Moral rules are part of the moral experience. When they are broken, the behavior involved is likely immoral. But moral experience is not limited to moral rules. Ideals and principles, even roles and practices, may demand that we break a moral rule. A lie to save one's parent, stealing to save a life, breaking a promise to help someone in need: all may be commendable or even morally obligatory. Morality is not an all or nothing affair. We need moral rules, but we should reject rule worship.

Further Reading

Bernard Gert's work provides the best introduction and overall view of rule morality: *Morality: A New Justification of the Moral Rules* (New York: Oxford University Press, 1988). David A. J. Richards, in *A Theory of Reasons for Action* (Oxford: Clarendon Press, 1971), offers a list of principles, in effect a rule morality, that he believes are reasonable to follow. J. D. Mabbott examines the use of rules in ethical theory in "Moral Rules," *Proceedings of the British Academy* 39 (1953): 97–117; and John Rawls explores the status rules in "Two Concepts of Rules," *Philosophical Review* 44 (1955): 3–32, as does M. G. Singer in "Moral Rules and Principles," in A. I. Melden, ed., *Essays in Moral Philosophy* (Seattle: University of Washington Press, 1958).

Endnotes

1. Bernard Gert, *Morality: A New Justification of the Moral Rules* (New York: Oxford University Press, 1988).
2. Kurt Baier, *From the Moral Point of View* (Ithaca, N.Y.: Cornell University Press, 1958).
3. David Gauthier, *Morals by Agreement* (New York: Oxford University Press, 1986).
4. W. D. Ross, *The Right and the Good* (Oxford: Oxford University Press, 1930).
5. R. B. Brandt, "Fairness to Indirect Optimific Theories in Ethics," *Ethics* 98 (2): 341–360.
6. R. M. Hare, *Moral Thinking* (Oxford: Clarendon Press, 1981).

7

Norms and Morality

7.1 The Moral Status of Norms

Moral rules are traditionally considered to be part of morality, with much of their status coming from the social importance placed upon them. The recognition of the need for moral rules is nearly universal; killing, stealing, lying, and breaking promises are generally thought to be morally wrong. We may think of moral rules as *universal norms*. A *norm* is a rule that regulates voluntary behavior. While some moral rules are almost universally accepted, other norms regulate behavior more locally, using arbitrary standards. For example, people in some societies generally walk to the right. This is a norm, but whether people walk to the left or to the right is not thought of as morally important in itself. More important is that some form of behavior is adopted, even though the direction is arbitrary. The same is true with driving a car; in some countries people drive to the left, in some to the right. While it is crucial to pick a direction, the direction picked is not. We also need some sense of property, public and private. Virtually all groups have some conception of property, even though these notions differ from place to place.

The fact that a norm is arbitrary, in its initial formulation, makes that norm a *convention*. Moral rules are not thought to be conventional, but many other norms, because they are partly arbitrary, are considered to be based on the fact that one way rather than another has been established as the correct way to do something in a particular environment.

Conventions are used to establish many ways of acting in a society, some of which are thought to be very basic. The American philosopher W. V. Quine concludes that two classes of moral value exist: one involving altruistic motivation to help others, and the other based on "practices of one's society or social group."[1] The British philosopher David Hume believed that many moral obligations, including obligations involving justice and keeping promises, stem from human conventions. Conventions regulate the way we act in a movie theater and in a classroom. They also define the way we address people in authority, and how we address younger people and older people. Conventions regulate how we eat and how we sleep, our notion of property, and the kind of money we use. Even marriage and religious practice are largely conventional. The importance placed on many conventions, even though they are partly arbitrary, suggests that conventions, at least some conventions, have a moral standing—that they are part of moral experience.

Some conventions are quite trivial and are frequently broken without any thought of moral violation. Eating lunch around noon may be conventional, but failure to eat lunch, under normal circumstances, is not thought to be a violation of morality. But other conventions have a moral standing. In her recent study of social norms, the American game theorist and philosopher Edna Ullmann-Margalit quotes the British philosopher H. L. A. Hart in presenting her own view that norms have a moral force. "[Norms] are conceived and spoken of as imposing obligations when the general demand for conformity is insistent and the social pressure brought to bear upon those who deviate or threaten to deviate is great."[2] This definition may be too broad, because some forms of behavior, like table manners, are not thought to have moral force, yet social pressure is brought upon those who deviate. Yet the definition correctly suggests that norms are widespread in a society. A local rule, like how to log on to a computer system, is not a norm in Ullmann-Margalit's sense, even if violating that rule leads to error or serious reprimand. It is not a norm because the demand is too specific. The widespread nature of a norm is suggested by the inclusion of "the general demand for conformity."

Though table manners may not have moral force, many conventional norms do. Ullmann-Margalit gives a reason for this: norms establish expectations and regulate behavior even among agents who do not know each other.[3] Norms establish dependencies and help solve social problems by encouraging people to coordinate their behavior. Driving on the right helps establish expectations, makes driving safer, and allows for the smooth flow of traffic. Not speaking out during a lecture, playing music at a proper level, respecting established property in conventional ways, and taking care of one's children at a shopping mall all help to make social living more tolerable. When such norms are violated, people are often thought to be acting immorally. (Do you agree that such actions are typically thought of as immoral?)

David Lewis, a contemporary American philosopher, considers conventions to be arbitrary because many different norms could serve the same function. Lewis understands that effective norms are stable, and he presents conditions that a norm must meet in order to be stable. A norm is *stable*, or likely to last, when most people are better off by following it.[4] That stable norms are in the interest of most people adds to their standing as morally binding. When a norm is violated, then people may suffer.

A norm has moral standing when (1) people typically directly suffer when the norm is violated, (2) the norm is regularly followed, (3) it is widely thought that violating the norm is immoral, and (4) the norm is well defined.

We may have difficulty determining which conventions have a binding moral standing partly because having a moral standing is not an isolated phenomenon. Moral experience includes rules, principles, and ideals. When breaking a norm also violates a well-established moral principle, like the prohibition against harm, then we have greater confidence that a norm is a moral norm. This is not to say that a norm can be derived from a principle. Remember, norms always have an arbitrary feature. From a nonharm principle alone, we cannot conclude that cars should be driven on the right, or that we need some form of private ownership of property. We have norms about which side to drive on and well-established property rules; we know that harm can be done if people do not follow these norms.

We must be careful when we talk about harm done by failure to follow a norm. "Harm" is sometimes used in a normative sense. This means that specific types of harm are considered morally offensive. Under the normative sense, other harms are not considered as harmful. The pain caused by a dentist is not thought to be covered under the moral prohibition against harming. Some people are offended, and thereby harmed, when others do the morally correct thing. Some people are harmed when someone does not put the fork on the correct side of the plate. If people are harmed in an unusual way, a way that most people would not be, we have reason to believe that the harm experienced is not reasonable. Part of the moral use of harm deals with whether a reasonable person in the same situation would be harmed by an action. So when it is claimed that failure to follow a moral requirement leads to harm, the harm involved should be interpreted as that experienced by a reasonable person. So a harm involved in violating a convention is given serious moral consideration when that harm is reasonable.

As we saw in the previous chapter, John Rawls claims that promising constitutes a social practice; it is, then, governed conventionally by social norms. Hume also argues that promising is conventional; promises are "human inventions, founded on the necessities and interests of society."[5] According to Hume, our sense of disapproval when a promise is broken depends not on a natural sentiment but on a sentiment based on a prior convention designed to fill some human need. To the extent that this is true, promising does create serious moral obligations. Suppose promising was not governed by norms. In that case, the words "I promise" would not effectively ensure behavior. Few would reasonably rely on promises. If promises simply meant that a person will try to do something, then the promisor should feel morally free to break a promise when it is difficult to comply. But if promising is a well-defined practice establishing a firm assurance, then a promise has more moral weight, and a promise should be made only with the intention that the promised act will be done, short of very serious reasons against doing it.

Conventional norms, like the norms governing promises, do create expectations; people rely on behavior in conformity with conventions, and such norms do allow for the smooth functioning of the social order. Many conventional norms are thought to have a significant moral standing. In short, conventional norms, aside from moral rules, are part of moral experience and thereby have some moral standing.

Study Questions 7.1

1. Identify four norms operative in your school, work, or home environment. Do these norms have a moral standing? Describe a situation in which nonadherence to a norm would be a violation of morality.
2. How do conventional norms differ from moral rules? Is this difference clear? That is, do people sometimes have difficulty telling whether an obligation comes from a conventional norm or from a moral rule? In answering, consider the status of promising: Is it a norm or a moral rule? Do we have well-established conventions about promise making?
3. How can we tell whether a norm has moral standing? (Consider the importance of the norm, its acceptance, and the way it fits in with other parts of moral experience.) Is the distinction between a moral norm and other norms clear?
4. Suppose violating the conventional norms of a person's society is immoral. In that case, is violating the norms of another society when visiting or living in that other society also immoral? Defend your answer.

7.2 The Prisoner's Dilemma

Norms are thought to have a moral standing partly because they are needed in society, and without a moral standing they would be ineffective. Evidence of this occurs in neighborhoods and institutions when ordinarily accepted norms of proper behavior begin to break down. Laws are not effective in guaranteeing smooth social functioning partly because the police cannot be everywhere. Instead, it is essential that people adopt ways of behaving, including conventional behavior, to ensure a healthy environment. Unless people accept basic social norms—including, for example, norms about property—social life becomes difficult.

We have little trouble realizing that norms are needed to ensure safety and security. But theorists examining norms argue that they pervade social life. Norms establish job expectations, required educational experience, basic social communication (like how far we stand from people we engage in conversation), how we drive an automobile, whether we talk in the theater, and so on. The argument is that we need many norms to coordinate behavior; norms help us to form expectations about how other people will behave, and this allows us to adjust our behavior. Furthermore, without norms, rational people, each independently doing the "right" thing or the rational act, produce irrational results—that is, results that deprive each of some good. Genuinely beneficial results are sometimes only secure when norms regulate behavior, so that behavior can be adequately coordinated. The proof of this comes from an example from the mathematically oriented study of "games," or formalized sequences of human actions.

In game theory, the *Prisoner's Dilemma* shows that two people, each acting "rationally," can produce undesirable results. The setting for the dilemma is a police interrogation. Two prisoners are taken and interrogated separately. The police offer each the same deal, in terms of prison time, to get them to confess, and each knows that the same offer has been made to the other. Both prisoners are assumed to be individually rational. They want the most for themselves, without thought about social norms or moral obligations. As we will see, the dilemma underscores the need for such norms.

In game theory, to be individually rational means basically that an individual does what most benefits him or her. The dilemma is set up using simple numbers to reflect individual interests, although these numbers may be varied to include special concerns, fears, and the like. In the Prisoner's Dilemma, individuals are assumed to want to avoid a jail sentence. So the numbers represent the number of years that each prisoner will be sentenced to depending on whether the prisoners confess or refuse to confess. So getting more jail time is worse than getting less. We assume that each prisoner only has two choices: confess or do not confess. These two options are represented by a matrix containing four boxes. The prisoners are called A and B. The top two boxes of the matrix represent outcomes when A confesses. Likewise, the two left-hand boxes represent outcomes when B confesses. Thus, the upper-left-hand box represents the outcome when both prisoners confess, while the upper-right box represents the outcome when A confesses and B does not. (Identify what the other two boxes represent.)

Choices of B

Confess   Don't Confess

	Confess	Don't Confess
Confess	(7, 7)	(2, 10)
Don't Confess	(10, 2)	(4, 4)

Choices of A

The outcomes are listed within the boxes. The upper-left-hand box shows what happens when each prisoner confesses: each gets a seven-year sentence. The first number in each box represents the sentence of A, and the second number the sentence of B. So if A does not confess and B does, then A gets ten years in prison, and B gets two years.

The rational thing to do is confess. This is the case because *no matter what the other does,* each prisoner is better off by confessing. We will work this out for A, showing that no matter what B does, A is better off by confessing. Afterward, you should work this out for B, showing that no matter what A does, B is better off by confessing. Keep in mind that in this simple example, being better off means serving less time in jail.

B can either confess or not confess. Suppose that B confesses. A should confess as well, because by confessing, A can serve three years less jail time. If B confesses, A gets seven years by confessing, but ten years by not confessing. So if B confesses, *A should confess* as well.

If B does not confess, what should A do? Once again, by confessing A gets a better deal. If A confesses, A gets two years in jail, but by not confessing, A gets four years. So if B does not confess, *A should confess* in order to get less time.

No matter what B does, confess or not confess, A gets less time by confessing.

As you can tell, the same analysis works to show that B should confess. If A and B are both rational, then they both should confess. Of course, the prosecutor sets up the game this way, attempting to get a confession from each.

According to the received view of rationality, both should confess. If the players are rational, this will be the outcome. But check out the box representing what happens when both confess: each gets seven years. Now suppose the prisoners are not rational. They act foolishly, or perhaps they act from an "irrational" sense of loyalty, and both do not confess. Each selects the irrational action. Now examine the box where neither confesses. After a plea bargain, both get four years. In this example, if both do the irrational thing, they each come out better! Here's the dilemma: rational action produces a worse result for both prisoners than irrational action.

In reflecting on the dilemma, we should be willing to generalize. The dilemma is presented under particular and unusual circumstances, but many more common situations are like the Prisoner's Dilemma in form. For example, it might be rational for me as an individual to walk across the lawn, violating a rule set up to prevent the establishment of an ugly dirt path. Even though I would rather walk around than see this path, I understand that my own action, as an individual, has little bearing on the formation of a path. So I save the time and walk on the lawn, understanding that if others do the same, a path will form regardless of my actions, and if others do not, I won't have a noticeable effect on the lawn. No matter what others do, I am better off taking the shortcut. If all of us act irrationally, no path is formed, but if we all act rationally, a path occurs, which we all would have preferred to avoid.

The Prisoner's Dilemma is a dramatic way to show that uncoordinated individual action can lead to less than optimal results. Solving the problem by an appeal to norms will not help unless those norms effectively serve as constraints on individual action. This is seen in the problem of the *free-rider*, which is also involved in the example of the lawn. Suppose not confessing is held as a norm. A knows that B is an honorable person, but A refuses to be guided by norms. A confesses, while B follows the norm and does not confess. In this way A gains from the norm without following it. A is a free-rider because A does not pay the price involved in conforming to the norm, yet A reaps the benefits involved in having a norm. The result: A gets two years while B gets ten. This is certainly not a desirable outcome for B.

Norms need to have the social power that generally keeps people from acting against them. Perhaps this power is backed by moral education, by social sanction, or by the manipulation of general institutional arrangements. The last way occurs when an institution is organized so that people generally gain by being moral or by following moral norms and lose by being immoral. The institution thereby carries much of the burden of supporting moral behavior.

One way to enforce solutions to Prisoner's Dilemma problems is through laws, but we know that unless laws are internalized to some degree, enforcement lags behind violations. Norms help to secure the effectiveness of the law; norms, including moral norms, do get taught and do get internalized. They provide a way to solve problems suggested by the Prisoner's Dilemma.

Study Questions 7.2

1. (For class discussion.) Suppose the prisoners promise to each other beforehand that they will not confess. Does that promise solve the problem they face? Suppose the agreement involves some sanction, say retaliation against anyone who breaks the promise. This changes the benefits and burdens involved, and so confessing might turn out to be a poor choice. Try to design a new matrix with this in mind; the numbers used will now reflect both the prison sentence and the retaliation. Keep in mind the definition of individual rationality. Does this additional agreement provide a general way to solve the Prisoner's Dilemma?

2. Is it rational for a mother and a father to sacrifice their income or even their health for their children? Keep in mind that in the received view, the happiness of another is an externality and is not a valid consideration in an individual's preference ordering. Does the answer about the parents affect your evaluation of the received view of rationality?

3. Is loyalty to a norm, such that a person will follow the norm even if it is not in his or her best interests, consistent with the received view of rationality?

7.3 Types of Norms

Edna Ullmann-Margalit maintains that three basic types of norms can be identified: *Prisoner's Dilemma norms, coordination norms,* and *inequality norms.* Each responds to social problems or situations that have unsatisfactory results in the absence of norms. Morally compelling norms may be the solution in each type of problem. The Prisoner's Dilemma represents situations where the outcome, for all, of acting "irrationally" is more desirable than acting rationally. In these cases, people have conflicting payoffs, and so are tempted to take advantage of others. But by acting according to their own interests, when all or most others also act from individual interest, they select an undesirable action.

Coordination problems are different. Here the interests of people are the same. They have no special desire to act differently. In the previous section we saw a problem where each person finds it beneficial to walk across the lawn, but still wants a pristine lawn. The desired action, the individually rational action—to walk across the lawn—is different from the prescribed action: don't walk. There is a conflict between what an individual wants and what the norm calls for. In contrast, coordination norms, like driving on the right side of the road, involve no such conflict because people have little desire to do the opposite. We simply need some way to decide on the proper side. A norm solves the problem by providing information about the proper side.

Coordination problems are common in life. In small groups, group leaders often emerge when they are best at proposing a way to get to consensus about one way to do things, even though it may not be the best way. One of the purposes of authority is to secure a single way of acting, so that things get done. In a similar way, one of the purposes of social norms is to ensure that actions get done.

Coordination problems occur when a division of labor is needed. In raising a family, parents need ways to coordinate who will shop and when, who will take care of the children and when, and who will work outside the home and when. Social norms often offer solutions to such problems. Insofar as these are moral norms, they have a moral standing. But today some norms regulating family life are viewed as exploitative. Norms may be thought of as favoring men or as favoring women, depending on individual circumstances. Overall, however, such norms have been criticized as systematically favoring men over women.

To claim that a norm has a moral standing is not to claim that it is morally proper. Moral experience is complex. A moral norm may conflict with a principle, a norm may be a holdover from different times with different needs and so may no longer be needed, and a norm may conflict with an ideal or with a moral rule. The code of silence in some communities may conflict with the need to tell the truth. A code of honor may conflict with rules against killing. A norm of family raising may conflict with equal opportunity. To say that norms have a moral standing—are part of our moral experience—does not mean that they are always proper, or that they shouldn't be changed. It does say that we need a good reason to change or violate a norm. Even norms considered immoral, when measured against the weight of moral experience, establish expectations, which need to be taken into consideration when considering change. In short, norms are a real but limited part of the moral domain.

The need to evaluate norms is most apparent in Ullmann-Margalit's third type of norm: *inequality norms*, or, in her terminology, *norms of partiality*. Inequalities are pervasive in social life. Those with more want to keep it, but those with less may want to take what richer people have. Without norms, inequality leads to continual social fear and frequent social strife. This is the message of the seventeenth-century British philosopher Thomas Hobbes, who wrote, in his *Leviathan*, that without the systematic use of social control through a dominating state with its police power, people would be in a perpetual state of war. Without social control the outcome would be a life that is "solitary, poor, nasty, brutish, and short."

According to Ullmann-Margalit, inequality norms provide social stability by serving "to promote the interests of the party favored by the inequality."[6] Inequality norms are evident in relation to property, for example, laws about trespass. Of course, laws against trespass do not only protect the better-off. Even those who rent property are protected. Universal protection meliorates the "partiality" of the norm because it protects the poor from the rich as well. A norm may protect the rich more than the poor, but it may still protect the poor. Whether or not the norm is proper depends on how life would be without it, and on how the norm may be modified.

We may think of trespass laws as *mixed partiality norms*. They help the poor as well as the rich, although differently. A *pure partiality norm* helps only one group, typically the better-off. A pure partiality norm is difficult to defend as morally proper. It is usually harmful, and it violates a basic moral requirement of impartiality.

Pure partiality norms are not easy to think of, but as a norm moves more to the advantage of one group than another, it becomes more suspect, morally speaking. Circumstances may determine the extent to which a partiality norm favors one group more than another. Norms about gender differences, for example, may change as circumstances change, in their unequal impact or in the compensation given for unequal treatment. No matter what, unequal treatment, even compensated inequalities, is often thought to be morally suspect. Compensated inequalities may be required in certain circumstances, but circumstances may change or be changed. As we will see in Chapter 10, equality is a social ideal; it is part of moral experience. Taken seriously, equality as an ideal suggests that we move away from the inequalities sanctioned by social norms.

Study Questions 7.3

1. List three norms for each of the types that Ullmann-Margalit examines.
2. Suppose you are assigned the task of defending the three inequality norms you listed. How would you defend them?
3. Now suppose your job is to claim that those norms are offensive. How would you make this claim?
4. Can norms be used to clarify general principles? For example, if we follow the general principle against harm, can norms tell us which action can reasonably be thought to cause harm? In your answer, refer to specific norms.

7.4 Gauthier's Morals by Agreement

David Gauthier, a contemporary American philosopher, argues in *Morals by Agreement*[7] that all moral norms and principles must be acceptable to all rational persons. He supports the received view that rational persons attempt to maximize their self-interest, and so moral constraints, to be proper, must be in the actual self-interest of all people. Gauthier argues that it is rational to accept constraints when such constraints make all better off, as in the Prisoner's Dilemma. Assuming that many such situations exist, and that each can be solved with a moral norm that constrains action, Gauthier can recommend a basic morality based on rational self-interest.

But the problem of the free-rider intrudes. Why not fake compliance with a moral norm and take advantage of others? Gauthier insists that moral norms are rational, but that, to be effective, they must constrain self-interest. That is the problem: to make even a clever deceiver see that following moral constraints is in his or her self-interest. For norms to work, each person must make a prior commitment. Gauthier believes that such a commitment can be rational because a deceiver is often recognized, and punished, for what he or she is. When recognized, that person will not be able to participate in rational gains. So Gauthier's solution is that people are *translucent*—that is, we can often see through their behavior and understand that they are not being genuine.

This solution still is not adequate. A moral constraint is a moral constraint when it is not in a person's interest. If we can see through people, then they are more or less forced to act morally. These actions are not based on a moral constraint but on a social constraint. The social constraint may be one that we can morally endorse; even the faker may want to endorse social constraints. A social constraint may be designed to detect cheats, or to persecute them. This is not what Gauthier wishes; he wants an individual commitment to abide by a moral rule or norm, and one that all rational persons may be able to endorse as morally proper. Gauthier wants to show that it is rational for each individual to be constrained by moral norms. This argument fails because some individuals may believe that it is more rational to attempt to fake compliance. And when an individual truly believes that he or she will be detected, then the constraint is not a moral constraint, but a prudential constraint.

Gauthier's account is an attempt to use a nonmoral value, acting rationally, as a way to defend moral values. Such attempts generally fall under the rubric of *deriving an ought from what is*. That is, Gauthier attempts to derive moral values from nonmoral basic individual interest expressed as individual rationality. Such efforts run into a problem similar to that raised by G. E. Moore, a British philosopher writing after the turn of the twentieth century. (We will examine this argument more fully in Chapter 12.) Whenever a nonmoral value is offered as a defining feature of moral value, Moore tests the claim by determining if it makes sense to ask whether the nonmoral value is really good. If the nonmoral value defines goodness, then the question should make little sense. But if our sense of goodness goes beyond the nonmoral value, then the question makes good sense. We can indeed evaluate the nonmoral values in moral terms. When we find our-selves evaluating the proposed basic value, we then understand that the proposed definition does not provide the meaning of moral terms.

Gauthier does not attempt to define moral value in terms of rationality; instead, he seeks to derive moral values from his conception of rationality. We may still apply a test like Moore's. Is this value, rationality, really a basic value from which moral values may be derived? This question makes perfect sense, and calls for an answer. Once we give an answer, we tend to use other values, including nonmoral values, to defend the status of the basic value. In this process those other values gain a standing equal to that of the basic value, or perhaps even a higher standing.

Basic nonmoral values like rationality and pleasure are controversial. We can easily think of pleasures that appear to be evil. Rationality is more complex because it depends on preference fulfillment. But suppose a person is brainwashed into accepting a preference ranking that is coercively imposed from outside. Gauthier understands that some preferences are not morally acceptable. So he builds into his conception of rationality some standards by which preferences may be evaluated. Preferences must be autonomously formed, consistent, stable, and carefully considered. This complicates the analysis by introducing, within the basic nonmoral value, unevaluated and undefended moral values, like autonomy. Even after introducing these values, we may still question whether the individual rationality he supports can adequately serve as the basis for moral value, and this question continues to make good sense. The answer will lead to further use of values, moral and otherwise.

Philosophers frequently point out that the distinction between moral values and nonmoral values is arbitrary. Gauthier's conception of prefer-ences is a case in point. If a brainwashed person says, "I prefer to give all my money to the leader," we may say that the person doesn't really prefer that. This is not the *genuine* preference of the person. A moral evaluation has been added to the supposedly nonmoral status of a preference.

Moral experience includes many moral values that pervade our other experiences in subtle and not so subtle ways. Deriving a moral *ought* from a nonmoral *is* is difficult because the nonmoral value is likely to be infiltrated by a host of moral values. The best approach, the one that avoids both Moore's Open Question Test and derivation of moral values from nonmoral values, relies on the sum of moral experience to determine the status of any particular moral value.

Our analysis shows that norms cannot be readily derived as moral norms from any basic nonmoral value. Some norms are widely thought to be morally binding, and can be supported or rejected in terms of other moral values. The hope of finding some nonmoral touchstone from which to determine moral value has so far proved ineffective.

Study Questions 7.4

1. Suppose we evaluate a person as morally good for performing a good act, but did not know that the person performing did so out of self-interest, say to get money. Is this likely to change our evaluation? Think of cases where it would and where it would not.
2. Consider your preferences. Take one that you hold as most important. Suppose your friend argues that your preference is not autonomously formed, perhaps because of some social indoctrination. How would you respond?
3. Why do you think Gauthier believes that the preferences that count must be carefully considered? Is this a preference of his or can his view be defended as objective?
4. (For class discussion.) A *revealed preference* for x over y is known to exist when, and only when, x is selected when y is available and y is at most equally costly. Some theorists believe that only revealed preferences count as a basis for policy decisions or for moral judgments. Is this support for revealed preferences a moral or a nonmoral demand? Why are revealed preferences valued over stated preferences?
5. Suppose a moral norm is not generally in the interests of the people acting under its influence. Should that norm be rejected? In your answer be sure to carefully think through the meaning of being "generally in the interests of." This is not a well-defined notion, so consider several possible circumstances under which norms are not in the general interest. For example, a norm may be in a group's long-run interest but not in its short-run interest.

7.5 Norms and Game Theory

Both Gauthier and Ullmann-Margalit use *game theory*, implicitly or explicitly, to defend norms. This is helpful because game theory can dramatize circumstances that show the need for norms and instruct us about the way norms may be preserved. But the use of game theory can be taken too far. Game theory typically depends on assumptions that are not normative. In a game-theoretic approach, any power one person or group has over another person or group is usually taken as given and is not evaluated. In life, differences in power are sometimes compelling. We might be willing to give our money to a person making threats with a gun. Although we may defer to the use of power, this does not make the use of power morally acceptable. Ullmann-Margalit's partiality norms may or may not be morally acceptable, even if prudence dictates that those with less obey such norms.

In *Theory of Games as a Tool for the Moral Philosopher*,[8] the British philosopher R. B. Braithwaite uses game theory to give us a taste of a resort to power that he considers morally appropriate. Two musicians live in adjoining apartments and each desires to play when the other does not play. One player, A, would rather not play than play when the other, B, plays. B, on the other hand, would rather play alone, but will play even if the other also plays. This gives B a threat advantage. (Explain why.) Braithwaite gives the solution to the bargaining game. B plays on 26 days, while A plays on 17. (Think of why A gets to play fewer days, but yet gets to play on some days.) This solution may be thought of as the analogue of a norm, only on an individual level. The solution depends on the power B has over A. B may be able to threaten to practice on all nights. A has no such realistic threat. A loses in the bargaining process, but we may question whether the solution is morally fair. (What do you think?)

This solution appears to be a prudential solution on A's part, yet A may complain that it is immoral. Just because A plays a more delicate instrument or can only concentrate when playing alone does not mean that A ought to get less practice time than B. A may understand that this is the best deal that he or she is going to get, but that doesn't make it morally right. Braithwaite's use of game theory takes the moral dimension out of the bargaining situation. Morality cannot be derived from threats any more than it can be derived from the received view of rationality.

The solution is to view some social norms as morally charged, to accept them as part of moral experience and evaluate them in terms of other moral and practical values. Game theory may come in handy if we start with assumptions about the relative power of the players. If they are equally endowed, morally, physically, economically, and intellectually, then perhaps the bargains they strike are morally proper, and any norms based on their decisions may be considered morally compelling. This may provide a way, perhaps a hypothetical way, to judge the moral acceptability of norms. But the norms that come from a fair bargain, or what we consider a fair bargain, may not have a prior standing. Inventing norms may be difficult; people may refuse to accept them because they are too complex, foreign to them, or perceived as unfair even if developed from a fair perspective. The actual norms of a society do have a standing, even if morally "purer" norms are possible.

Study Questions 7.5

1. (For class discussion.) This section ended with the claim that invented norms, discovered by postulating a fair bargaining process, may be morally weak. They may, for example, go against established custom.

Think of a case where this could happen. Does the unfairness depend on the way we set up the bargain, perhaps unwittingly introducing some unfairness, or can it be the case that our notion of fairness is partly dependent on the way things are done, at least, on the part that is considered morally proper? For example, suppose we make a bargain between an eleven-year-old and his or her parents, starting from equal power. Would we consider the results of their bargain to be fair?

2. Bargains are often made where those with more end up receiving more. Better players, better qualified professionals, and stronger people may get more in a deal. Is this morally acceptable? If so, to what extent and under what conditions?

3. (For class discussion.) Suppose one person has a preference in favor of another's receiving more. Is this preference rational? Should the person with that preference receive less, morally speaking?

4. Are preferences molded by society, and if so to what degree? Gauthier argues that society needs to be organized so as to ensure that preferences are autonomously formed. What would society be like to ensure such autonomous formation of preferences? Is such a society realistic, or is it utopian?

7.6 The Lessons from Moral Norms

We need to have rules that guide behavior in society. Unlike moral rules, many such rules may be different from society to society because they are partly conventional. We need them because uncoordinated activity, even rational activity, can lead to unacceptable results. Life without norms would be disastrous. Norms solve coordination problems, establish expectations, and create reliance.

Morality is a form of social coordination designed to establish constraints on behavior; norms are one way of doing this. Many norms have a moral standing; for example, if Hume is correct that promising is conventional, then keeping a promise is one of our norms and it has a moral standing. Whether promising is a norm or a moral rule is difficult to establish; the difference depends on whether it is conventional. Part of the problem in determining whether a regular form of behavior is guided by moral norms is that we have no simple way to show how norms come about. Game theory provides some explanations about the origin of norms and hopes to tell us the conditions under which norms endure. But we cannot derive the whole moral status of norms from any other moral or nonmoral values. Instead, their moral standing comes from their place in moral experience.

In this chapter, we claim, perhaps controversially, that many norms have a moral standing, and that the burden of proof is on those who wish to argue against them. The most effective arguments in favor or against the moral binding power of a norm refer to other aspects of moral experience or to other norms. Also, an appeal to facts—such as that a norm, held over from the past, improperly responds to current realities—may be a good argument against a norm. That reliance is created by outmoded norms makes such argumentation weaker unless we can show that people will not be harmed by changes or that changes can minimize harm.

Norms depend on compliance. The easiest way to defeat the supposed moral power of a norm is to show that it is not generally followed. This may be the case with promises today. Few hold promises in the same strong way as many did in the past. Today the practice of promising, if there is such a practice, is weak and amorphous.

Norms are important in social life not only because they solve problems and create reliance, but because they give specificity to moral principles. Principles like "Do good," "Avoid harm," and "Be just" are not merely open to individual interpretation. They are also interpreted, in part, by aspects of moral experience like norms. Norms frequently instruct us in how to avoid harm and how to do good. Justice frequently involves actions performed in accordance with norms.

We can begin to see the complexity of moral experience. Norms are judged by, among other things, moral principles, yet moral principles get substance from norms. Moral experience has a limited, built-in coherence; the job of a moral theorist is to strengthen and guide moral experience to greater coherence. One aspect of morality should support another, and often does. When that coherence is disturbed, perhaps due to a change in circumstance, we have reason to believe that a change in moral views is required. Many other things besides norms give substance to moral principles—for example, individual judgments, other principles, practices, and moral rules. Principles are, in part, independent of any given norm. Relying on this independence, we may judge a norm. Nevertheless, principles may be judged or amended by our norms. A rationality principle, one that appeals to the received view of rationality, may be rejected if it conflicts too much with our norms, other principles, and moral rules. By understanding various aspects of moral experience, we are able to see how a coherent approach, a mutually supporting approach, to principles, ideals, norms, and rules can be developed.

In the following chapters we center on more abstract aspects of moral experience, like principles and ideals. As we do, keep in mind how principles may be used to judge norms, virtues, and particular judgments, and how these, in turn, may be used to give substance to principles and ideals.

Further Reading

Edna Ullmann-Margalit's book, *The Emergence of Norms* (Oxford: At the Clarendon Press, 1977), is a good place to begin an exploration of moral norms. David Lewis, in *Convention: A Philosophical Study* (Cambridge: Harvard University Press, 1969), provides a rigorous, and somewhat difficult to read, account of conventionalism generally. Francis Snare's study of Hume's use of conventions is also more advanced: *Morals, Motivation and Convention: Hume's Influential Doctrines* (Cambridge: Cambridge University Press, 1991). A recent edition of *Ethics*, a major philosophy journal in ethics, is devoted exclusively to norms: *Ethics* 100 (4) (July 1990); most of the articles are not especially difficult to read, and the issue does give a good overview of the use of norms in moral reasoning. Stanley Cavell, in *The Claims of Reason: Wittgenstein, Skepticism, Morality, and Tragedy* (New York: Oxford University Press, 1979), argues against using practices or conventions as the basis for morality. J. F. Scott examines moral norms from a sociological outlook in *Internalization of Norms: A Sociological Perspective* (Englewood Cliffs, N.J.: Prentice-Hall, 1971).

Endnotes

1. W. V. Quine, "On the Nature of Moral Values," in *Theories and Things* (Cambridge: Harvard University Press, 1981), p. 58.
2. Edna Ullmann-Margalit, *The Emergence of Norms* (Oxford: At the Clarendon Press, 1977), p. 12.
3. Ibid., p. 85.
4. David Lewis, *Convention: A Philosophical Study* (Cambridge: Harvard University Press, 1969).
5. David Hume, *A Treatise of Human Nature*, Book III, Of Morals; Section V, Of the Obligation of Promises, p. 222.
6. Ibid., p. 173.
7. David Gauthier, *Morals by Agreement* (New York: Oxford University Press, 1986). Also, see my critique "The Problems of Preference Based Morality: A Critique of `Morals by Agreement,'" *Journal of Social Philosophy* 20 (3) (Winter 1989): 77–91.
8. R. B. Braithwaite, *Theory of Games as a Tool for the Moral Philosopher* (Cambridge: Cambridge University Press, 1963).

8

Principles

8.1 The Nature of a Moral Principle

Principles in any field involve the field's basic rules, purpose, or goals. This is true of any organized activity, from basketball to physics. In a formal theory, such as physics, principles are often stated as laws or axioms from which many other statements, rules, laws, or theorems may be derived. A principled approach to ethics usually involves the expression of one or two basic rules that implicitly define the domain and range of the theory; by using the principles, judgments can be made in specific concrete cases. In this way principles are designed to provide the foundation for the rest of an ethical theory.

Because principles, using only a few words, do so much in ethics—setting the basic intent of the theory and offering instruction potentially on all moral problems—they must be abstract and very general. A principle is *abstract* when it leaves out concrete detail. A principle is *general* when it covers a broad domain, including many different types of actions as well as such other things as political organization and virtues. And a principle gives basic insight when it is able to produce results—to help us establish other, more concrete and less general, aspects of the field. We saw that a rule-utilitarian uses the demand to seek the greatest happiness to evaluate moral rules. Moral principles may be used to evaluate everything from social norms to personal ideals. A principle like "Do whatever you want unless it harms another person," if offered as the basic moral principle, establishes a libertarian perspective on moral theory, guides individual judgments, and covers many different activities by using broad terms, including "harm."

Some philosophers seem to think that moral principles provide precise guidance. If we apply a principle properly, we will determine the right course of action. Others believe that principles cannot, in most instances, be directly applied without further interpretation. Consider the principle about harming others. Suppose I decide to go to the movies, but this disappoints my colleague who hoped I would have some time to help with a difficult logic proof. Did this disappointment "harm" my colleague? We might decide that a harm must be serious to count, but this decision is not part of the principle. When we add this interpretation, the libertarian moral principle is amended; now it is more precise. The problem is that many similar amendments may be required before the principle provides adequate advice in real circumstances.

We previously briefly examined rule-utilitarianism. Under this view the utilitarian principle cannot be directly applied to individual cases due to limited knowledge and to offensive counterexamples. In rule-utilitarianism, the utilitarian principle, in its generality, is able to judge only in macro terms. It is not intended as a way to "micromanage" moral life; the principle needs to be mediated by a set of rules. These rules end up offering what we may think of as an extended interpretation of the utilitarian principle; they tell us how we can contribute most effectively to the greatest happiness for the greatest number of people, and who to take into account when making decisions. For example, if moral rules about charity indicate that charity starts at home, then we will give greater weight to those near us than to people in more remote places. Although rules help to specify the meaning of principles, they cannot offer a complete interpretation. After all, the principle must be used, without the help of rules, to determine which rules must be followed. Rule-utilitarians believe that the vagueness in the main principle is less of a liability at the macro level, where issues are more easily studied in general terms.

While the *rule* view maintains that principles are applied to individual cases through the use of derived rules, the other view, the *act* view, maintains that principles are to be applied directly to all moral concerns. Under either view, because principles are abstract and general, they require fuller explanation. What do key terms within the principle mean? How are principles to be applied? How can principles be justified?

In this chapter we will examine two influential ethical theories that claim that one or a few basic principles provide the only proper perspective from which moral decisions may be made: utilitarianism and Kant's moral theory. Each is a fundamentally influential view in the history of ethical theory, claiming to establish all the valid ingredients of the entire moral experience. We will attempt to determine whether the bold claims of these theories—that readily stated principles can direct and order moral experience—are correct, and if not, we will try to locate where they go wrong. Although we find flaws in each, we also recognize that both theories do represent very significant parts of moral experience.

Study Questions 8.1

1. Explain why moral rules—for example, those we examined in Chapter 5—are not called moral principles.
2. Are "Do good" and "Avoid harm" principles or moral rules? Explain your answer.
3. Is the Golden Rule, "Do unto others as you would have them do unto you," a principle or a moral rule? Explain your answer.
4. Since principles are more basic than rules, we often use principles to defend and explain moral rules. Does the Golden Rule offer support for Gert's rules? Would Gert's theory be improved if he used a small number of basic moral principles to defend his moral rules? Could the same be said about virtue theory? Feminist ethics?
5. (For class discussion.) "Avoid doing harm" is vague. Suppose this principle is accepted as the basic principle in a moral theory and is thought to be directly applicable under an act view. However, many philosophers recognize that applying a principle is usually difficult because a principle is so abstract. What are the difficulties, if any, in applying the principle about avoiding harm to the following problem?

> Anita, a research chemist, discovers that the company she works for is selling drugs, considered unsafe by the FDA, to a "third world" country. She strongly believes that the main principle of morality demands that all people do their best to avoid harm. Although she generally believes that the company does good, she is considering quitting because the company will be harming poor people in other countries. However, the job market is tight, and she fears that if she quits she will have to go on welfare to support her children.

8.2 Act-Utilitarianism

Utilitarianism is a *consequentialist* theory because it maintains that morally right actions, the actions we are obliged to do, are selected by considering the consequences that those actions tend to produce. In short, utilitarianism requires that we look to nonmoral effects of actions as the guide to making moral decisions. It advises us to always act so as to gain the greatest happiness possible, either indirectly by following the proper rules or directly by considering the happiness produced by each action we might perform. And happiness is defined, traditionally, as pleasure. In what follows, we will examine *act-utilitarianism*, which examines the consequences of each act. Jeremy Bentham and John Stuart Mill are considered the two greatest utilitarians; both were British philosophers writing in the eighteenth and nineteenth centuries.

The utilitarian principle is traditionally expressed: **Always act to produce the greatest happiness for the greatest number of people**. This principle is intended to establish moral obligations, to tell us what actions we are morally bound to perform. We are morally obliged to consider *all* our options, all the actions we might perform, and choose the one that most conforms to the demands of utilitarian principle. We must, morally speaking, always do the best thing available, where being best is decided according to the utilitarian principle; it is the action that produces the greatest happiness for the greatest number of people.

By its inclusion of the "greatest number of people," the utilitarian principle makes explicitly clear that it goes beyond *egoism*. An egoist is only concerned, morally speaking, with himself or herself; the utilitarian rejects this as immoral with the claim that morality demands that the happiness of all be given equal consideration. But by insisting on a general concern for the welfare of all, the utilitarian introduces some problems of interpretation. When we say "the greatest number" of people, do we mean to examine how many people are made happy and how many are made sad, and select the action that makes more people happy? Does the principle mean that we should look at the total *amount* of happiness by adding up everyone's pleasure and pain? Or does it instruct us to look for the greatest average amount of happiness that would be produced by each action? (*Carefully* consider these options and make sure you understand their different implications.) Does the principle include future people? Does it include all reasoning beings as people? If creatures from another galaxy appear on earth, are they covered by the principle? Does it include animals?

We may get different results when we analyze any given action depending on how we answer those questions. Different answers, in effect, mean that we are faced with *different principles*, each having a different meaning. (Explain why we have different principles.) For example, let's assume that we should make more people happy than sad. Suppose we are deciding what movie, A or B, to see tonight. Three people will be made happy by seeing A and two people will be sad. The only other choice, B, will make two people happy and three sad. So as good utilitarians we decide to make the greatest number of people happy by choosing A. But does this really establish the greatest happiness? Suppose we find out that the three people made happy by movie A will only be slightly happier seeing A than B, but the two people made sad by A will be miserable. By seeing B, they become very happy, instead of miserable, and the other three, while sad, are only slightly sad. Thus, the total amount of happiness may be improved by seeing movie B.

With the same number of people involved, when the total happiness increases, so does the average happiness. (Be sure you understand this; think of your test grades as an example.) But suppose now that movie A is closer, so that everyone can walk to it. Movie B is further away and can only be reached by the one available car. If A is chosen, then five brothers and sisters can be taken. This will make the little siblings happy, but only slightly more happy than they would otherwise be, because they can watch some good cartoons on TV. Taking them to a movie decreases the happiness of the original group. But it may increase the total amount of happiness. Now the total will be increased by movie A, but the average happiness might be decreased. This is an example of a way in which the average and the total happiness may differ. The difference is a serious problem when population issues are concerned. The next person born into a family may have a significant chance of having more happiness than sadness, but may diminish the happiness of all the other members of the family. So the total happiness may increase, while the average happiness decreases. If we include animals in utilitarian theory, even assuming that they have a lesser capacity than human beings to be happy or sad, we could get quite different answers than if we only count human beings.

The act-utilitarianism of Bentham takes into account the total amount of happiness for all people, not the average pleasure. Happiness is interpreted as pleasure, and all pleasures, in themselves, are equally good. For Bentham, unlike Mill, intellectual pleasures are no worse than bodily pleasures. In itself, the pleasure of wallowing in mud is no better than the pleasure some people get from solving a good logic proof. This sounds like an animalistic morality, but this inference leaves out the complexity of Bentham's position.

Bentham recognizes that pleasures are complex; they differ in ways that end up making some pleasures better than others. Although one type of pleasure is no better than another in itself, a *longer-lasting* pleasure is better than a shorter pleasure because it produces more pleasure; so the *duration* of a pleasure must be considered. How soon a pleasure is expected to be experienced is called the *propinquity* of a pleasure. A pleasure coming sooner is better than an equivalent pleasure coming later. Bentham claims that a *fruitful* pleasure, one that leads to other pleasures, is better than a pleasure that goes nowhere. (Does this help us to argue that refined forms of pleasure, like what some get from doing a logic proof, are better than less refined bodily pleasures?) Bentham continues: An *intense* pleasure is better than a dull pleasure. A more *certain* pleasure, one that we can reliably expect, should have a greater impact on our calculations about what to do than an uncertain one. A *pure* pleasure, one that is not mixed with pain, is better than a pleasure that is tainted with pain. For example, the pleasure many get from jogging is sometimes mixed with significant pain.[1] Added to all of this, the absence of pain counts as a pleasure.

Now we can argue that the pleasure of solving a logic proof is a better pleasure if it satisfies Bentham's standards. We are made more skillful by logic and can enjoy a new set of experiences that the less skillful cannot enjoy. It is a reliable pleasure and one that usually is long-lived. It does come mixed with some pain, the hard work to learn how to do the proof and the struggle to solve it, though the pain is usually not intense. All in all, the negative features of doing logic may be compensated by its long-run, positive, happiness-producing qualities. And these may produce, for many, more than enough happiness to outpace the happiness from a low-level physical pleasure. (Does this solve the problem that a mindless bodily pleasure may win out over a refined intellectual pleasure?)

Bentham proposes a *calculus of utility*. To decide which actions to do, we add up all the pleasure and pain each possible action leads to. We must be careful to evaluate all the aspects of pleasure: intensity, fruitfulness, duration, certainty, propinquity, and purity. After we consider all the totals, we should do the action that produces the most happiness.

Mill objects to such a procedure. Some pleasures, he thought, are more admirable than others. The pleasure from doing mathematical proofs is a more admirable pleasure, in itself, than the pleasure we may get from eating a good meal. Furthermore, some actions so fundamentally disrupt pleasure, like injustice and censorship, that they are virtually always forbidden. Under his view, injustice is a name we assign to those actions that upset people's lives in basic ways. These are forbidden in a strict way by most theories because they involve such a serious amount of pain and a consistent forfeit of pleasure; typically, no calculation is needed to condemn acts of injustice.

Mill's reaction to injustice and censorship helps to show one of the advantages claimed for the utilitarian theory, that it can account for or explain the values supported in other theories. If a deontologist claims that it is always immoral to violate justice, the utilitarian claims that this is a good insight, because justice promotes happiness, but one carried to an extreme. The deontologist properly claims that violating justice or freedom is a serious offense. It virtually always causes a loss of utility, but by making this a strict, unexceptional moral requirement, the deontologist loses sight of the base of the concern, that injustice robs us of happiness. The deontologist is mistaken because he or she ends up making justice more crucial in human life than happiness. Keeping happiness in mind, the utilitarian can explain our typical objection to injustice without making the objection into an absolute requirement.

Utilitarianism is also considered a superior theory because happiness is fundamentally desirable, something thought to be desired by all people. (Do you agree?) A moral theory focusing on the attainment of the greatest happiness for the greatest number of people gives good guidance. If we all seek the greatest happiness, then we should live in a better world and a better society. The utilitarian objects to racial and sexual exploitation, to vengeful punishment, to war, and to pollution. These things deprive us of happiness. We may sometimes be fooled into thinking that they produce happiness, but a careful analysis of the hostility caused, the harm inflicted, in relation to the gains, will show that the utilitarian is able to insist upon social reform. A utilitarian not only objects, typically, to many of the things we consider wrong, but gives us a reason to believe why they are wrong. And when that reason doesn't hold, then the utilitarian theoretically is willing to agree that something is not wrong. Far from being a vice, the utilitarian believes moral life requires that we carefully consider all actions to determine whether we are doing the right thing. In the past we have rejected actions, like those involving homosexuality, as immoral, when those negative attitudes themselves cause more pain than pleasure. Other actions, such as racist acts, we rightly reject as producing more unhappiness.

Study Questions 8.2

1. Suppose a utilitarian objected to the use of addicting drugs, and someone counters that drugs produce pleasure and therefore should be approved by the utilitarian. How would a utilitarian respond?
2. (For class discussion.) Some philosophers believe we can measure happiness in units, called *utils*. A negative number represents pain. As utilitarians with this belief, we are to decide between four possible actions, A, B, C, D, each affecting three people, Alicia, Shaq, and Leslie. The following table indicates the utils that Alicia, Shaq, and Leslie get from these actions.

	Alicia	Shaq	Leslie
A	15	−2	−2
B	5	4	1
C	−2	11	0
D	6	6	−2

This means that action A produces 15 utils for Alicia, −2 utils for Shaq, and −2 for Leslie, and action B produces 5 utils for Alicia, 4 for Shaq, and 1 for Leslie, etc. Which action would the utilitarian accept? Even though we are given so little information, do you agree with the utilitarian's choice? Based solely on this information, which action would you select and why?

3. Can you think of any obligations, supported by many people, that do not produce more happiness than unhappiness? State what they are. What would the utilitarian say about these supposed obligations? For example, how would a utilitarian explain that so many people believe in such obligations?

4. What position would you expect a utilitarian to take on the following

issues: abortion, free speech, laws regulating drugs, antipornography laws, the production and sale of fur coats, welfare reform in the United States?

8.3 Problems with Act-Utilitarianism

Although utilitarians are thoughtful, sincere, and socially concerned, and underscore the crucial moral value of happiness and nonharm, their doctrine has been attacked as impractical, unidimensional, and unfair. Furthermore, some philosophers complain that act-utilitarianism is an overly demanding morality because we are always obliged to choose from among the actions that exactly produce the most happiness. Under this moral view there is no room for morally extraordinary actions. Actions that go beyond the ordinary demands of morality are called *supererogatory*. For the utilitarian no actions are supererogatory. In this section, we examine each of these complaints.

In study questions 8.2, the table of values offers a neat set of numbers, each assigning an outcome in utils to an action. Action A produces 15 utils for Alicia, –2 utils for Shaq, and –2 for Leslie. This may sound plausible. We might know that going out to dinner for ribs will terribly upset Shaq, the vegetarian, and please Alicia due to her upbringing in Texas. Numbers like –2 and 15 may be a good relative guess at the outcome, but it is a guess and might be quite wrong. Shaq may overstate his objection to eating meat. Subconsciously or consciously he may desire meat and get great happiness from it. Our estimates may be wrong, even when we know each person well, which, of course, is not always the case.

Let's examine a case where we would have difficulty figuring how happy a decision would make the people involved. Suppose we are dealing with an issue about which we have a little previous knowledge. We have noticed that Alicia gets excited over a small gift, but that Shaq only gives a clear response to a valuable gift. Since we have only $100 to spend, we decide to divide it up as $5 for Alicia and $95 for Shaq. This seems to produce a great deal of happiness. Alicia responds well, and so does Shaq.

Did we do the right thing? Alicia might not be so happy with the gift and may respond out of courtesy. If we knew more about her, we might have interpreted her approval differently. Shaq may have been delighted with a $50 present, even without much expression. The added delight he shows with a $95 present might not indicate much additional pleasure. If we had spent $50 on each, perhaps the amount of pleasure would have been significantly increased.

Some people are more expressive than others about equally strong feelings. Regardless, no one really knows how to compare the pleasure one person receives with the pleasure of another. This is called the problem of *interpersonal utility calculations.* We can observe the behavior of two people, but this behavior may not give us an accurate reading of the pleasure either one receives. Though pleasure is an internal state, even a single person, after two experiences, may not be able to specify the degree to which one pleasure surpasses the other. The problem of interpersonal utility calculations is, to many utilitarians, an insurmountable problem because pleasure is too problematic.

A better way to determine "happiness" is through observable situations. Since pleasure is unobservable, some utilitarians have decided that what matters is the satisfaction of *preferences.* Those who measure pleasure by utils believe that an exact number represents happiness attained, which appears to be unrealistic. Using utils is a mistake; all we can really know with assurance is that some one state of affairs, say A, is preferred to another, say B. When people rate outcomes *ordinally*—that is, as long as they rate outcomes as first, second, third, etc., without saying how much better one outcome is than another—then the utilitarian can more realistically claim that decisions should be made that, insofar as we can, give people their most preferred outcomes. This scheme, theoretically at least, is favored by economists. They believe that preferences can be revealed through actions; if we purchase A rather than B, and A costs more than B, we reveal that we prefer A to B. This, those economists claim, is all it means to say that A makes you happier than B: you have a *revealed preference* for A.

Using revealed preferences sounds more realistic than the assignment of precise *cardinal* numbers to utility. Cardinal numbers indicate the exact amount of utils in an experience, as in the question about Alicia, Shaq, and Leslie. These numbers can be compared in the utilitarian scheme. If experience A produces 3 utils and B produces 6 for Alicia, then B makes Alicia twice as happy as A. This does sound unrealistic. But revealed preferences are also difficult (if not impossible) to determine, may be contradictory, and may not remain constant for long.

We can show that preferences are inconsistent when a person prefers A to B, and B to C, but C to A. For example, I might prefer a five percent return on a certificate of deposit (CD) to a three percent return on a tax-free bond, and a three percent return on a tax-free bond to a mutual fund, but, surprisingly, I might prefer a mutual fund to a five percent return on a CD. In this way I either am considered inconsistent or have, over possibly a short period of time, changed my preferences. Either way, the utilitarian faces problems because the intent is to produce more happiness or more preference fulfillment. If preferences change easily, then the opposite outcome may be unintentionally produced; that is, by the time we make and carry out our decision, preferences may have changed enough so that we end up hindering preference attainment by securing things that people do not want. Furthermore, we might reveal preference for something out of ignorance about it. We all know about wanting something we think will make us happy, only to find, when we get it, that its real appeal was less than its imagined appeal. Preferences are tricky because we might be ignorant about our preferences or we may find situations incomparable. How do we decide what we prefer when comparing a short-term pleasure, like going to a movie, with the long-term rewards that we get from studying moral theory? (If you don't like this example, make up your own.)

The difficulty of determining what makes people happy suggests that applying the utility principle is impractical. But let us assume that we can make interpersonal utility calculations, or that we can determine, after careful observation, what people prefer. These are heroic assumptions. But even under this hypothesis, the principle is impractical. We don't know how many people will be affected by our actions. We do not know how an action performed today affects a person's behavior tomorrow. Doing good today, say helping a sick person, might create psychological dependencies. We do not have adequate knowledge about habit formation in general, let alone habit formation in particular cases. But we do know that what is done today may create habits, good or bad, tomorrow. Because our actions may affect many people, problems about determining long-run happiness are compounded. When we think about the items Bentham would have us consider, we begin to see how impractical anything but a rough and ready utility calculation can be. (Do you think a rough and ready calculation is enough?)

We might be able to overcome these problems by resorting to common sense. In this way, especially when we deal with events that involve a large number of people, we might be able to make good utility estimates. Up to a point, better health care clearly makes people happy. Some want no care, and others are hypochondriacs. These idiosyncratic traits are balanced out in large numbers of people. Typically, or on the average, people want better health care. The utilitarian properly argues that a better system of care is a good thing. But utilitarians are not good at specifying the details of what constitutes better care. So even in terms of large-scale action, the best a utilitarian can hope to do, practically speaking, is make suggestions about basic policy.

If practicality were the only problem, the utilitarian might feel more at ease. After all, abstract principles do not give specifics; instead, they tell us what to give careful consideration. Although we might not be able to make precise calculations, we are to do the best we can. The impracticality of making a new calculation for every action might also need to give way to making our best estimates for significant actions. We may hope for more direction from a theory, but if this is the best that can be done, the utilitarian may claim that in practice we are forced to do second best: make approximations, and risky predictions, and take calculation shortcuts.

The critic may persist: the whole idea of determining who is made happy is an illusion. If this is the only criterion, if we have no theory about human needs, morally proper rules, moral commitment, or moral conventions, we will always be chasing a mythical point of maximal happiness. We know that, in our personal lives, the more we try to pursue our happiness, without commitments and tough choices, the more we are likely to fail. Instead, if we become loyal to a cause (recall Royce's suggestion) and act in ways we know to be responsible independent of utility, we will end up satisfied, fulfilled, and probably happy.

The practicality debate goes round and round. Whether utilitarianism is impractical, it suffers from a greater problem, morally speaking. It often seems to be an immoral doctrine, suffering from serious *moral counterexamples.* A moral counterexample has this structure: We accept a moral principle as a hypothesis. Then we examine the actions that the principle demands under various circumstances. If a theory clearly demands actions that are *generally* considered to be *basically* immoral—serious moral infractions— then that theory is considered to be disproved or weakened by those counterexamples. For a counterexample to be strong, the theory must clearly claim it is required, and that required thing must be widely, and obviously, considered quite wrong.

Utilitarianism is subject to many easily produced counterexamples. These are cases where the greatest happiness could be produced by an institution or a situation, yet the happiness is immorally produced. The most famous counterexamples to utilitarianism deal with slavery and punishment of the innocent. They are usually presented as hypothetical cases:

(1) Imagine a society where ten percent of the people are slaves. They are miserable, but because of the benefits from slavery, the other ninety percent are much happier. Those who are not slaves may feel superior, avoid difficult work, and have a larger share of the economic pie. In this example, if the slaves are freed, they become happier, but the population generally suffers. The sum total of happiness goes down with freedom. If all of this turns out to be true, the utilitarian is forced to accept slavery, a blatantly immoral institution.

(2)   Imagine a town faced with a crime wave. Unless the police get a suspect soon, nervous, gun-carrying townspeople will start to shoot at each other in fear, and the police investigation will be hampered. All of this can be stopped if some habitual criminal, an undesirable person anyway, is framed. Indeed, the town will be made more peaceful, an undesirable person will be put out of commission, and the police can get on with business—but only if an innocent person is framed. Given these

circumstances, the utilitarian principle supports framing the innocent person, but this appears immoral.

Both counterexamples involve sacrificing the well-being of some people for the good of the rest. This seems unjust. But utilitarians rightly claim that they support social reforms, especially against social institutions such as slavery that produce so much misery. By and large, utilitarians support a well-regulated police, a fair judicial system, and just punishment. But the point remains: *if* the opposite provides more happiness, then slavery and punishment of the innocent must be done. Utilitarians are *theoretically* committed to the claim that, in these counterexamples, the apparently immoral action is the proper action.

Utilitarians may counter that these counterexamples are improbable. We do not generally judge theories by far-fetched examples. The critic persists, saying that cases like these often happen in social life. A disadvantaged youth is ridiculed to the greater happiness of the elementary school students. A convict is given a heavier sentence due to political pressure. Rights, like the right to free speech, are infringed because it is the acceptable thing to do. The tyranny of the majority, or of an influential minority, may sway utility calculations in an immoral direction. The act-utilitarian rejects counterexample scenarios with the claim that such circumstances only *appear* to cause more happiness. In reality, more pain is produced, and that is why such things are wrong. Others claim that this is merely a utilitarian assumption, and that more happiness can be produced by immoral actions. (Consider where you stand on this debate.)

Some utilitarians accepted the force of the counterexample argument. They responded by developing rule-utilitarianism (which we examined in Chapter 5), so that instead of evaluating particular cases of slavery or punishing the innocent, rules about these things need to be evaluated. The individual case is not judged: that is too impractical and too susceptible to counterexamples. By judging general issues, the rule-utilitarian believes that both problems, impracticality and counterexamples, can be solved. The act-utilitarian rejects this approach. If happiness counts as the main value, it is immoral rule worship to accept a less happy outcome in an individual case merely because the general application of a rule results in greater happiness. And utility calculations made about a rule may be even more difficult than those made about a particular action. After all, we are closer to the current circumstances than we are to actions done in the future, or in far-away places, under a rule.

The debate between act-utilitarians and rule-utilitarians may be mediated. Perhaps we should have rules, but allow exceptions. Rules may serve especially well in institutions, like the government, bureaucracies, or the law, but perhaps in family life actions should not come under binding rules, so that in each case happiness may be the main consideration. In more local environments we know more about those involved, and so can calculate happiness or preference satisfaction more directly, even if only approximately. If this observation is correct, then utilitarianism must more carefully specify the domain over which calculations are made. Over broader domains, say those involving governmental action, a rule orientation may be more appropriate, while in a narrower domain such as family activities, covering actions affecting fewer people, a more direct, act approach may be in order.

Utilitarians are subject to counterexamples because their theory is unidimensional. The moral domain is vast, so it is easy to select some well-supported rule or principle with which act-utilitarianism conflicts. The sacrifice of an innocent person for the good of the community appears unjust. When we think of each person as having a unique moral value, then the fact that people achieve happiness at another person's expense doesn't compensate morally for the sacrificed person's misery.

The unidimensional quality of utilitarianism is evident in its attitude to *moral praise* and *blame*. Since all actions are morally regulated, for the utilitarian, by the sum of happiness, whether moral praise and blame is to be given is also determined by the sum of happiness that results. If we knowingly praise an evil person for being morally good and this produces enough happiness for enough people, then praising an evil person is morally obligated. This appears to be an embarrassing position for a moral theorist. But the utilitarian is only concerned with outcomes, so the character traits of people, their virtues, are only significant insofar as they produce happiness. Others view traits, such as integrity, as inherently valuable. We praise a person for having integrity because we value integrity. The utilitarian believes that nothing but happiness has intrinsic value. Others wonder why this exalted state is only given to pleasure. Aren't moral rectitude, courage, integrity, honesty, loyalty, and beauty as valuable as happiness? Of course, the utilitarian answers that we value virtues because they produce happiness, and those who value them apart from happiness put instrumental values over the final goal, the production of happiness. (Make sure you understand the utilitarian's reply, which deals with the reasons we value things.)

Utilitarianism, paradoxically, turns out to be a somber or demanding theory. This is paradoxical because it begins by supporting the production of happiness. We are always obligated to the action that, of all our choices, produces the most happiness. Even though this is the case, the utilitarian places extreme burdens on us all. Whether you should be reading these lines now, or helping a friend or a family member, or working, or studying biology, should be determined by the amount of happiness such actions produce. The American philosopher Shelly Kagan challenges us to consider whether what we are doing now actually does produce the most happiness. If I go to a movie, couldn't the seven dollars I spend do more good if I gave them to UNICEF? In fact, wouldn't it be better yet to dedicate my life to some social cause designed to save lives? The reply—that demands about my life, how I spend my money, or what I do—are unfair, and may make my life miserable doesn't hold status in the utilitarian calculation; if giving money to charity creates more good than going to a movie, this is what I must do. The initial enthusiasm of the appeal to happiness soon results, at least according to Kagan, in a somber commitment to universal, or near universal, sacrifice. You should do the action that produces the most happiness for the greatest number of people, no matter what that action is.

In calculating utility your own happiness doesn't count more than the happiness of anyone else. Everyone's happiness counts equally. The main question is about how much happiness is produced. So if I give my money to a good cause, the unhappiness that the loss of money causes me doesn't count for any more or less than the unhappiness avoided by the charitable gift. Your actions probably affect you, and those close to you, more than others. Those you cannot affect don't count in your calculations, but those close may gain or lose happiness depending on your actions. So in this sense we may believe that by getting a good grade in a course, or learning ethical theory, we are doing the best thing possible. But this is doubtful. Given the misery around the world, Kagan is probably right that utilitarianism demands that we all become slaves to the demands of morality. (Consider whether you think Kagan is correct about this.)

The demands of utilitarianism are extreme. You are to do the action that produces the most happiness. If this demands self-sacrifice, or saintly actions, you must act like a saint. And if this involves selfish actions, then we are morally required to be selfish. But most believe that morality is not so thoroughly demanding; we are not required to act like a saint, no matter how praiseworthy that is. Saintly actions, in this view, are supererogatory—they go beyond the demands of morality. Perhaps the problem is that utilitarianism has limited the moral range. Utilitarians make only narrow distinctions between morally permitted, morally encouraged, and morally required actions. We are permitted but not required to do an action that is equal to another in its potential for satisfying the utilitarian principle. But one or another of the actions that promise to *maximally satisfy* the principle must be selected. The utilitarian restricts this option, permitted actions, to cases in which prospective outcomes are tied. When the range is limited— in this case, allowing permitted action only in the case of ties—we want a solid justification. Utilitarians think they have such a justification, for what we all want, happiness, is at stake. Although we all may want happiness, we want other things as well: freedom, fairness, and even complacency.

Of course, happiness and pleasure count. If everyone pursued each other's happiness, we would surely face a better world. This is the appeal of the utilitarian. But the critic points out that pleasure is derivative. We get pleasure when we are loving, caring, concerned, dedicated, capable, successful, creative, courageous, etc. These things matter, and we are happy because they have independent value, the value we give them. The utilitarian answers that since such things make us happy, they are often required by the utilitarian calculus.

Study Questions 8.3

1. Think of a situation in which you have several options, and you believe that you can easily calculate the utility gained or lost by the few people involved in each option. Do the same for a set of options where making calculations would be difficult. Explain why in one situation you can make the calculations more easily than in the other.

2. How serious is the charge that utilitarians are subject to counterexamples? Explain how a situation you are familiar with, at school, at work, or at home, might be considered a counterexample.

3. Is happiness the only value that should be given weight in a moral theory? Is it the main value?

4. (For class discussion.) Can a utilitarian successfully defend the theory by claiming that in application the problems discussed, e.g., interpersonal utility calculations and counterexamples, are not significant because if they were they would produce unhappiness and defeat themselves? That is, we do not have to calculate exactly because such calculations produce unhappiness.

5. Does the utilitarian principle really make us all into moral slaves? In your answer refer back to question 4, which claims that when something makes us unhappy, utilitarians begin to reject it.

6. (For class discussion.) The demand that we give our movie money to charity instead of using it for our own gain makes sense in terms of the utilitarian calculation. But it makes best sense given that other people do not give. If we all used "extra" money to do good, the need for each person to sacrifice might be very low. How should we make utility calculation? Should we consider a counterfactual world in which all make and live by utility calculations, or should we consider the actual world, in which people are selfish and often immoral, especially under the utilitarian principle? If we choose the latter, because it is more realistic, does this create a moral unfairness, making some pay for the moral failings of others? If so, what would the utilitarian claim about this unfairness? If we choose to calculate under full compliance, doesn't this involve a loss of utility?

8.4 Kantian Deontology

Utilitarianism is a consequentialism, centering on the production of a good, happiness. Most of the problems with it center around the use of a nonmoral good, happiness, to dominate moral deliberation. Many who find this objectionable believe instead that moral requirements are often valid whether or not they produce more good. These people propose a *deontological* moral theory. The most influential deontology is the work of the eighteenth century Prussian philosopher Immanuel Kant, who many believe to be the greatest philosopher ever. Kant's greatness as a philosopher comes because of his originality, the depth of his thinking, and the influence he has had. This is true of his basic theories of knowledge and reality, and also of his influential moral theory. In each aspect of his thought, Kant moved to a position centering on human contribution. We contribute, he believed, to the "reality" of the world around us by our mental activities; likewise, morality does not come from outside us, by divine command or by cultural conditioning, but from human freedom and creativity. Students and philosophers also know that Kant is as difficult to follow as he is great. So we will approach his moral view slowly and carefully, seeing how well it accords with some of our basic beliefs about moral experience.

We have all read reports about people who act heroically. We typically believe that such people deserve moral praise. But if we find out that they did the deed for a reward, or for praise, or by accident, or were somehow forced to do it, our sense of respect is diminished. Some acts that look morally praiseworthy may turn out to be self-interested or even vicious in intention. We do not want to give people praise when people act out of improper motive; we feel more comfortable in assigning praise when they act from a morally correct motive. (Think of other motives that would make you believe that a person who did a brave thing—say, swimming into Lake Erie in the winter to save a drowning child—does not really deserve moral praise.)

Kant's moral deontology is developed around a notion of a good will (acting from the morally proper motive) as the basis for considering an action morally correct. From basic questions about a good will, Kant quickly moves to a fascinating set of principles. These principles delineate a realm of moral obligation. Thus, his theory moves from his reasoning about what a good will is, what makes us deserving of moral praise, to a specification of moral requirements.

Kant begins his speculation on ethics by considering whether a person deserves moral praise for a given action. This depends on the person's intentions. If the person is acting from some ulterior motive, for personal gain, out of embarrassment, under coercion, etc., that person does not deserve moral praise, even for an action that otherwise appears morally good.

When a person acts for some personal gain, that person does not deserve moral praise because the action is a self-interested action, not a moral action. It was not done to be morally proper; it was done *for gain*. Kant argues that no actions done for personal gain deserve moral praise. They are not *morally* good actions, although they might be good from some other point of view, and might be morally permitted. Only actions done from a morally proper motive deserve moral praise.

One by one Kant considers motivations for actions and decides that they are not moral motivations. If an action is simply done to make money, it is not a morally inspired action. But what if a person does an action out of care for a family member? Remember Nel Noddings's sense of care, which we studied in Chapter 5. In her theory, an action done out of natural care is not a moral action. Only by extending care to those with whom we are not emotionally involved do we get, in her view, an ethical or moral care. Kant would agree that natural caring, as the motive for actions, is not a moral motive. In this case our actions based on care do not derive from moral motivation, that is, from a sense that we are doing the right thing, but are done because we care, because we are involved with the person. Kant would go further by claiming that even acting from a sense of care extended to those with whom we are not emotionally involved based on a recollection of natural care is not a moral motivation. When we act out of a remembered care, or out of a sense of extending care, as Noddings suggests, we are still not acting under a moral motivation, because it is the morally right thing to do, but are acting because, in some sense, we care. Kant insists that any external motivation—from a desire for general happiness to a caring attitude—is not a moral motivation. All of these motivations are like the desire for money. They are external to a moral concern.

Imagine a college student turning in a poor logic test. At the bottom of the test the student writes: "At least I didn't cheat." What might be the intention behind the remark? Perhaps it is an attempt to impress the instructor with the student's honesty. Perhaps it is an attempt to make himself or herself feel better after failing. Perhaps it is a stab at humor in a painful situation. Perhaps he or she couldn't cheat, knowing the instructor was watching, and thought he or she would make the most of that fact. Perhaps his or her friends were watching and would have thought badly of cheating. To avoid their scorn he or she may have taken the "F." None of these motivations would fill us with moral admiration for the student. But suppose the student believed he or she could have passed by cheating and needed the passing grade badly. Suppose the student didn't cheat because he or she believed it is morally wrong to cheat.

One still wonders why he or she bothered telling the professor. So perhaps some other unannounced student in the class did poorly but didn't cheat out of a sense of moral obligation. Now we start to feel that this person deserves moral praise, more than the person who announced the action. We might inquire into this person's motivation. He or she may have avoided cheating for utilitarian reasons: cheating leads to a sense of guilt and creates bad habits. This is fine, but Kant would say it is still an external nonmoral motivation. The only proper *moral* motivation is that it is *wrong* to cheat. If the student did not cheat *because* it was morally wrong, then that student deserves moral praise. Any other motivation is not a moral motivation, is not acting from a good will, and does not deserve moral praise.

When someone does not cheat simply because it is morally wrong to cheat, we may say that the person acted solely out of respect for the moral law. Kant contends that a will is good only when actions are done of *respect for the moral law*. Morality is not about happiness, personal gain, care, general advantage, or the like. Kant has stripped morality of every motivating factor except that something is the right thing to do.

The right thing to do is *categorical,* not *hypothetical*. A hypothetical requirement involves an "if." If I want to be good at logic, I should practice and study regularly. There is no general, or categorical, demand that I be good at logic. Instead, my sense of obligation about logic stems from my desire to succeed. A categorical imperative is a simple demand, "You must not cheat." Kantians demand that the rule against cheating is not hypothetical. It does not say that if you don't want to be embarrassed, don't cheat. That is a *hypothetical imperative,* or hypothetical command, one that involves some external motivation. Since Kant has taken all externals from morality, moral commands must be categorical.

A good will is not oriented to externals; morality is not about externals. Morality is about categorical commands that we ought to follow simply because doing so is the right thing. Here comes Kant's genius, and the part of his theory people find difficult to follow. He seems to have robbed morality of all content. Morality is not about happiness, pride, self-fulfillment, care, devotion, etc. What is it about? Nothing but following moral laws expressed in categorical imperatives. But his laws seem to have no content. What are the correct moral laws, and how are they established? Kant gets the answer, and brings content into his theory, by examining the nature of a moral law. A law is universally binding. A morally good action is done out of respect for the moral law, solely because it is a moral law and not for any other reason. This provides Kant the needed clue. *All* actions ought to be done that are required by a moral law, and all actions forbidden by a moral law should not be done. The one thing we know about a law is that it makes universal requirements. Some actions cannot be thought of as required by a moral law because they cannot be universally required. Others can. The test is simple. Ask whether your action can be made into a universal moral law. If it can, the action is permitted. If it cannot, you should not do it.

The law must be universal because all features about you or me are external to moral rules. The only proper moral question is whether an act is permitted by the moral law. So we universalize an action, getting rid of all specifics about our situation, to determine whether the moral law permits it.

Kant argues that the test of morality is the *categorical imperative: Can I consistently will that my action be made into a universal law?* The question is not whether I *want* such a law. The question is whether a universal law about the action is *consistent*. Suppose I find myself in a circumstance where a lie saves considerable trouble and makes all parties, especially me, happier. Morally, am I permitted to lie? Kant proposes that we answer this question by turning our action into a universal law: All people should be permitted to lie. Is this a consistent law? The law tells people to lie. If any of you are acquainted with a person who chronically or pathologically lies, you know that you no longer believe anything that person says. Lies become ineffective. A lie works when people expect the truth. If everyone followed the law and lied, no one would be able to tell a believable lie. Lies depend on the belief that most people most of the time do not lie, on the expectation of the truth. A liar is making an exception of himself or herself. For the Kantian, a willingness to make oneself an exception is the mark of immorality. We conclude that telling a lie cannot be made into a universal law and so is always morally forbidden.

We all know people who always excuse their own behavior. They are exceptional so they park in the handicap spot, cheat on their taxes, take money that doesn't belong to them, cheat on tests, take a longer lunch break, talk in the theater, or write on the walls. We respond with disdain to such behavior and wonder what would happen if everyone acted that way. Kant's moral theory explores this sense of morality, which may be read as an interpretation of the Golden Rule: Do unto others as you would have them do unto you.

So far Kant accounts for two widespread moral beliefs: (1) A person who does something because it is the morally right thing to do is especially commendable, more than a person who does something for some sort of gain; and (2) a moral person is willing to live by the same rules all others ought to follow. Kant produces this moral theory by freeing morality from everything but the moral law. Kant, the revolutionary thinker, has even freed morality from the laws of God. If we act because God commands, that itself is an externality; it is not an action done out of respect for the moral law, but out of respect for God's commands. So an action done out of respect for God's commands is not entitled to moral praise. Only the intention to follow the demands of a *universal* moral law makes an action worthy of moral praise.

Human beings often act out of self-interest. Many thinkers claim that we are programmed, or determined, to act that way. They say that we are not really free to respond to the moral law; instead, we follow the path that we are psychologically conditioned to follow. This is a form of *determinism*. Many philosophers believe that if we are determined, if we have no real choice in our actions, then morality is a sham. Kant believes that the moral experience, the fact that the person taking the logic text could have said "no" to cheating despite his or her interest in cheating, shows that determinism is false. People are not like animals; we are free to follow the moral law even against all our fondest desires.

This makes human beings special. As followers of the moral law, human beings stand apart from other species. People are moral-law makers; the moral law flows from our ability to reason about whether a moral law is consistent. The moral law originates in our ability to universalize and to follow universal maxims. When we act out of respect for the moral law, we stand apart from all external features; we overcome the conditioning power of environmental influence. By acting morally, we perform a special action, one that comes from our free response to moral laws, one that is unconditioned by external factors. In following the moral law we become ends-in-ourselves. We are not being used by something or someone else. We are acting freely, as *autonomous* moral agents. We are following the moral law we created out of our own ability to reason about the universalizability of an action. We make the moral law for ourselves, divorced from the conditioning power of the emotions, external rewards, or selfish gain.

Because people are special—as free ends-in-themselves—Kant supports a moral command in addition to the categorical imperative. People should be treated as special, as the source of morality and free action, as ends-in-themselves. This is Kant's *respect principle: Never treat a person merely as a means, but always as an end.*

This does not mean that we cannot use people. We rely on each other, socially and personally, all the time. It means that we should not *merely* use each other. We must treat one another with respect even if we rely on each other. Those of you who have worked as waiters or waitresses know the difference. Some people do not recognize the humanity in others; they are rude or else ignore the person offering a service. Others are considerate and polite. In this way they recognize the humanity of the other.

The respect principle rejects as immoral the kinds of circumstances we examined as counterexamples to utilitarianism. We cannot use part of the population as slaves: this treats them merely as means. We cannot exploit a part of the population for the gain of the rest, and we cannot exploit a single individual.

The categorical imperative and the respect principle are the two principles in Kant's moral theory. Both have had tremendous influence. Today, many believe that immoral behavior is precisely the behavior that involves making an exception of oneself, one's family, one's group, one's religion, or one's nation. Moral behavior involves the willingness to allow others to do what we permit ourselves to do. And a moral position that does not respect the humanity in others hardly seems capable of claiming a status as a moral theory.

Study Questions 8.4

1. Someone braved the cold of Lake Erie in the winter to save a drowning child. Would you be willing to praise this person's morality, if he or she acted out of a desire for a money reward? For fame? Out of love for the child?
2. (For class discussion.) If Harriet acted to save the life of another because she thought the other person was inherently valuable, would Harriet be entitled to moral praise under Kant's theory? Explain your answer.
3. How does Kant's categorical imperative differ from the Golden Rule?
4. Aristotle claimed that a moral person gains happiness from doing the morally right thing, but Kant thinks that when we gain happiness from doing the right thing, we have reason to believe we did not act out of respect for the moral law. Present reasons for and against each position. Argue in favor of the one you believe to be correct.
5. (For class discussion.) Which actions would be forbidden by Kant's moral principles: suicide, preventing homosexuals from serving in the military, abortion, capital punishment, favoring one social group for admission to college, sexual harassment, becoming a farmer, saving one's own child instead of saving two other children, failing to give food to a starving person?
6. To what degree, if any, could we consider rule-utilitarianism a Kantian view?
7. Imagine two worlds. In one world everyone is a utilitarian, and in the other everyone is a Kantian. Which world would you prefer to live in?

8.5 Problems with Kantian Morality

Kant proposes a stern morality. When we universalize we do it in the most general way. Suppose I'm faced with an unreasonable request for information, say about something personal. I might be forced to answer, so I lie, believing that the person asking the question has overstepped his or her rights. Although I may believe it is generally wrong to lie, I may also believe that some circumstances are exceptional. And I may be willing to make this into a universal law: Everyone facing coercion can lie. From a Kantian perspective, such a law may fail because if all follow the law, it ceases to be possible to lie under coercion. Kant would claim that I cannot lie. No matter how serious the situation, since lying is generally wrong, no exceptions can be made. But this seems like a form of rule worship—an overly strict morality allowing no exceptions.

To solve this problem we may try to generalize differently, and more precisely. Suppose your landlord in Shaker Heights wants information about you that is intrusive. You consider lying, but do not want to violate the categorical imperative. Should people in a mid-sized suburban city who are asked by a landlord for intrusive information be allowed to lie? It may not be inconsistent to require such lies, but it does seem as though our "universality" is a sham. We have not really generalized but instead offered a rule tailored to fit people in exactly our own situation. Kantians believe, instead, that we must generalize at a broad level.

Suppose a handicapped person wants to go to the head of a lunch line, and generalizes that all those with physical problems should go to the head of a line. This makes an exception of handicapped people, but seems perfectly acceptable. If Kant rejects such a generalization, we may argue that he is wrong. This seems to be a permissible generalization while the lie to the landlord may not seem to be. How do we determine an acceptable generalization from an unacceptable one? How do we answer such questions without becoming overly subjective? If we generalize in the broadest way, without including special features, Kant's morality looks like a rule-worshipping morality, one supporting immoral treatment of people with special needs or in special circumstances. If we allow special conditions to be included in the generalization, we have no guidance about what makes for an acceptable generalization.

The problem that we are discussing with Kantian morality arises because there are many ways to generalize. When we generalize we attribute something to all in a class. We may make a general statement about all seniors in your college. This is a generalization, but it is not about all seniors in the nation, or the world, or about all students at your college. It is about a restricted class of people. We may restrict our generalization by taking special circumstances into account, like being a senior. But which circumstances are morally relevant? We cannot merely look to universalization to answer this question because the question concerns how we may properly universalize. Kant does not provide the answer, but in moral experience we find many clues to which factors are morally relevant. Conventions give guidance, as do virtuous character and accepted moral rules.

Suppose I want to universalize about doing some writing on my computer. I ask, "Can I consistently will that everyone spend five hours a day writing with a computer word processor?" This is probably not consistent because with so many writers we would have no computers produced. It takes resources to build computers. Resources come from human beings who need to eat, who need health care, and so on. If everyone writes, no one would be an adequate producer. Should we generalize that all people who have the skill, support, equipment, and desire should be allowed to write five hours a day? This seems acceptable because there is little in our moral experience to suggest such a generalization is immoral. We accept the fact as morally proper that different people have different responsibilities, and we have established practices, norms, rules, and principles to regulate and guide those activities. We do need to make exceptions, but Kant's theory does not help us decide on morally valid exceptions.

On the other hand, some apparently acceptable broad universalizations seem to involve immoral behavior. It might be consistent to have all parents beat their children for telling lies. But is this morally right? We might believe that beating a child does not show respect for the child. But the respect principle is not precise. It says not to *merely* treat a person as a means. By acting brutally, I may respect the child's freedom because I may believe that the child could have chosen not to lie. In this way I am perhaps minimally respecting the child. Or I may use appropriate words of respect, even indicating sorrow at being forced to act brutally. Kant did believe that failure to punish a criminal, even failure to execute a person, represented a lack of respect for the criminal. Such failure treats the criminal as a child who was not free to do otherwise, and this indicates disrespect for the criminal as a responsible agent.

Unfortunately, we often don't know what respect requires, so we need more guidance on the meaning of respect. Perhaps failing to act to gain happiness for the other, or failure to act in a caring way, treats the other as a means. Kant would reject these as outside the bounds of morality. Yet merely acting to recognize the humanity in another, perhaps by some sort of polite behavior, is consistent with all sorts of disrespectful behavior, perhaps even slavery.

Kant's morality leaves us without guidance on too many issues. What social institutions do we require? How can we avoid exploitation and discrimination? What punishment is acceptable? How do we know when to give moral praise? How can we distinguish the moral saint from the person who follows the proper moral rules?

While the utilitarian narrows the moral range, the Kantian narrows both the range and the domain. For Kant all actions are morally obligatory or morally permitted. This gives a larger range than does the utilitarian, but it still excludes judgments about which actions are morally recommended but not required, and it does not allow us to compare the moral value of different actions. Kant also restricts the moral domain. We cannot readily use Kantian principles to determine which institutions are morally superior, and we face difficulty in using Kant's theory to support virtues. His theory contains one virtue, to follow the moral law, and only supports other virtues, like courage, when these help us to act out of respect for moral principles. Some virtues, like care, seem out of place in a Kantian perspective.

Kant's view is overly strict in not permitting exceptions and too vague in not specifying more clearly how to generalize and how to act with respect. Kant unacceptably limits the moral range and the moral domain. Although his theory reflects part of moral experience, and although it firmly insists on the creative human dimension of morality, it appears, to many philosophers, to be too restricted to offer a fully comprehensive moral perspective.

Study Questions 8.5

1. Can exceptions be built into universal moral laws? If so, can a law be made that is about one person? Are all such laws morally unacceptable?
2. How do people typically determine whether an exception is morally proper?
3. Can people respect those they are punishing?
4. Can Kant make his respect principle more specific? If so, how?
5. (For class discussion.) John Rawls believes his theory of justice is Kantian in outlook. He claims that people in his contrived original position—made up of a group of hypothetical free and equal people who are ignorant of their own special circumstances, including race, sex, intelligence, and class status—can create categorical moral principles. Would Kant agree?

8.6 The Lessons of Utilitarianism and Kantian Morality

Utilitarians and Kantians take into account only part of the moral experience. The utilitarian rightly points out that morality is about making a better life for all, and the Kantian insists that we are wrong to disrespect others and to make exceptions of ourselves. But both fail to recognize that following a simple principle leads us to results that are sometimes in conflict with other equally valid moral views. Utilitarians and Kantians would have developed better theories if they took seriously existing rules, virtues, practices and conventions, ideals, and principles. By limiting themselves to one or two principles, each appears rigid and unidimensional, inadequate in relation to the richness of moral experience. Even the rule-utilitarian fails to properly integrate the need for exceptions that arise out of the moral demands of a given context. We may learn from each theory, and apply them when appropriate, but we should understand that neither is the last word.

Further Reading

Jeremy Bentham's *An Introduction to the Principles of Morals and Legislation* (1789) and John Stuart Mill's *Utilitarianism* (1861) are the classic sources for an initial inquiry into utilitarianism. J. Smart and B. Williams, in *Utilitarianism: For and Against* (Cambridge: Cambridge University Press, 1973), can help to bring the account more up-to-date. Kant is difficult to read but worth the effort; try his *Fundamental Principles of the Metaphysics of Morals*. Sir David Ross's *Kant's Ethical Theory* (New York: Oxford University Press, 1954) should provide some help in understanding Kant's position.

Endnote

1. Jeremy Bentham, *An Introduction to the Principles of Morals and Legislation,* Chapter 4, first published in 1789.

9

Moral Values: Welfare, Freedom, and Justice

9.1 Moral Values

In the preceding chapter we examined a consequential moral theory based on a single moral principle, the utilitarian principle, and Kant's deontology, expressed by the categorical imperative and the respect principle. These principles implicitly or explicitly appeal to values, moral and nonmoral: happiness or pleasure in the case of utilitarianism, and fairness and respect in Kant's deontology. Such moral values are presented within main principles, which also tell us how such values should be treated. For example, the utilitarian wants happiness to be maximized for all. When we examined these theories, we also explored how the values in those theories may be defined—happiness or pleasure may be expressed in an ordinal measure or in a preference scale—and we found that we may universalize with more or less precision.

Principles often refer to basic values, but values may be explored independently, without considering principles. In this chapter we explore three values, *welfare, freedom,* and *justice.* All three have been used in basic moral principles and are considered desirable, things we typically want more of rather than less. In this way, these values guide moral inquiry. Freedom, justice, and welfare have been defined in many different ways; each is sometimes given a dominant role in moral decision making but sometimes is considered subordinate to other values. All three values are well supported in moral experience; most people prefer a world with greater freedom, justice, and welfare even when we recognize that one or the other must take precedence over the rest. In social life these values are the central concern of basic political debate, and they often play a leading role in individual decision making.

Contemporary moral philosophers have presented and debated theories about what these terms mean. Different views on a single term are often conflicting, and theorists debate which value should be given priority and the role each should play in moral decision making. We examine some of these views, hoping to lay the foundation for basic conceptions that may help us in our moral decision making. Each basic value represents a needed and desired feature of human social life. The task of the moral theorist should be to guide human actions so that the world we live in has more freedom, justice, and welfare. Because each is highly valued, we need to find ways to bring about circumstances where these values are mutually supporting rather than conflicting, as is often the case today.

9.2 Welfare and Nonharm

We first examine the notion of *welfare*. According to many moral theorists, we have a responsibility to promote welfare. But how we do that depends on our notion of what welfare entails, and which aspects of general welfare are to be given priority.

Welfare generally signifies all those features of life that make life worth living. The utilitarian believes that welfare is reducible to happiness or pleasure. For the utilitarian, all worthwhile things, such as food, education, sex, security, the arts, recreation, wealth, income, and longevity, are measured by how much pain they avoid or how much pleasure they produce. But as we have seen, theorists debate whether and how such a notion of welfare can be measured. Economists focus on revealed preference, and seek to promote welfare by securing what people prefer. But others insist that *interests* count more than preferences. The American philosopher Joel Feinberg defines an interest as something a person has a stake in because that person stands to gain or lose depending on what happens to that thing.[1] Thus, welfare may be gained by promoting and protecting what people have an *interest in*. Interests are somewhat more objective than preferences, which are defined in an entirely personal or subjective way. For example, one cannot have a *preference* for something one does not know about, but one may have an *interest* in it. If I inherited a million dollars yesterday but was not informed about it, I still have an interest in that money. Although we may not prefer the things that promote good health, we can have, unknowingly, an interest in them. We may claim that interests are more objective because they may exist independent of our knowledge, and others may know better than we what our interests are. (When preferences and interests conflict, which do you believe should be taken as primary?)

One approach to welfare is defined in terms of satisfying human interests. This approach, however, is subject to criticism because people have interests in odd, sometimes elaborate, sometimes harmful things, such as extreme wealth or illegal drugs. A theorist is inclined to rank interests; some are more important than others, some more valuable (however "valuable" is defined). Without health, for example, little else matters. Health is a fundamental interest, while owning 30 shares of a Fortune 500 stock is less fundamental. Morally speaking, we may have greater obligations in relation to basic needs (food, clothing, medical care, basic education) than to less basic goods. So if all of us have an obligation to be charitable, then that obligation might focus less on contributions to a college than those to a food-for-the-poor program. And if we have a general political obligation to promote welfare, then in ranking goods our efforts ought to be directed first of all to meeting basic needs.

Depending on the order of priority among interests, a different form of utilitarianism may be developed. We might add to Bentham's list of standards used to judge pleasures, which we covered in the previous chapter (duration, intensity, propinquity, certainty, fruitfulness, and purity), that a more basic interest is to be given priority over a less basic interest, regardless of how subjectively pleased this makes a person. Subjective pleasure may be considered a faulty indicator of genuine, long-run pleasure. We can justify this by claiming that actions now affect people in the future. Because we cannot predict the future with accuracy, basic needs are arguably a better indicator of future happiness than less basic goods.

Welfare is often extended to include the absence of harm, which, together with the injunction against committing harm, is often singled out for special consideration. Some theorists believe that a prohibition against harm is the most important thing in moral life. Many are tempted to say that as long as I don't harm anyone else, I should morally be free to do what I want. Compared to nebulous concepts like freedom and justice, nonharm sounds like a term that should be easy to define. Although the difficulties are not as great, defining nonharm is not as straightforward as it first appears. (Before going on, you should try to formulate what you mean by not harming someone else.)

Joel Feinberg completed in 1988 a massive, four-volume study of "harm," *The Moral Limits of the Criminal Law*.[2] Anyone interested in this concept is well advised to consult this careful and thorough study. Feinberg's work is about the limitations we should place on governmental use of the coercion involved in the application of criminal law. He argues that criminal law should only be employed to protect against harm. In this way, Feinberg is a liberal, meaning that he assumes that individual freedom is a basic value and should only be infringed, in this case by imprisonment, as a last resort. Use of the coercive power of criminal law requires a strict moral defense. Feinberg believes that imprisonment is only justified if it can be shown to prevent harm, and for this reason he offers his conception of harm. We are not going to study his examination of the criminal law; instead, we will focus on how he develops his notion of harm.

In Feinberg's account, *harm* means a setback to an interest. This typically includes physical and emotional harm, as well as setbacks to interests like financial gain. If we extend Feinberg's analysis beyond the criminal law and introduce a *nonharm principle,* claiming that we all have a basic moral responsibility not to harm, then difficulties become apparent. On a daily basis, we all are harmed in ways that are not morally offensive. When an instructor gives a grade, students may be harmed, even seriously harmed. Yet this is not usually considered to be covered by a nonharm principle. (Even ethics instructors routinely give grades without giving much credence to the idea that they are doing harm.) Feinberg deals with such accepted cases of harm by adding that nonharm really refers to "wrongful" harms. A *wrongful harm* is a harm that violates a person's rights. But this leads to problems about what rights a person has, a moral issue that must be solved before we know what kinds of harm count as wrongful. When we question whether harms are wrongful, the whole idea of using nonharm as a basic value begins to look suspect because some harms, those that do not violate rights, are not considered to be wrong. There must be some values included in our notion of what rights we have that turn harms into wrongful or nonwrongful; these values serve to evaluate harm. In their evaluative role, these values seem to take primacy over harm as a basic value; if nonharm were the basic value, then all harms would be wrongful.

Problems continue. Feinberg begins to extend the notion of harm. The simple claim—that as long as I don't harm anyone else, I can do what I want—looks more complex as he extends the notion. Harm starts out involving an individual doing something against another, and the first extension involves the failure to do something. In some cases, a *failure to act* is, in Feinberg's view, *the moral equivalent of actually doing harm.*

Feinberg's extension of his conception of harm comes by way of an analysis of a *bad Samaritan.* We know that a good Samaritan helps another in need. A bad Samaritan refuses to help. To make matters worse, this person refuses to help even when helping involves little or no personal effort or cost. Imagine a person sitting by the side of a swimming pool watching a small child drown when the child could easily have been pulled from the pool and saved. Without even getting wet, this bad Samaritan could have saved a life. By refusing to help the child, does the bad Samaritan *cause* harm? Whether or not the person is the cause, Feinberg believes that he or she does contribute to harm. Not helping the child is the moral equivalent of causing harm. So he calls for bad-Samaritan laws that make it a crime to fail to help when giving help involves little personal cost. Feinberg believes that a harmed person is harmed by those who could have prevented the harm at little personal cost. This sense of harm, preventing harm at little personal cost, extends the nonharm principle; we cannot simply do what we want unless it harms someone else, but now we must also seek to prevent harm when that comes at little personal cost.

If we agree that preventing harm, when at little personal cost, is a basic moral responsibility, we begin to see the need to extend the nonharm principle even further. Acting together, we may have a responsibility to prevent harm because through collective action personal cost can be minimized. If you or I are given the responsibility, individually, to prevent harm, we may be able to do very little. But through social cooperation, with pooled resources, we have prevented harm with programs ranging from medical vaccination to fire and police protection. We do this through organized intervention: police and fire departments, the maintenance of a social infrastructure, health care, education, and the like. For example, through taxation, we are able to supply the money necessary to fund many activities designed to avoid harm, including disability and unemployment insurance. Feinberg comments: "Part of the reason why I don't have a duty to maximize the harm-preventing I can achieve on my own is that society collectively has preempted that duty and reassigned it in fair shares to private individuals. Collectively there is hardly any limit to how far we are prepared to go to prevent serious harms to individuals."[3] By using cooperative techniques, we, together, can prevent harm at comparatively little personal cost. From a moral point of view, refusal to prevent harm at little personal cost may be as offensive as doing harm. (Do you agree?)

Feinberg's willingness to use the government to prevent harm adds a utilitarian note to his sense of nonharm, yet he insists on a fair division of social burdens. The utilitarian is willing to place great burdens on you and me. We may be required to sacrifice all we have and become moral saints. This may be commendable, but it seems to go beyond the ordinary demands of moral requirements. The utilitarian shrinks the moral range by making nearly all recommended actions obligatory. Feinberg, on the other hand, does not require individually heroic action; by organizing socially we can spread the burdens of harm-avoidance. Many social problems attacked by the government involve such harms as poverty, lack of education and health care, unemployment or underemployment, and pollution. Under Feinberg's analysis, people may be morally guilty of doing harm when they prevent governmental power from being used to avoid harm in these crucial areas.

In Feinberg's conception of harm, the nonharm principle moves well beyond prohibiting direct personal harm. Now it dictates a social attempt to prevent harm. Thus we move into the realm of political morality. Today, the ability to do good and to do evil largely rests with governments. Governmental action is part of the moral domain. When it is considered as a way to guide us, collectively, in fulfilling the moral responsibility to prevent harm, the evaluation of governmental action becomes a crucial part of morality. Governments may act wisely or foolishly in attempting to avoid harm. Once government is entrusted with much of the collective response to harm-prevention, the government should come under frequent and careful moral evaluation.

The move to large-scale social action to avoid harm leads to difficulties; the problem of defining and locating harm becomes more difficult and perhaps more crucial. We now ask questions about who, or what group, is suffering harm and to what degree. Philosophers understand the difficulties in determining when harm is done because judgments about harm are made from different perspectives. For example, suppose Sammie has been ridiculed all her life. Now she has grown accustomed to that ridicule. Tammy comes along and subjects Sammie to serious verbal harassment, but Sammie seems unaware of Tammy's attempt to offend. Is Tammy's action harmful? We don't want to excuse Tammy because Sammie is accustomed to ridicule, so we might not judge the action by the actual harm done, but by a different standard: what would reasonably harm a typical person. We might reasonably expect that the typical person would be harmed by Tammy's abusive remarks, and thus label the remarks as harmful. But in the actual case, Sammie is not harmed by Tammy's abuse.

The question is, should we judge the harm done in relation to a general standard, based on a typical or normal situation, or judge it in terms of the actual condition of Tammy and Sammie? This is a question of the proper *baseline* for determining harm. The conception of harm used in any moral theory must give serious attention to the selection of a proper baseline because, depending on the baseline used, different moral judgments will be made.

If we take money away from a rich person, we harm that person. But is a less wealthy person harmed by not having as much money as the rich person? The baseline is the point from which we make such judgments. If the current situation is the baseline, then we assume that people rightly have what they have. The poor may be harmed because they lack health care, or jobs, or education, but not because they do not have enough money to buy the things they want. On the other hand, suppose we take equality as the proper baseline. Then those with more must justify having more. Because we believe that the rich are harmed if they lose money, we may also believe that the poor are harmed by not having money. People may grow accustomed to some things in the environment of poverty; they might not be harmed in the same way others would be harmed by offensive or ugly conditions. But this may be like the case of Sammie. We may want to judge harm by how a typical person would react, and not by the way someone reacts who has become accustomed to a bad environment. Poor housing, ugly and polluted neighborhoods, poor health, crime, and lack of opportunity are best measured, one may argue, from a baseline of equality. That is, using the notion of equality as a baseline, we can determine the extent of harm done by the environment of poverty better than by simply looking at the way people are currently harmed.

Another alternative is that the proper baseline is the point at which all basic needs are satisfied; thus anyone whose basic needs are not met is harmed, and people above the baseline are not socially harmed, even when someone else has more. Using basic needs as a baseline will support different judgments than using either the status quo or equality. (Be sure you understand why this is so.)

A baseline is needed because people's interests, a key ingredient in the conception of harm, are partly formed by the social process. People might routinely accept harm because they are socially conditioned to believe that the harm is proper, or perhaps because they do not notice the harm. But when a baseline is established, we may better understand the harm done by the social process. For example, as long as we do not have a baseline for comparison, we have difficulty deciding which kinds of social roles are exploitative. Does the fact that black people or men have a significantly lower life expectancy than white people or women indicate social harm? Suppose the baseline is equality. Under this assumption, we answer the question about men living shorter lives this way: if the social roles of men and women were equal, would men still show the same difference in life expectancy? Suppose that the difference in life expectancy would be less under equality. Then we argue that men are socially harmed. But if equality is not the baseline, we may argue that men have chosen activities that lead to shorter life expectancy—for example, smoking. In this case, men have hurt themselves and are not socially harmed. This example should show that the baseline we accept makes a difference in how we view harm, especially social harm. The baseline helps pose the question. But answering such questions is difficult, no matter what the baseline. (How do you think the issue should be approached?)

Harm started out as a simple notion, but we found significant room for disagreement about the role it should play in a basic moral principle. Some would prefer a narrow notion, defined in relation to direct individual action that wrongfully affects the interests of another. Others want a broad conception of harm, relying on the baseline of equality, and so they include in their moral evaluations social influences and socially organized actions that foster harm-avoidance. Moral experience is broad enough to include both, depending on the circumstances. From an individual's day-to-day point of view, nonharm is best thought of in a more restricted way; in evaluating social institutions, a broader notion of harm may be more appropriate.

Study Questions 9.2

1. Is failure to act to prevent harm properly called a "cause" of harm? In your answer consider analogous circumstances—for example, whether the failure to rain is considered the cause of crop failure.

2. Suppose a parent fails to get proper medical attention for a child. Is this failure to act a cause of harm? Can social roles—health care professionals, teachers, parents—establish special obligations to prevent harm? If so, can failure to act in those situations cause harm?

3. Suppose someone claims that the current welfare system in the United States causes more harm than good. But the welfare system is designed to prevent harm, and often does. On balance, harm done by the withdrawal of welfare payments may be great. Can someone consistently maintain that all three claims are true? (You might want to claim that different baselines are used in the three claims.)

4. Is offensive behavior harmful? Offensive behavior includes such things as obscene language, unusual dress, poor personal hygiene, poor grammar, desecration of religious symbols, and racist language. In your answer, be sure to differentiate between the various forms of offensive behavior because some may be thought to cause harm while others may not. You may want to refer to Feinberg's definition of harm and to the notion of what a reasonable person would expect or be harmed by. Does your answer depend on the acceptance of a particular baseline?

5. Consider whether an alternate baseline makes a difference in answering the following question: Is it socially harmful to women to have separate-gender public toilet facilities? (Remember that toilet facilities in private homes are almost never separate.) Now answer the same question substituting homosexuals for women.

6. Does Feinberg's analysis contain a clue to how far the state should go to prevent harm to its citizens? For example, suppose taxation and laws begin to become oppressive and unfair. Would Feinberg recommend governmental action supported by such taxation and laws?

7. (For class discussion.) Baseline arguments are often used without explicitly mentioning the baseline. Making the baseline explicit may help to defend some social policies. For example, someone defending the morality of affirmative action might claim that the baseline for judgments about the way skills are measured or about needed access must be based on where a group would be if it had not faced previous discrimination. Evaluate the claim considering the use of different baselines.

9.3 Freedom

Harm is not as clear-cut an issue as it first seems. *Freedom* (also called *liberty* or *autonomy*) is a more abstract notion, so we might expect it to be more difficult to define. Actually, arriving at a proper definition is notoriously difficult. Yet freedom is often considered a basic value in moral and political decision making, so it is given heavier weight than many other values, including nonharm. We will examine several attempts to develop a conception of freedom that can be used to guide moral evaluation, including the use of the freedom in a moral principle. A freedom principle may be expressed as "promote freedom," or, negatively, as "do not interfere with freedom." Because it is a basic value in moral experience, all theorists are under obligation to explain how freedom fits in their view, whether it is given a dominant position, and how failure to give it a basic role can be explained. (How would a utilitarian explain that freedom is not given a basic role?)

Philosophers distinguish between two types of freedom: positive freedom and negative freedom. *Negative freedom* occurs whenever no external restrictions are imposed on a person by others. *Positive freedom* goes further by focusing on the ability of a person to do what he or she wants to do. A person is free, in the positive sense, when that person has the ability to do what he or she desires. For example, you are free to travel, in the negative sense, if no one places a prohibition on your right to travel. While you may have the right to travel (negatively speaking), you may not have the positive freedom to travel if you have little opportunity or insufficient funds.

The categories of freedom, positive and negative, seem clear at first, but like many distinctions, even tall and short, we are often not sure where one begins and the other ends. If someone takes money from me as I am about to take a trip, does that person violate my positive or my negative freedom to travel? If negative freedom, then does a past injustice to the head of a family that deprives that family of money violate its positive or negative freedom? What about social conditioning, or the effect on an adult of proper care as a child? If a past negative violation of freedom interferes with a person's ability to act today, we face a significant intermingling of positive and negative freedoms. Social life molds our abilities, yet the extent to which this is done is difficult to determine. When something is done to us that affects our ability to function, we think of it as an infringement on our negative freedom. If the influence of social life is pervasive (which seems to be the case), then all of our actions may be affected by external interference. The influence of social life may lead people to internalize many past external influences, so today what appears to be an infringement of positive freedom (a person is not able to do something) may actually be an infringement of negative freedom (a person was deprived, by others, of the ability to act). (Do you agree that the influence of social life on our abilities is pervasive?)

Freedom, as a moral value, often is used within moral principles. Given that freedom is desirable, a principle can direct us to ensure that freedom reigns. Freedom principles will differ insofar as they center on positive or negative freedom. F. A. Hayek, for example, is concerned with a negative sense of liberty, and he wants, in a principled way, for negative freedom to be optimized: "We are concerned . . . with that condition of men in which coercion of some by others is reduced as much as is possible in society. This state we shall describe . . . as a state of liberty or freedom."[4] He defines coercion to include the manipulation of the circumstances of one person by another so as to force that person to depart from his or her own coherent life plan.[5]

Hayek wants people to pursue their coherent life plans without coercion by others. Although Hayek does not make this clear, his view presumes that a coherent life plan is valuable and that people can autonomously develop such a plan. But our social milieu may, either in subtle or not so subtle ways, diminish our autonomy. (Consider ways in which social life makes people dependent.) Given Hayek's basic concern, he should reject such social coercion. But when social coercion is rejected, given that it may be wide-ranging, we seem to move more and more to a positive conception of freedom. For people to be autonomous they may need enabling features of life: general well-being, good health care, a solid education, real choices, etc.

Hayek recognizes the power that social life may have over the individual. He claims:

> There is the fact that man's mind is itself a product of the civilization in which he has grown up and that it is unaware of much of the experience which has shaped it—experience that assists it by being embodied in the habits, conventions, language, and moral beliefs which are part of its makeup.[6]

Talk about a person's mind being a social product refers to control over a person. The control may be benevolent, or it may be harmful, but either way it may curtail autonomy. Since control may be pervasive, Hayek's definition of freedom is not as much help in guiding actions as it first seems; now we might attempt to coerce people in order to weaken the coercive interference of socialized conditioning. In effect, Hayek's broad view of the power of social control opens speculation about actions needed to reduce coercion.

But Hayek is not done. No matter how we are constituted, by whatever social forces, we are what we are. We have plans, hopes, desires, and needs. No one knows exactly how we got these features of our lives. Social and individual life is shrouded in ignorance. Individual freedom is needed because of ignorance; no one knows enough to know what another genuinely needs.[7] By default, this leaves the individual as the one best placed to control, insofar as feasible, his or her own life. Hayek understands that social life involves interaction and control, but wants to limit that control so that the individual can be left alone, free to do what he or she wants, no matter how those desires came about.

Let's call the area over which an individual is free to act as he or she wishes an *envelope of security*. Hayek believes that society should make clear what things we are free to control ourselves; our envelope of security should be stable and clearly defined within our society. Once we have a good sense of where we may act freely, we can organize our lives around that freedom. Oddly, Hayek doesn't seem to care how that envelope is drawn, how broadly or how narrowly, so long as it is secure. For him, the way to secure the envelope is through the rule of law.[8] Once the legal system establishes the areas in which we may do what we want, an individual may feel secure in his or her actions and may depend on gains made, may keep the fruits of his or her labor, within that envelope. In this way, an individual can pursue a coherent or rational life plan. Once an envelope of security is provided, Hayek is willing to allow for state action, with its interference and force, to solve social problems. As long as a secure realm exists, he recognizes that state action is proper and may be helpful.[9]

The envelope of security is a metaphor for negative freedom. This negative freedom, for Hayek, can be consistent with taxation, economic control, and collective action. (Explain why.) It points out the need for space in which we may reliably pursue our own plans while recognizing the need for social action outside that envelope. Unfortunately, Hayek does not specify what should be in the envelope. John Stuart Mill would insist on free speech, others would insist on control over property, and still others would insist on personal privacy and freedom from police action. A private sphere is a powerful notion in moral theory. We need and want a realm over which we have control and in which we may do what we want. Ethics is a social enterprise. It establishes the boundaries of acceptable action, and it establishes the need for mutual support and mutual cooperation. Both limitations on what we may do and positive direction for actions we should perform for the good of others are consistent with having a private sphere defined by an envelope of security. Indeed, as long as the aims and purposes of a moral theory can be accomplished, the envelope should be as large as feasible.

The rule of law protecting an envelope of security is offered by Hayek as the best expression of negative freedom. But this is not enough. Positive freedom is a conception that also responds to the moral experience. Even the envelope of security is empty, or not fruitful, unless people are enabled to act rationally in that envelope. The negative conception of freedom needs to be balanced by an appropriate positive conception.

The twentieth-century American pragmatist John Dewey presents a conception of freedom that is rich enough to serve as a model of positive freedom.[10] For him, the idea of liberty focuses on freed intelligence and individuality. Dewey rejects economic and political restrictions that prevent most people from attaining "voluntary intelligent action."[11] According to Dewey, the liberal must attempt to overcome social oppression, regardless of its source. A concern with human individuality entails concern with "the structure of human association. For the latter operates to affect, negatively and positively, the development of individuals."[12] Wherever social oppression exists, regardless of the systematic source, liberalism should stand opposed to it. Oppression occurs whenever some group or class "is suffering in a special way from some form of constraint exercised by the distribution of powers that exists in contemporary society."[13]

Dewey believes that genuine development and knowledge involves social cooperation. Social life is cooperative. As individuals, people, including you and me, are dependent on social structures. A notion of freedom that sets individuals up as purely autonomous is illusory; even an envelope of security lacks significance except within proper social context. For example, in *Brave New World*, where all are brainwashed and crudely socially controlled, actions within a secure zone are no more free than actions anywhere else. (What would Hayek say about this?) Freedom will not be found in the context of unequal power and unequal control. Effective freedom requires supportive social structures that direct and promote human cooperation and mutual aid.

Dewey seeks group equality and supportive social structures. Both are required if freedom is to be more than a sham. But group equality, in current circumstances, is utopian. And supportive social structures present an open-ended demand. We can aid people with increasingly higher levels of support, and people can grow dependent on that support. Perhaps we should consider the full statement of positive freedom to be a social ideal, not a principle. In the next chapter we discuss how ideals differ from principles. At that point we can think again about how a full, positive notion of freedom, as an ideal, may function in social life.

Study Questions 9.3

1. (For class discussion.) John Rawls gives social priority to liberty. The liberties he mentions concern basic constitutional rights, such as the right to freedom of speech, assembly, and religion. He believes that these rights must be equal, that they must be secured for all people, yet he understands that some people may be unable to exercise them. Therefore, basic liberty may have a different *worth* for some people. Is the notion of the *worth of freedom* the same as positive freedom?

Suppose a freedom is not worth much to a person, say a poor person, yet that person lives in a society with basic constitutional rights. Is it fair to say that the person lives in a free society?

2. Do Hayek's and Dewey's positions on freedom conflict (as Hayek believed), or are they complementary?

3. Do individuals in most advanced industrial societies have secure zones, envelopes of security? If so, what are they like, and how do they differ from society to society? Answer the same question about yourself.

4. Does education promote freedom? If so, in what ways?

5. To prepare for the following chapter, on ideals, think of an ideal—for example, to love your neighbor as yourself. How does the ideal you have in mind differ from a principle, like Kant's categorical imperative? (Think about the use of the term "ideal," the sense we have that it is not fully attainable.) With this difference in mind, do you believe positive freedom serves as an ideal or as a principle?

6. (For class discussion.) Sometimes actions done to enhance the freedom of another might actually diminish overall freedom. Social debates about the protection of the rights of criminals, the right of free speech, and so on, often make the claim that one person's freedom comes at the expense of another's. Is this a significant social problem? Which best helps to minimize conflicts over freedom, Hayek's notion of an envelope of security or Dewey's notion of social empowerment?

9.4 Justice

A theory of justice is intended to provide an interpretation of justice and to offer principles by which human interaction—involving the exchange of goods and basic rights—ought to be governed. *Justice* occurs when the benefits and burdens of social life are properly distributed and when each person gets his or her due. We know that some people make more money than others, that some inherit tremendous wealth, that others are born into poverty, that various groups face discrimination, and that the administration of the law favors the financially advantaged. These problems provoke questions about the correct conception of justice: what is a person due, and how are society's benefits and burdens to be distributed?

If a person does not play by the accepted rules, that person is often called *unjust*. If a professor does not assign the grade a student earns, that professor may be called unjust. If an employer does not pay minimum wage, or makes an employee work extra hours, that employer is considered unjust. Laws, customs, and conventions establish expectations. When these are not met, injustice is often the result. We might consider following the established rules to be the justice of the status quo. But the rules themselves might be unjust. Why is the minimum wage so low? Why does the instructor insist on asking overly difficult questions? Still, failure to follow generally accepted rules is part of what justice involves, though only a part.

Whether the status quo is just is controversial; we can judge it using a basic conception of justice that attempts to show who *ought* to get what. Philosophers have presented many ways to answer this by proposing standards we may use to determine what is due to a person. For example, a person who contributes a great deal may be entitled to more than people who contribute little. A conception of justice may hold that **each person should be rewarded in proportion to his or her contribution.** But this is vague because contributions can be measured in many ways: time spent, the significance of the contribution to a project, the scarcity or value of the contribution. Maybe someone is needed for a small role in a large project, yet without that person's contribution the project may not be completed. If the contribution would be difficult to replace, that person, who holds the key to a unique and valuable contribution, has great *bargaining power*. Some philosophers believe that rewarding people in relation to their bargaining power is morally proper, while others believe that bargaining power is typically morally arbitrary and that rewarding it is the antithesis of morally proper behavior.

A person's contribution and bargaining power may be large because of past exploitation, past unjust reward, or present luck. If a past wrong makes someone more productive, rewarding that person may be wrong. And it may be unfair that some people are luckier than others. So some philosophers reject contribution as an appropriate standard of justice. Instead, they focus on *effort*. I once overheard students complain that a grade in swimming should be given on improvement rather than on ability. Perhaps all grades should be given on effort. After all, regardless of what skill or knowledge a person has, almost all people can choose to work hard. (Is this is true?) The proper rewards should then be measured by how hard someone works. On this view, **people are to be rewarded in proportion to their effort.**

Effort is sometimes rejected as itself socially determined. Some are able to work harder than others because of their social background, including the attitudes they adopted as children. Our social roles, our place in society, and our physical and psychological makeup may determine how hard we typically work. Past injustices and present luck may work together to affect our work ethic. (What evidence can be offered to show whether this is true or false?) Even though we find it difficult to determine who currently suffers from past injustices, especially injustices perpetrated against groups of people, it is apparent that many currently suffer disadvantage stemming from past injustices, perhaps including the stultification of effort. So another standard may be morally superior, one that is sensitive to luck, special need, and past injustice. One standard proposed is *need*. **Each person should receive in proportion to his or her need.**

Need is difficult to define. Some needs are immoral, like the need for certain drugs. Other needs are idiosyncratic and self-stultifying, like a need to attain the unattainable. Needs may be selected or learned: a person may teach himself or herself to need elaborate and expensive food, an expensive car, or a rare violin. These things may then be genuinely needed; without them life might be intolerable for that person. Even so, rewarding such needs seems to be wrong, perhaps unjust.

Moral worth has also been suggested as a proper standard for distributing rewards; **each person should receive the society's goods in proportion to his or her moral worth.** Something like this goes on in local elections for political office, or for an office in an organization, where a person may receive more votes because voters mark a ballot for those they think are morally trustworthy or morally good. A morally good person may be thought to deserve the job over someone who is not trusted. However, using moral worth to distribute *goods* seems strained; using moral goodness as a general standard of justice has had little support. When people cooperate to do a job, or work for someone else, or exchange money for goods, the whole point of the transaction is to get the job done. Whether a person is more moral than another is often irrelevant to the question of the person's just reward. Furthermore, establishing relative moral worth is tricky to the point of impossible.

None of these standards—contribution, bargaining power, need, effort, or moral worth—appears to be the sole standard, or the sole morally proper standard, to determine proper social compensation. Each does play a role, depending on the circumstance. Need is often used as the standard for the distribution of resources within a family. Perhaps it should be the only standard for the distribution of medical care. Moral worth might help us make some distribution decisions, especially if we are distributing sensitive positions or moral praise. Bargaining power may indicate a scarce resource that, because of its scarcity, should have a high price so that it is most efficiently used. That high price may offer an incentive to use the resource in a proper way.

The question about who gets what in an individual transaction is different from questions about who pays what taxes or who has what responsibility. A person with a scarce resource may be required to pay high taxes on the gains from that resource. In this way we can separate, to some degree, questions about such issues as bargaining power and gain. Although those with more bargaining power may receive more in an economic transaction, they may also pay more taxes. Other standards may then be used to determine who is to be subject to various levels of taxation. *Ability to pay* has been suggested as a morally proper standard for determining taxes, even though it may not be the only proper standard. As we watch political debates, we notice that all the standards mentioned above have been proposed as ways to determine who deserves the benefits and burdens of social programs and social taxation.

These standards have been presented as ways to determine who gets what within current basic social arrangements. That is, we assume that the basic structure is in place, and then ask how much people within that structure deserve. By *current basic social arrangements* we mean the basic organization of the economy, the government, the legal system, family structure, and education. This includes the basic ways people are related to each other based on their social identity and the roles they occupy in major social institutions. A person's ethnic group, job, or social class often influences his or her income, wealth, and opportunity. It also influences how much that person can contribute and how much effort will be expended. All of this depends on basic social arrangements.

Questions about justice do not always assume the existence of basic social arrangements. Philosophers since Plato have also questioned the justice of the basic structure. In his *Republic,* one of the greatest works in the history of Western philosophy, Plato spelled out in detail what a just state would be like. He paints a picture of the ideal state from start to end by refusing to accept the justice of any current practice. His intention in describing the ideal state is to show what a just individual would be like; he assumes that an individual and the state have analogous structures: economic need, the need for guidance, for protection, and so on. For Plato, the virtues of a good state are easier to understand than the virtues of a good individual. (Why do you think he says this? Do you agree?)

A key job of the theory of justice is to provide a critique of current structures, independent of the way things are now. Plato does this by imagining a state in which each person does, as his or her social role, what he or she is innately best suited to do. He wants children raised in common so that family life would not influence the way people function; instead, each child would be selected to do the job the child can do best, by nature, and not according to social category, including gender. The state would be divided by function, establishing social classes of workers, warriors, and rulers. However, this promises to be a state divided by class loyalty. Plato argues that a common upbringing would help to unify the state. People would not know their biological family members, but instead would view everyone as members of an extended family.

According to Plato, the state ought to be led by a philosopher-king, exercising the main control of the community; other rulers would do certain tasks under the king's direction. The rulers ought to be the wisest and most dedicated people in the community. The rulers and the philosopher-king are entrusted with all basic decision making. The wisest person ought to be selected as philosopher-king and then use that wisdom to properly guide the entire state. In this way, Plato believed that the state could embody justice, because the philosopher-king would rule based on his or her insight into the ideals of goodness, truth, and beauty.

Plato presents his state as a utopia; he does not believe it could exist. Human greed and desire for power militate against ideal conditions. Instead, he presented an *ideal*. (We will examine Plato's use of the Republic as an ideal more fully in Chapter 10.) Nevertheless, his ideal is too hierarchical and dictatorial for many. Raising children in common and selecting them at an early age for life in one social class, even though selection is based on ability and not on race, gender, or other irrelevant traits, is far from a conception of democratic participation. In a democracy, even those without special wisdom, abilities, or indeed even moral goodness are allowed a voice in government because the actions of a ruling party affect their lives. Though Plato presents an overly rigid utopia, he did lead the way in applying philosophical theory to the justice of basic social arrangements.

John Rawls engages in a similar enterprise today by trying to determine the correct principles of justice to use in organizing and changing basic social structures. He concludes that we should apply the method of the social contract tradition to an examination of fundamental social structures. The *social contract tradition,* in the writing of Hobbes, Locke, and Rousseau, examines the question of proper social arrangements by considering what people in a *state of nature* —a place without political power—would accept. Considered as hypothetical people (which the early theorists may not have done), those in the state of nature have never lived under any social control. This means they cannot be prejudiced by any current power relations. We may put ourselves in that imaginary point of view and ask what kind of social organization we would select. In order to pose this question, the classic social contract theorists define the people in the state of nature according to their views on human nature. Such views differ from theorist to theorist. Hobbes, for example, believes humans to be greedy and dominating. He thinks that a dictatorial monarch is needed to keep people under control. Locke believes that people could, by and large, participate cooperatively in social life. For him, a limited government is needed to do what people cannot do for themselves, like provide military protection and an independent judiciary. Rousseau believes in a natural inclination for cooperation that could be unleashed by proper community structures.

These conflicting views on human nature suggest that the state of nature can function as a way to introduce one's own bias about a just state. Hobbes wants a dictatorship, and his description of the inhabitants supports his version of justice. Locke thinks a limited state is most just, and Rousseau insists on communal governing structures involving full participation of nearly all. Each view depends on how the theorist defines human nature, from their own perspective, itself influenced by their past participation in basic social structures.

Rawls believes that this introduction of concrete views about human nature is invalid. Instead he wants to define an original position populated by imaginary people who have only the traits that support the production of a good theory of just social structures. For example, if the people know who they are, they might be prejudiced enough to believe that people like themselves deserve more than others. Instead, if the occupants of the original position are under a *veil of ignorance*—meaning that they do not know their personal and social traits—they will protect all people no matter what people are like. For example, hypothetical people who do not know whether they are male or female are unlikely to design a society to the systematic benefit of one gender.

According to Rawls the traits of the people in the original position enable *us* to decide what such hypothetical people would want in a society, and the kinds of principles of justice they would develop. If the people in Rawls's original position are defined under the proper constraints, then we can decide, through them, on the nature of proper principles of justice. Rawls defines the people in the original position as wanting the most for themselves, as devoid of jealousy over the gains of others, and as risk-adverse because they would not take a chance on being in a disadvantaged social class. They are under the veil of ignorance by lacking knowledge of their personal characteristics, such as race, sex, and intelligence. With these constraints in mind, Rawls believes that such people would adopt the following principles: (1) society ought to have as much equal freedom as possible; and (2) provided the presence of equal maximal freedom and equal opportunity, social goods such as income, wealth, and self-respect must be distributed equally to all representative individuals unless an unequal distribution is to the greatest benefit of the least well-off. (Do you believe that hypothetical people described as Rawls describes them would select these principles?)

Rawls claims that the benefits of social cooperation, involving the production of goods and services, must be cooperatively distributed. The best-off can get more only if their gain also helps the least well-off. If not, then the social cooperation required in a society is not reflected in the distribution of the goods produced in the society.

Among philosophers, Rawls's theory is well known and carefully studied, yet he has not attracted many disciples. Instead, philosophers continue to offer widely divergent theories about the justice of basic institutions. Some philosophers, such as Robert Nozick, a Harvard colleague of Rawls, believe that a just society respects the *entitlements* of those who worked to gain what they have without exploiting others, and that those entitlements may be used in any way people see fit. Kai Nielsen, currently teaching in Canada, concludes that distribution should be equal. Michael Walzer argues that all goods should be restricted to their proper use, their proper spheres, and distributed based on that use. Medical care should go to the sick, but money may go to those who work hard.

Although many questions about the justice of basic social structures remain to be settled, most people agree that inequality based merely on racial or gender differences is unjust. But determining the extent to which inequalities are based on race or gender is not always easy. Some thinkers make the assumption that any inequalities across large social groups cannot be based on individual differences; when considering a group we are not talking about individuals, but about an average person. In all groups, individuals differ. We should expect many similar variations among women and men, blacks and whites, etc. Where key social variations are not similar between groups—for example, that blacks have a lower average income than whites and that women have a lower income than men—racism or sexism is suspected. Faced with such disparities among groups, the demand is sometimes made that social action should ensure that such social groups are equal, on the average, in terms of goods like income and wealth.

We have been examining theories of justice relating to the way the social structure should be judged. This goes beyond the minimal sense of justice. In the minimal sense, justice involves acting consistently and according to the established rules. Sometimes the established rules are in flux, not well-established, vague, in conflict with other established rules, inconsistently applied, or morally objectionable. In such cases, a theory about the justice of basic structures may help us change the rules, or else help establish what is fair. However, once we leave the established rules, the standards of justice are quite debatable. Strong support for one standard of justice over the others, claiming that it is the only proper standard, is not appropriate. The standards suggested all make some sense. We need to explore how they may be integrated so that they may be thought of as complementary, rather than antagonistic. For example, one standard may be more applicable in one circumstance than in another, or one standard may be used to try to foster another, so that, for example, needs may be better met when people become more productive.

Many standards of justice used to evaluate basic social action are imprecise and might be used to hide injustices. Rawls's theory, for example, is intended to protect the least well-off class of people. This, in one way, is utopian, because it will require significant redistribution to make sure that all benefits help those with less; carrying through on Rawls's principles would require an unusually high level of social rearrangement. In another way, Rawls capitulates to the status quo; the least well-off are called upon to accept as fair that they have less than what other groups have. Rawls considers this to be proper even when differences are defined at birth in terms of expectations about what will be received. Since the least well-off cannot get more equality without a loss, this is called just. But their inability to get more seems to be based on the unwillingness of the better-off to contribute unless they benefit by inequality. The assumption is that if the better-off get more, then they contribute more. This inability or unwillingness to contribute should be evaluated. Even a subconscious unwillingness to contribute or structures that work only when some have more—for example, structures dependent on the investments of the rich—may be unjust. Rawls's theory might not permit this evaluation. Perhaps we should not read Rawls as presenting a utopia, or an ideal version of justice, but a view of justice that depends upon the best use of current talents, skills, and dependencies.

We do need theories that evaluate changes needed in the way things are done, accepting the status quo as the starting place, and we also need theories willing to evaluate all basic aspects of society. Utopian theories, showing us the ideal society, will be examined in the following chapter.

Study Questions 9.4

1. Rawls claims that the current family structure may not permit equal opportunity. Some are born into luxury and a supportive environment, while others are born into hostility and poverty. Comment on this and evaluate Plato's idea that a just society would raise children in common.
2. Comment on the following claims: (1) If blacks and whites have a different expected income at birth, then some injustice is behind this inequality. (2) If women and men have a different expected income at birth, then some injustice is behind this inequality. (3) If women and men have different life expectancies at birth, then some injustice is behind this inequality.
3. Rawls proposes that a free society should be judged by how well the least well-off class does. Is this a proper standard?
4. (For class discussion.) Would people different from us because they are behind the veil of ignorance agree that the position of the least well-off should be maximized? Supposing the people in the original position were not risk-adverse or selfish, would they still insist on judging a society from the point of view of the least well-off?
5. (For class discussion.) In economic theory the *long run* is the time during which all economic factors are variable. Is Rawls's difference principle valid in the long run? Or does it depend on current structures of dependencies and current class identities?
6. Is it possible that social equality is impractical and harmful? If so, how

can it be harmful? If harmful, can it still serve as a social ideal?

7. In a *meritocracy* people are rewarded with social positions and income in relation to their skills. Do Rawls's principles recommend a meritocracy? Is Plato's theory a meritocracy? How would Plato evaluate Rawls's theory?

9.5 The Lessons from Moral Values

Moral values sometimes function in private and social debate in a way that suggests that people consider them well-defined. We found in this chapter that disagreement exists over the nature of basic values and how these should be incorporated into principles. Most basic values have a narrow definition and an extended definition. The narrow definition of harm, for instance, is in terms of direct personal causation of a wrongful setback to a personal interest. This sense of harm supports a negative principle: Do not harm. But when the notion is extended, its principle becomes either "Prevent harm" or "Provide for welfare." As values take on a more positive role in moral theory, they also become more vague. Who should prevent harm and at what burden? How much welfare should be provided?

When principles are positively stated, like "Do good" or "Promote justice," they do not give specific commands to specific people. Instead of giving precise direction, the positive statement of the values in principles may be thought of as establishing an ideal, toward which we may progress a little at a time when conditions are right. We cannot do good for others all the time, but we can support institutions, including the government, that do significant good, and we can do good for many others. A sense of justice can help us direct our own activities, from our attitudes toward others to the selection of our neighborhood. We might never live in a completely just environment, or even establish a single well-defined and generally accepted conception of justice, but we can use the various theories proposed as a way to determine the impact of our actions, and to determine the actions that help to move toward the attainment of the circumstances that produce more moral value rather than less.

When basic values are broadly stated, they often do not conflict. Viewing society in terms of a variety of values tells us how far the society needs to go in order to be consistent with welfare, freedom, and justice. We may evaluate a society even if we can do little, in the short run, to bring it closer to full embodiment of these moral values. Any theory that sets moral values into permanent conflict should be viewed with suspicion. All the values we explored in this chapter are part of the moral experience; we should find the ways to realize all of them, in our social and personal lives, and moral theory should support and guide this attempt.

Further Reading

Joel Feinberg's *The Moral Limits of the Criminal Law,* four volumes (New York: Oxford University Press, 1984–1988), is an excellent place to begin study of the complexities involved in harm and welfare. F. A. Hayek's *The Constitution of Liberty* (Chicago: University of Chicago Press, 1960) provides a rich overview of a conservative view on freedom. John Dewey's *Liberalism and Social Action* (1935; reprint, New York: Capricorn Books, 1963) offers a statement and defense of the liberal perspective. In "Freedom, Autonomy, and the Concept of a Person," *Proceedings of the Aristotelian Society*, New Series, 76 (1975–76), S. I. Benn examines the basic concept of freedom.

Plato's *Republic* is the classic work on justice, and John Rawls, in *A Theory of Justice* (Cambridge: Harvard University Press, 1971), provides the best contemporary account of justice. Richard B. Brandt gathered five essays by philosophers and economists on justice and its relation to equality in *Social Justice* (Englewood Cliffs, N.J.: Prentice-Hall, 1962)

Endnotes

1. Joel Feinberg, *The Moral Limits of the Criminal Law* (New York: Oxford University Press, 1984–1988). Volume One: *Harm to Others* (1984), pp. 33–4.
2. Joel Feinberg, *The Moral Limits of the Criminal Law,* op. cit. Volume One: *Harm to Others* (1984); Volume Two: *Offense to Others* (1985); Volume Three: *Harm to Self* (1986); Volume Four: *Harmless Wrong-Doing* (1988).
3. Ibid.
4. F. A. Hayek, *The Constitution of Liberty* (Chicago: University of Chicago Press, 1960), p. 11.
5. Ibid., pp. 20–21.
6. Ibid., p. 24.
7. Ibid., p. 29.
8. Ibid., p. 140.
9. Ibid., p. 257.
10. John Dewey, *Liberalism and Social Action* (1935; reprint, New York: Capricorn Books, 1963).
11. Ibid., pp. 25–26.
12. Ibid., p. 41.
13. Ibid., p. 48.

10

Moral Ideals, Moral Exemplars, and Social Equality

10.1 Introduction

In this chapter we examine a part of moral theory that has often been ignored by philosophers. Just as philosophers are more comfortable examining actions rather than character traits, many also limit the moral range to three judgments: permitted, obligatory, or forbidden. Sometimes philosophers also claim that an action is *supererogatory*, that it goes beyond basic moral demands. In this chapter we examine judgments about things that go beyond supererogatory status to a more exalted position, the judgment that, for example, an action is *exemplary*, a family is *ideal* or near ideal, or a person is a moral *saint*.

Such judgments are part of moral experience, and they can help to regulate and guide human behavior. What is unclear is whether such judgments can be adequately derived from traditional theories like utilitarianism or Kantianism. We explore several ideals, including the notion of moral sainthood, primarily to determine their meaning and value in moral evaluation, but also with an eye to the way judgments about morally exemplary things and people fit in with traditional perspectives.

Philosophers also present ideal versions, or ideal models, of some of the things that we want. We all want to live in a good society or under a good government, we want to be treated equally, and we want freedom. Some models of ideal conditions, *utopias*, are presented to help us see the flaws in our own situation. Utopian views are impractical and extreme, and because they are "ideal," many overlook their significance. But it is clear that, as a model, an ideal can motivate and instruct moral behavior and can help us to make moral judgments.

Moral ideals are not like principles or rules. Instead they indicate what things would be like under perfect, or extraordinarily good, conditions.

Perfect or near perfect conditions will probably never exist. In fact, if we begin to approach a situation thought to be utopian, we will either drop, or redefine, our ideal as an ideal. After the four-minute mile became more common, it ceased to be held as an ideal. An ideal in current use has a suggestion of unattainability.

Moral ideals are sometimes the full expression of more ordinary basic values. Some moral ideals, like ideal freedom, justice, and welfare, have initial statements that are not utopian. We can have an envelope of security, a horizon of freedom, without living in a fully free society. Freedom in its full sense, including full positive freedom, is a moral ideal, while having this or that freedom is a practical directive expressible in a moral principle or rule.

Moral ideals may be expressed by moral values, but they may also be expressed by descriptions of the ideal life, the ideal society, the ideal teacher, or the ideal parent. As ideals, the described states are unattainable, but they are valuable as models and as goals toward which we may move. In distinction, *moral exemplars* are typically thought to be attainable. They are actual examples of someone or something that is considered especially morally good, perhaps a person we should in some way imitate. A moral exemplar, as we shall see, may be far from ideal. A moral saint, on the other hand, comes close to being ideal, especially in terms of self-sacrifice. As we shall see, philosophers have debated whether being a moral saint is a good thing.

In this chapter we present some ideals and moral exemplars. Ideals are controversial. People are often bothered by ideals, partly because ideals are presented in unrealistic terms. But many utopian views contain some truth and some helpful guidance about what is morally proper. Insofar as ideals may help to guide conduct and to develop institutions, clarifying moral ideals and moral exemplars is a helpful way to strengthen moral decision making.

Study Questions 10.1

1. (For class discussion.) Religions often use moral ideals as models of proper behavior. Are religious figures—Jesus, Buddha, or Moses—considered morally perfect? If they have faults, do these faults involve moral violations, doing what is morally prohibited, or merely moral weaknesses, doing the less perfect thing or being tempted to do something evil?
2. What is the relationship between moral virtues and moral ideals? For example, must an ideal person have all virtues or most virtues? Suppose a particular form of government is considered ideal. Does

this judgment have anything to do with individual virtues? For example, would an ideal government instill virtue or moral sensitivity?

3. Are ideals frequently used to judge people and institutions? Give examples.

4. Explain the difference (if you agree that there is a difference) between making the judgment that an act exhibits some ideal characteristic and saying that an action is obligatory, permitted, or forbidden.

5. (For class discussion.) Describe an ideal Kantian personality and an ideal utilitarian. Which of these ideals is more appealing? Which is more consistent with our moral experience?

10.2 Moral Saints and Moral Exemplars

A conception of the *ideal person* incorporates our idea of a person who is best able to make morally proper decisions, has all or most virtues, and may be thoroughly happy or fulfilled in his or her moral worthiness. Each of us may propose a different description of the ideal person; in doing so, we clarify our moral views. A conception of the ideal person may also illustrate how different values can be assimilated into a person's life. Differing ideals, some emphasizing concern with individual perfection while others focus on concern for others or on love of God, may produce different judgments about the value of different lives. An ideal cannot be fully realized, but we can incorporate aspects from many ideals, even conflicting ones, into our own lives. (Explain how this is possible.) Most of us will find some proposed ideals more attractive than others. Ideals do embody our values; as we bring more values into our lives, and into our definition of the ideal person, we express a richer conception of an ideal life.

We can think of real people who we believe come close to being ideal: Mother Teresa, Martin Luther King, Jr., Mahatma Gandhi, Albert Schweitzer. These people had faults; they are not ideal but real people. But many believe that they did lead exemplary lives approaching an ideal. As models they may inspire moral action, and give us reason to reconsider what we take to be morally right. Other figures, like demonic cult leaders, are mistakenly thought by some to lead an ideal life. We can evaluate the lives of people thought to be nearly ideal, and we can evaluate moral ideals, ours or those of others, through the weight of our moral experience. Those that militate against moral values, against personal freedom, justice, or welfare, are improper ideals. Those that reject the moral rules—say, rules about telling the truth—are not likely moral models. Moral experience helps us locate ideal behavior, but ideals can, in turn, instruct us about our moral experience and modify our sense of moral value.

Virtue ethics concentrates on a virtuous character and what it involves. An actual person presented as a moral *exemplar*—an example, held up as a model, of a person with especially fine moral characteristics—gives life to the virtues, and allows us to understand how they are developed and the kinds of rewards and sacrifices they may entail. Although notions of the ideal person vary, most conceptions include integrity, honesty, reliability, and courage. Other virtues, like kindness, care, compassion, and altruism, are not always thought of as ideal traits. Yet many people argue that these characteristics should be included in our notion of an ideal person.

A moral exemplar may be selected by the extent to which he or she exhibits ideal characteristics. The ideal person is not merely a bundle of virtues, but has some personal traits that attend a virtuous disposition. We expect an ideal person to be peaceful, contented, satisfied, fulfilled, and perhaps charismatic. Control is crucial; although the ideal person may be pulled by temptation, ultimately temptation does not win. *Weakness of will* is not an ideal trait. Control involves the proper use of emotion, the direction of emotion toward proper goals. A *saintly* person, clearly a moral exemplar, comes close to being a morally ideal person. The British philosopher J. O. Urmson, in "Saints and Heroes,"[1] emphasizes that a saintly person does act from self-control in situations where others would "be led astray by inclination or self-interest."[2] Sometimes such control is not easy and involves genuine self-deprivation, but this is not an essential part of being a moral saint. Urmson believes that a person is called a "saint" even if he or she has no contrary inclination or interest, and in this case all saintly actions are done without effort. The notion that a moral saint gives up some of the finer things in life is well ingrained, so much so that, in a recent article, Susan Wolf[3] claims: "I don't know whether there are any moral saints. But if there are, I am glad that neither I nor those about whom I care most are among them. By *moral saint* I mean a person whose every action is as morally good as possible, a person, that is, who is as morally worthy as can be."[4]

Wolf's view of a moral saint is extreme: surely nobody was ever as "morally good as possible." (Do you agree?) Her view represents an "ideal" statement, but one she finds in some ways unattractive. In effect, she believes that moral values must be balanced by nonmoral personal values involving self-interested behavior. Others argue that this position understates the moral value of personal enjoyment. The utilitarian counts one's own pleasure as well as the pleasure of others. In response to Wolf, R. M. Adams[5] claims that concern for personal interest does not disqualify a person as a moral saint:

> Albert Schweitzer, whom many have honored as a twentieth-century saint, was one who felt keenly the tension between artistic and intellectual achievement on the one hand and a higher claim of humanitarian commit-

ment on the other. Yet in the midst of his humanitarian activities in Africa, he kept a piano and spent some time playing it—even before he realized that keeping up this skill would help him raise money for his mission.[6]

Perhaps Wolf's definition of a moral saint is mistaken; recall that she claims that a saint is as morally good as can be. Perhaps a saint is simply someone who reaches some plateau of goodness, but still with room for moral improvement. Real saints are not as good as can be, so it is only in the ideal realm that Wolf's definition applies. We have already argued that ideals are helpful in the guidance they offer even though they cannot realistically be achieved. But typically we think that ideal conditions would be good to achieve, or at least good for someone to achieve. If Wolf is correct, being a moral saint doesn't look so good. It could be that she has incorrectly deprived a saint of all the nonmoral goods you and I often seek. However, it could be that the expression of an ideal typically involves negative features because ideals are stated in extreme language. An ideal might provide direction and guidance, even if attaining an ideal state is less than fully desirable. (Can you think of someone you want to be like, but not exactly like?)

Wolf's point is that an examination of the meaning of moral sainthood shows that morality should not always override other values. I think this is a mistake; it takes a narrow view of moral experience. When we say that someone is as morally good as possible, we assume a moral scale that only exists in extreme moral positions, such as utilitarianism. In a comprehensive moral view, taking into account various principles, obligations, judgments, and commitments, to claim that someone is as morally good as can be makes little sense. Someone who acts for the good of others may be morally no better than Einstein, who toiled for science. To say that someone is a moral saint may mean that that person has much courage, works diligently for others, and tends to put off the satisfaction of his or her own interests. Yet a moral saint may do other things as well that are no less morally worthy. To fail to be a moral saint need not involve putting morality into a secondary position, but may instead result from choosing to do things in a way different from—but perhaps no less morally worthy than—what we expect of a moral saint.

Wolf's view suggests that our conception of a moral saint is not fixed because people disagree about whether a moral saint needs to be a good as possible. We can readily locate other contentious beliefs about what it takes to be a moral saint or a moral ideal. We sometimes think of an ideal person as fighting against suffering and sometimes against immorality. In this way we may add anxiety and frustration to the notion of being a moral saint. Even religious saints often experience inner turmoil along with their special inner peace. We find it difficult to determine that such struggle is part of the ideal. Also unclear is whether the ideal person reflects on his or her ideal qualities. Do they know, for example, whether they are ideal and take satisfaction in that knowledge, or do they struggle to be good and believe they fall short?

How knowledgeable is an ideal person? In some moral theories, being good is a function of knowledge. Plato believed that with full knowledge we would appreciate the beauty and value of moral goodness. As we noted in Chapter 4, at one point in his life, W. E. B. DuBois claimed that much evil, at least social evil, is propelled by ignorance. (Suppose all citizens had more knowledge about the causes of social problems. Would they be more likely to vote in ways that better helped to resolve problems?) Utilitarian doctrine puts a premium on knowledge of what makes people happy, and Aristotle's good person is wise in a practical way. Yet, in religious traditions, the ideal person often has difficulty gaining knowledge of God. Plato's philosopher-king engages in a lifetime of struggle to gain knowledge of the ideal of goodness. Since knowledge is a part of so many moral perspectives, should we claim that the moral saint has special moral knowledge?

While many people include knowledge in the definition of the ideal person, others reject this. Mother Teresa may or may not be highly intelligent. Intelligence is not why she is valued: her goodness rather stems from kindness, care, and sincerity. Some people may argue that she falls short of the ideal because she lacks knowledge about the consequences of some of her beliefs. For example, some believe that her rejection of contraception, through a lack of awareness, may be antithetical to her general care. Others see her rejection of contraception as part of the unconditional value she places on human life. Also, Mother Teresa's sensitivity seems to be selective. She will not accept certain donations, sometimes offending those who make offers. After being renovated, a home in the United States was donated to her. She insisted that the carpets be removed, perhaps to the offense of those who went to the expense of having them installed. Her valued sensitivity, perhaps rightly, is to the poor and to their suffering. Once again, the issue of whether her rejection of the carpeting was as morally good as could be is strange. Her action was consistent with her life commitments, not part of some objective scale of moral perfection.

Philosophers have not spent much effort identifying the characteristics of an ideal or a saintly person. This is more common in religious presentations and in literature. But much of what philosophers say can be incorporated into an ideal. Socially, we select exemplars and pay homage to them. Elie Wiesel, the holocaust survivor and novelist, is sometimes thought to be a clear example of a person who behaves in a morally proper way. We select such people in the belief that they have more morally praiseworthy qualities than most of us and have probably sacrificed individual nonmoral concerns more than the rest of us.

A person may be a moral exemplar over a limited domain. That is, a person may do some extraordinary things, yet in other ways be unexceptional or even morally lacking. If those virtuous actions are significant enough, despite other shortcomings, that person may be thought of as a moral exemplar. In his thoughtful study, "Moral Exemplars," Lawrence A. Blum[7] offers Oskar Schindler as an example of what he calls a *moral hero*. As you will recall from the movie *Schindler's List*, Schindler was a German industrialist who saved thousands of Jews from the holocaust, yet he had his share of moral flaws. Blum presents Schindler's love of pleasure, his unfaithfulness to his wife, his willingness to lie and to take unnecessary risks, and his attachment to power as features that detract from his "moral excellence." Despite these traits, Blum believes that Schindler meets his five criteria of a moral hero:

> (1) bringing about a great good (or preventing a great evil); (2) acting to a great extent from morally worthy motives; (3) substantial embeddedness of those motives in the agent's psychology; (4) carrying out one's moral project in the face of risk or danger; and (5) relative "faultlessness," or absence of unworthy desires, dispositions, sentiments, attitudes.[8]

A moral exemplar may be far from ideal. Schindler may be an exemplar under Blum's standards, depending on whether or not his behavior violates the fifth point about relative faultlessness. Yet Schindler's morally exemplary actions came in a specific way at a particular point in his life. He had a kind of good *moral luck*, by being at the right time and place to become a moral hero. Moral luck can be good or bad; many people who live good lives, if faced with certain circumstances, would have done evil. The difference between you and me, and someone who has cooperated in evil may be good moral luck, the fortunate circumstances that have kept us from facing the temptation to do immoral things. Others become moral heroes only when the circumstances arise, rather than making the circumstances by finding the good to be done. Blum believes that moral luck—that the circumstances find the person—should not disqualify a person from being a moral exemplar, one we can emulate.

Folk heroes, religious figures, and literary creations are commonly used to promote moral behavior by presenting moral exemplars and moral heroes. Young children learn to be moral in many ways. Certainly parental guidance, religious conviction, social convention, and institutional rewards and punishments promote morally desirable behavior. But examples of personal moral excellence are also important. Having proper moral exemplars is part of forming a morally good world.

Study Questions 10.2

1. Are there any special virtues that must be present in morally ideal persons? In effect, you should present the *necessary conditions* for being a morally ideal person. Is it possible that all of the traits you list are the traits of a particular person and yet that person is not a moral ideal? In other words, are there *sufficient conditions* for a moral ideal as well as necessary conditions?

2. Select three well-known historical figures who in your opinion come closest to being moral exemplars. Are these figures generally thought to be near ideal? What features make them exemplars? Does your notion of a moral exemplar agree with Blum's?

3. We may face hazards in presenting models. For example, the moral ideal encourages dedication to that person. This may curtail moral autonomy. List some other dangers and explain how they may be avoided.

4. Should knowledge be included in the concept of a morally ideal person?

5. (For class discussion.) Is Oskar Schindler a proper moral exemplar? To answer this, carefully examine Blum's analysis of Schindler in "Moral Exemplars," or Thomas Keneally's account, *Schindler's List* (New York: Penguin Books, 1983).

10.3 The Ideal State

Many different types of ideals have been proposed, e.g., the ideal family, the ideal school, the ideal physician. All may be helpful in leading a moral life, though we keep in mind that an ideal selects certain features for emphasis that given excessive weight, as Wolf points out, may prove overbearing. Regardless, the value of ideals in terms of the guidance they offer suggests that more effort should be spent in developing them. Because they are ideals and therefore cannot be achieved, the temptation is to label such speculation as utopian or futile. An ideal can, however, be used to mark a goal toward which we may progress, and it can clarify our moral values and help in moral decision making.

Political theorists have presented ideals, *political utopias*, and even *anti-utopias* or political nightmares, to help clarify political thinking. *1984*, *Brave New World*, and *Animal Farm* are examples of anti-utopias. *Walden Two*, by the American behavioral psychologist B. F. Skinner, is an attempt to specify the ideal community. Here Skinner advocates social conditioning to ensure that people lead healthy, productive, fulfilled, and happy lives.

Although we do have recent utopian models, the most famous political utopias are found in the history of philosophy. We will examine two influential examples of utopian thinking: Plato's *Republic* and Karl Marx's nineteenth-century political doctrines.

(1) Plato's *Republic*

Plato's ideal state serves two functions. First, Plato hopes to instruct us on the value of competence, equal opportunity, and the need for a hierarchical structure. Though he believes that the state he designs, his Republic, is utopian—we can never have such a state, at least in a stable way—Plato believes that from his account we can understand the need for and the value of the structures he presents. Plato, however, had more in mind. The state and the person are, he thought, analogous; the state is the individual written large. We can more easily detect desirable properties in a state, he thought, because the basic structures of a state are free from idiosyncratic features and special individual needs. This is the second function: once we understand the ideal state, we better understand the ideal individual, and can accordingly better guide our behavior.

Plato begins his account of the ideal state when the charge is made that a person is foolish to be good or to be just. The ideal state, like the ideal person, is just. But why be just? Why be morally good? In the *Republic*, the "Myth of Gyges' Ring" pounds home this question: Why not be immoral if you can get away with it? In the myth, Gyges' ancestor, a fine example of a morally proper person, finds a magic ring that allows him to become invisible. Once he realizes that his invisibility permits him to get away with evil, his character changes. He kills the king and takes over the kingdom. Wouldn't everyone act in a similar way, doing immoral actions if all sanctions could be avoided? When immorality is to a person's advantage, and he or she can get away with it, wouldn't the reasonable person act immorally?

In answer to this challenge, Plato has Socrates explain, in great detail, what the just state would be like. His conclusion is that the ideal state would be productive, secure, beautiful, and good. In short, it would be a healthy state. The moral or just individual is, by analogy, personally happy and productive and leads a life of beauty and goodness. This healthy life, a reward in itself, would be followed as more beneficial than the unhealthy life of the immoral person.

Plato emphasizes knowledge. He believes that goodness is an absolute, unchanging ideal that we only know through constant effort, solid education, and nearly overwhelming desire. He portrays this knowledge, and how it differs from what ordinarily passes as knowledge, in another myth, the "Myth of the Cave," which may well be the most famous piece in Western philosophical literature. The myth is about people chained from birth in a dark cave, forced to face forward; the only source of light is from a fire behind them. In front of the fire, but behind the captives, cut-out figures of the things we see—trees, cows, houses—are passed, projecting shadow figures on the wall. The shadow figures the prisoners see on the cave wall provide their only knowledge of reality. The prisoners name those figures and, in what passes as science, speculate about them. One of the prisoners is released and brought out into the daylight. The passage is frightening, and the sun causes pain. When the freed prisoner adjusts his sight, he sees the reality behind the shadow figures. He is overjoyed at the beauty of reality. However, instead of staying in his newfound world, his social instincts compel him to go back to the cave to tell the others about his experiences and to set them free. They find him incomprehensible, made crazy by his experience, and would kill him if they were not in chains.

Plato wants to show that our world is the world of the cave because we are generally ignorant of the truth, including the nature of proper values, and that people like Socrates who attain true knowledge of the ideals lead a life of beauty and goodness, but are generally misunderstood, even executed. Most of Plato's dialogues have Socrates, Plato's teacher and the paradigm of philosophical wisdom, as the leading figure. Socrates was executed by the state for heresy and for corrupting the morals of the youth.

Plato constructs his Republic as a meritocracy based on knowledge. The philosopher-king knows the ideal world, knows what is right, productive, efficient, and beautiful. If this person leads and others follow his or her directives, the state functions properly. Each person does what he or she does best, and participates fully in the life of the state. Each gains from the production of goods by those who are best at it, including shoes and beds from the best cobblers and carpenters, protection by the best warriors, and guidance from guardians who are genuinely wise. The state embodies philosophical wisdom through the ultimate leader, the philosopher-king. This is a healthy, happy, and just state, a properly ordered state. Those best at leadership have genuine knowledge; those best at protection, the warriors, have a "spirited" nature, much like a contemporary athlete; and the workers produce the items that best suit their talents. The essential thing, for Plato, is to ensure that the workers and the warriors are under the control of the wisdom of the leaders who act according to their knowledge of the ideals of truth, goodness, and beauty.

Plato believes that we also have a productive aspect, a spirited aspect, and an intellectual aspect. When we are guided, in all aspects of our personalities, by genuine insight into the truth, we also will be healthy and happy and live beautiful, productive lives, thus answering the claim, expressed through the "Myth of Gyges' Ring," that doing evil is better than doing good.

Plato's emphasis on skill and knowledge is thorough, perhaps dictatorial. The rulers are to decide, based on their insights into truth and beauty, who is to have children and at what time, the professions of other people, and the nature of the ideals and values toward which the state is directed. This means, for example, that the art, literature, and history in the state are decided by the ruling class. This is an *aristocracy*, albeit an aristocracy of merit, and is used to support aristocratic thinking. Though presented as an ideal, Plato's state is extreme in many ways, including his notion that only a select few have knowledge enough to lead the state.

(2) Democracy

Democracy is an alternate ideal. In a complete democracy all decisions that affect the lives of people should be made jointly. In an ideal democracy all have the minimum knowledge to make informed decisions about social and individual policy, and have special knowledge about their own needs and desires that makes each vote especially valuable. An ideal democracy includes the workplace, where all should have a voice about the jobs they perform; it is an industrial democracy as well as a political democracy. Talent may have a large role in the ideal democratic state, but the knowledgeable person functions with the advice and consent of those who are affected by his or her decisions.

An ideal democracy seems unattainable if only because of the difficulties involved in voting intelligently. People are not well informed about all aspects of their society and often vote on illusory information. Plato rejects democracy because it leaves social rule in the hands of the ignorant, who are susceptible to the persuasion of the *demagogue*—to someone with appealing but false answers to difficult social problems. Democracy assumes that the typical person can be well enough informed about basic arrangements; people's interests are at stake and each is expert in his or her own needs and concerns. The dispute between a meritocracy and a democracy is fundamental in political thought. Although many advanced industrial societies boast of a democratic base, much decision making is not democratic. Industrial and political decisions are frequently made without any vote, either by representatives or directly by the people. Many decisions are made by experts, but many other decisions are made by people with power and without general knowledge about how those decisions affect others, or even themselves. Democracy expressed as an ideal can help us to detect the ways in which advanced industrial societies fail to be democratic. This may help to critique social structures and to guide social reform.

(3) Marx's Communism

Communism is another ideal political order. The nineteenth-century German philosopher-economist Karl Marx speculated on the ideal version of communism and focused on the way he thought it would be achieved. Yet most of what Marx wrote centered on his critique of capitalism. He believed that economic forces would cause capitalism to fail, ushering in a *dictatorship of the proletariat,* where the working class would rule with the aim of eventually developing full communism, a classless society without the need for political control.

Marx's greatest intellectual influence probably rests in his doctrine of *economic determinism.* For him social institutions, such as the state, law, marriage, family structures, and education, are molded by economic forces, meaning that the way goods are produced and distributed determines the nature of social institutions. Capitalism comes about through the development of large-scale production in factories made possible by the productive power of machines. The factories and the machines are the factors of production. They are owned by the capitalist class, the *bourgeoisie.* Marx argues that there is hostility between the working class, called the *proletariat,* and the bourgeoisie. The proletariat is the only productive class; they make things, including machines, using the tools and the factories of the bourgeoisie. Although they are the productive class, they and the means of production they use are controlled by the bourgeoisie. The hostility between these classes is so serious that it moves a capitalistic society toward violent revolution. *Class struggle* is the label Marx gives to the hostility between the classes. Class struggle is the driving force behind the change of social organization. When a hostile, dominated class has the opportunity and the power to rebel, it will. So Marx confidently predicted that the proletariat would rebel once it was able.

Economic conditions create classes, including the relative power of those classes. When economic conditions change, relative class power changes. With the advent of large-scale production, economic arrangements gave power to the bourgeoisie, and so the power of the nobility in Europe decreased. Through class struggle, with the bourgeoisie becoming dominant, the power of the nobility was destroyed. Marx believed that class struggle would provide the force needed to destroy the bourgeoisie. This would happen as soon as the proletariat gained in power through changing economic conditions.

Marx attempted to prove four things, all pointing to a future successful revolution. (1) The bourgeoisie is superfluous, or unneeded in the production process. (2) Economic depressions make the bourgeoisie numerically smaller and more vulnerable to violent overthrow. (3) Capitalism continually forces the proletariat, in general, to live at a level of bare economic subsistence, and that workers become even more miserable in a depression. (4) The structure of capitalism fosters periodic cycles of depression and recovery, progressively increasing the chance of revolution because each depression diminishes the power of the bourgeoisie.

Although the economic position Marx stakes out is complex, we can briefly give its main features. Economic depression comes, paradoxically, because capitalism unleashes tremendous economic productivity. This productivity is not centrally planned, so in expectation of profits, individual capitalists produce more than can be consumed. Overproduction leads to layoffs, and layoffs mean less spending. These spiraling consequences lead to depression, with capitalists forced out of production and out of the bourgeoisie. When production bottoms out, not enough is produced, causing a spiraling increase in productivity, and, eventually, a booming economy. However, the structure is changed; now fewer capitalists exist, because some were forced to sell out in the depression. In this way units of production become larger and larger. The capitalist class, now fewer in number, becomes more isolated from the production process.

Marx examined the notion of economic value in a capitalistic society to show that the bourgeoisie is unnecessary and that labor lives at the edge of subsistence. Marx argued that in an economy everything sells for what it is worth. And the worth of an item depends on the labor that goes into it. This is the classic *labor theory of value*. Labor extracts raw materials, mixes raw material and machine productivity with its labor to build factories and machines, and then makes consumer goods in factories. Everything eventually is produced by labor, with machines and factories that are considered stored labor. Marx considered the labor theory of value to be a scientific theory, but many believe it a philosophical or political doctrine. It proclaims that labor produces everything, and that capitalists are unnecessary.

The labor theory of value also shows that labor, an economic good under capitalism, will be paid what it is worth—that is, an amount equal to the cost of goods needed to keep the laboring class alive. The goods that keep labor alive cost an amount equal to the labor in them; for example, 30 hours' labor a week may be required to make the goods needed to keep labor alive. An equal exchange would be 30 hours of work for the goods that it took 30 hours to produce. But labor must eat to live, so the capitalist can bargain for extra hours, say 40 hours' work for the equivalent, in money, of 30 hours' worth of goods. The capitalist thus exploits labor. In this example, 10 *surplus* hours are gained, which help to make the capitalist rich without contributing, in Marx's view, to the production process.

The labor theory of value shows that the bourgeoisie is unnecessary, that labor is driven by its low wages to subsistence, and that labor is exploited. All this, together with the weakened numerical status of the bourgeoisie, leads to overthrow. Where social classes are found, Marx claims exploitation exists. The exploitation in capitalism is unpaid labor, or *wage slavery*. That exploitation leads to class struggle, and eventually to a revolution. This process only stops at a classless society, in which exploitation makes no sense. A classless society can succeed, Marx thought, when production is so abundant that exploiting others makes no sense. This classless society would come with advanced communism, Marx's utopia.

In Marx's view, once the proletariat rebels and a new social order is developed, the state, laws, police, and even ethics will not be needed. All of these are part of what Marx calls the *superstructure*. The superstructure is made up of the features of society designed to protect the interests of the dominant social class, a class that has power because of the economic structure, the *substructure*. Marx scorned ethics and religion because he believed that both served the interests of exploitation. Once exploitation is eliminated, through the elimination of the exploiting bourgeoisie class, only one class would exist, or, because there would be no class structure, no separate classes would exist; it would be a *classless society*. Since everyone is united in interest, oppression ends. Marx thought that under communism people would produce things based on their ability, and receive whatever they need. Production would not be a problem, because capitalism paved the way for abundance. Each person could work a few hours a day, and use the other hours for productive leisure time.

Marx's image of communism does not square with actual communist societies. This may be the failure of those societies, or it may indicate that Marx's hope was unrealistic and too utopian. Many economists reject Marx's labor theory of value as old-fashioned, and they reject his claim that labor is the only productive class. Marx's theories are now aging. We expect them to be wrong in numerous ways. Yet he does offer a vision, sometimes a dangerous vision, of the way things could be. He also instructs us to carefully examine the influence of economic arrangements on the way we live our lives, for better or worse.

The history of contemporary Marxist states shows that utopian ideals, however good they sound, can be destructive, just as charismatic "ideal" leaders can be. We should never give up a full vision of moral experience, including rules, principles, and conventions, as well as ideals. When one dominates the others, say an attractive social ideal over our basic moral principles, we may find ourselves in tragic circumstances.

Study Questions 10.3

1. (For class discussion.) Plato assumes that the state and the individual are analogous. Each, in effect, has physical and mental needs, and each requires protection and leadership. More than this, he seems to claim that we are what we are, to a degree, because of the social life we lead. When we know more about our society, we know more about ourselves. Do you agree with this view? Argue for or against it. Does your view affect the value of a utopian perspective on the state? That is, if you agree, does this make a utopian model more effective as a way

to guide individual behavior? Even if we disagree, we may still believe that a utopia is helpful in guiding our lives as individuals. So you may reject Plato's basic claim about the analogical relation between an individual and a state and still value utopian political thought.

2. Can political utopias help us to specify the best sort of social life for us?
3. What would you do if you found Gyges' ring? That is, would the ability to do evil without being detected cause people like me and you to act differently than we act now? How adequate is Plato's answer to the concerns raised by the "Myth of Gyges' Ring"? How would you answer that myth?
4. (For class discussion.) Suppose a person was blind for life and could only feel and imagine what things are like. If that person's sight were medically restored, would he or she find reality as beautiful as the freed person in the "Myth of the Cave"?
5. Plato challenges our awareness of reality in the "Myth of the Cave." Can you answer the Platonic charge that you are blind to reality?
6. Is knowledge a highly valued social commodity? Should it be valued? Would we be better or worse off if social leaders were also technical experts on social problems?
7. What is the strongest point in favor of meritocracy? In favor of democracy?
8. Why has communism failed in the old Soviet Union and Eastern Europe?
9. (For class discussion.) Workers in advanced industrial countries do not generally live at a subsistence level. Those who accept Marx's views argue that this is because foreign labor is exploited by both the bourgeoisie and the proletariat in advanced industrial societies. Indeed, most of labor in the world seems to live in poverty. Does this reply validate or help to disprove Marx's beliefs?

10.4 Social Equality as an Ideal

We have examined personal and political ideals, expressed as a full picture of an "ideal" person or state, that highlight and perhaps exaggerate desirable features. As we saw in Chapter 9, social values like freedom and justice shade into ideals as they become more demanding. In this section, we examine an ideal social value that is different from freedom and justice. Freedom and justice can be presented in limited, or negative ways, falling short of ideal conceptions. Negative freedom means that we are left to do what we want, but it does not demand positive actions. And justice, in a limited conception, involves following existing rules or practices. *Social equality* differs from freedom or justice because it is a more basic value in moral theory and does not have a limited sense. (Explain why.)

Equality (not *social* equality) is given a regulative role in moral experience insofar as it constrains the application of moral rules and principles; moral rules and principles ought to be equally applied. (This is not the same as limited justice, which involves following the rules. Established rules may not be equally applied.) Utilitarians, for example, believe that everyone's happiness counts equally. No matter whether a person is highly valued, or discriminated against, the utility of that person counts in the same way, in proportion to the strength of the happiness involved. Kantian theory makes the categorical imperative—a prohibition against making exceptions—the main principle of morality. The immoral person considers himself or herself to be more valuable than others, a kind of moral inequality.

Equality also serves as a *baseline* in moral theory. You may recall, from Chapter 9, that a baseline establishes a point of comparison. For example, suppose some person was harmed through negligence, and we want to decide how much compensation he or she should receive. Should we decide to bring the person back to the level he or she was at when harmed or to the level he or she would be at now if no harm occurred? Different levels of compensation may result depending on whether the baseline is the past or the present. As we saw in the previous chapter, equality is often used as a moral baseline from which we may judge whether harm has been done. If another baseline is suggested, it has the burden of proof; it must show why equality is inappropriate. We tend to question why people are unequal in terms of wealth, income, life expectancy, and educational attainment. We might find a proper explanation, but inequality invites moral inquiry, while equality typically does not call for justification.

We can only fully understand notions like harm, freedom, justice, or morality itself when we place them in the context of equal treatment. For this reason equality appears as a *metavalue,* a value that stands behind other values, ready to give direction, calling for inquiry, pointing out when justification is required. A socially equal society will never exist, but the assumptions of moral experience—the equal moral consideration given to people and the burden of proof against inequality—tend to push us toward the endorsement of more equal social practices. The unique value of the individual, the social creation and variability of values that limit equality, the moral demands that each be given equal consideration, and the whole notion of the advances gained through genuine social cooperation highlight the emphasis we put on equal participation and on equal rewards and burdens, except where unequal rewards and burdens are fully justified. (Be sure you understand all these features of social life and why they call for greater equality. For example, the variability of social values means that many of the factors defending inequality may be unneeded or that society may be rearranged, through social intervention, to make those things unnecessary. Since the burden of proof is on inequality, we must show that an inequality is genuinely required. You may want to consider the way inequalities have been defended, say gender or race inequality, and whether these defenses involve variable features of social life.)

While social freedom has a limited and a full sense, social equality does not. A society may have less inequality than another, but only a fully equal society can claim to be equal. Social equality is an ideal. We have no negative expression of it. Even so, the ideal notion of social equality is in dispute. In this section we examine several suggestions about the proper conception of social equality.

Philosophers want to determine the "best" conception of equality, so it is reasonable to put some demands on any proposed conception of social equality. First of all, a notion of equality that permits large and significant social inequalities is self-destructive. We want a genuine notion of equality, a genuine ideal. If in its ideal expression social equality ends up supporting large social inequalities, it will not serve its function as a guide to a more equal society. Secondly, we need a notion that admits empirical detection. To claim that a society is equal, despite the fact that it always appears to be unequal, is not helpful. Third, we need a conception of equality that allows us to determine whether we are on the right path toward the ideal. We need to know whether our society at one time is closer or further from equality than at another time. Fourth, the conception must take into account individual needs. Some people need more than others, legitimately so. A sense of social equality must account for those differences in some way. If those who legitimately need more than others are given the same amount, they may properly claim that they have been treated unequally.

An acceptable notion of equality as a social ideal is not easy to find. Those who attempt a solution often fall to a charge recently made by Douglas Rae. In *Equalities*,[9] he argues that any equality claim may be satisfied by increasing inequality somewhere else. In this way, equality is an amorphous concept, its own worst enemy. For example, the demand for equal opportunity, the opportunity to show one's talents, may be formally met, even guaranteed, while an increase in unequal wealth makes those with less wealth unable to compete. Over the last ten years people in the United States have become more unequal, in terms of income and wealth, while at the same time more emphasis has been placed on equal opportunity, formally defined. When we examine definitions of equality offered by philosophers, we need to consider whether Rae's lament holds. Does the proposed definition of equality permit compensating inequalities?

Social equality deals with distribution of social goods and burdens. Although we may claim that all people are equal—say, equally valuable in the eyes of God—this is not a conception of social equality but a call for equal moral treatment. Social equality occurs when some good, like income, wealth, or happiness, is equally attained. Say the good is freedom. Social equality will then mean that freedom should be equally distributed. The problem of defining social equality involves the specification of the goods that should be equally distributed and the units to which those goods are distributed.

Should we claim that basic political rights should be equally distributed, or income, workload, wealth, health care, or opportunity? Which should be included in our ideal of social equality? The units to which these goods are to be equally distributed is also problematic. Many believe that all proposals should be in terms of individuals. All people should have an equal right to good X. Suppose we use income as the good. Should we really insist on all individuals having a right to the same income when many people are infants, or share expenses with others in the same household? We may believe that a proper mark of social equality will call for equal distribution of income to all *households*. This example shows that the question about the unit to be equally provided with a good is not properly answered by the quick claim that individuals constitute the unit.

We turn to three attempts to define social equality. Many other answers have been suggested; these three have been selected because their dramatic difference in perspectives show us the options and difficulties involved in supporting a proper conception of social equality. Each conception we explore involves the proposal of an ideal version of equality. Perhaps a completely equal society is undesirable, but considering the harmful inequalities history has forced on people, the ideal version of an equal society can serve as a helpful moral guide to morally needed political, social, and individual reform.

(1) Ronald Dworkin's Equality of Resources

The contemporary philosopher Ronald Dworkin explores whether welfare (perhaps measured by happiness) or resources should be equally distributed.[10] Dworkin assumes that the goods involved will go to individuals, so the problems he seriously examines only concern the sort of good involved. He rejects narrowly defined goods, even goods like income and wealth. Different incomes may compensate for unequal burdens, while wealth, like the farmer's wealth in land, may not be easily translated into a genuine inequality. Instead, Dworkin first examines welfare. Does it make good sense to claim that everyone, regardless of income or wealth or anything else, should be counted as equal when they have the same happiness, utility, preference satisfaction, or, more generally, the same welfare?

Welfare gets to the reason for having wealth, income, and all other goods. Dworkin believes that the best notion of welfare, the one best suited to current economic theories, involves *success* at gaining what is preferred. But this leads to problems because some people have preferences for things that are difficult to attain; they may need amazingly large amounts of resources to gain what they want. So, Dworkin concludes, if everyone is equally successful, they will be, in other ways, grossly unequal. This is not equality; it violates one of the constraints we already put on any conception of equality. (Which one, and why?)

The problem with welfare theories of equality is that they permit gross inequalities in the name of equality. A standard independent of people's personal sense of attainment is required. Dworkin turns to an examination of *equality of resources*. Resources come in different kinds, so we need a way to think of them as equally divided. Dworkin offers a hypothetical scheme that helps us set the ideal of equally distributed resources. He imagines an original auction, with each person being given an equal amount of bidding money. Then all the goods will be bid upon. What is received in the fair auction counts as an equal distribution of resources. After that, whatever each person does with his or her goods is permitted. Keep in mind that Dworkin is proposing a hypothetical standard. Is the distribution of resources in our society consistent with the kind of distribution that would follow, over time, from an original auction where people have equal amounts of bidding money? If the answer is "yes," then our society is equal in resources.

Dworkin argues that equality is consistent with people using their resources as they see fit, unless more adequate use is based on natural talent. Unequal natural talent introduces a morally unacceptable inequality, he thinks, because it is based on genetic luck. He proposes a scheme of social insurance to protect people against bad genetic luck, like the way we currently insure against accidents. This insurance level is set by how we would expect people to bid on it in an initial auction. Dworkin speculates that the level of insurance would not be very high, because a high level of insurance would be expensive.[11]

Dworkin's plan may be better than equal welfare at holding down extraordinary inequalities, but it might not be. People may be lucky about the resources they select, might work harder, and might amass fortunes that could then be used, over time, to ensure unequal consideration, politically, legally, and socially—much the way things are now. This plan would then meet the same fate as equality of welfare because its notion of equality might involve tremendous inequalities. Rae would maintain that Dworkin has not refuted the claim that providing equality in one way may increase inequalities in other ways. Equality of resources may be its own worst enemy; it eventually leads to great inequality of resources based on genetic luck (with a small insurance), resource luck, and hard work. We may believe that such inequalities are morally acceptable. But now we are examining the attempt to define an *ideal* notion of equality, and ideal equality, like Wolf's moral saint, may not be fully desirable. Nevertheless, if that ideal involves great inequalities, it might be ideal, but not an equality ideal.

(2) Michael Walzer's Complex Equality

Perhaps the trouble involves reliance on the distribution of the same or similar goods to all people as individuals. Michael Walzer[12] tries an approach that focuses on the type of goods distributed but doesn't worry much about the exact amounts people get. Inequality is oppressive when one type of good, like money, dominates other goods. He proposes that goods be allowed to be unequally distributed within their proper spheres of influence. But one type of good should not influence who has another type. Money should buy many things, but not such things as health care or political power. Each good is allowed to be unequal in its own sphere; unequal wealth is not offensive when it does not have power over the things money should not buy. Walzer calls this *complex equality*.

He has a point here. Today wealthy people bid up the price of fine violins, causing difficulties for excellent musicians who want to play them. When musical instruments, health care, education, and access to good lawyers go to those who need them, inequalities of wealth have a smaller social impact. Walzer claims: "So long as yachts and hi-fi sets and rugs have only use value and individualized symbolic value, their unequal distribution doesn't matter."[13]

While we worry whether unequal distribution of goods is really a conception of social equality, we see another problem. What keeps Walzer's spheres separate? Doesn't wealth affect educational attainment, political power, health care, and leisure time? Allowing income and wealth to be greatly unequal, while prohibiting spheres from overlapping, is unrealistic. Walzer's analysis does not adequately take into account the overlap of spheres. Regardless, we may call his complex equality "complex inequality." Nothing in it needs to be equally distributed. We seem, again, to fall short of an equality ideal.

(3) R. H. Tawney's Group Equality

The British social critic R. H. Tawney rejects the notion of individual equality. Instead, he rejects unequal attainment of any goods that may lead to significantly unequal class status. He states his ideal:

> It is to hold that, while natural endowments differ profoundly, it is the work of a civilized society to aim at eliminating such inequalities as have their source, not in individual differences, but in its own organization, and that individual differences, which are a source of social energy, are more

likely to ripen and find expression if social inequalities are, as far as practicable, eliminated.[14]

Tawney rejects inequalities among social groups. When, for example, blacks and whites and men and women are judged on individual merit and receive goods and burdens based on that merit, and not on initial group status, then social equality among these groups is achieved.

I believe that Tawney's message comes closest to an adequate ideal of social equality. Unfortunately, his proposal is vague. He does not tell us how we are to determine whether group traits are used to determine inequality, and he does not specify the sorts of goods to be used in the measurement.

Equality is a crucial moral and political ideal, but it is difficult to settle on a conception of equality and the criteria for recognizing its presence. More work needs to be done to clarify the issues involved, the way equality can be measured, the impact of inequality, and the extent to which inequalities are socially engineered. Notions, even vague notions, of equality as a social ideal have been influential in guiding moral decision making. Philosophers are called upon to propose and critique equality ideals; they have done so, but so far without the success of a consensus around any conception. Although we may believe that a fully equal society is unattainable, and perhaps even less than fully desirable, we do need to understand inequalities in our societies, how they arise and their consequences. With a full understanding of social inequalities, moral decision making holds the promise of being more equitable and impartial.

Study Questions 10.4

1. (For class discussion.) This section assumes that moral rules cannot be equally applied under social inequality. Do you believe this is true? Consider rules like "Do not steal," "Do not break promises," and "Do not lie."
2. Is an equality ideal of use today in discussions of gender, race, and ethnic inequality? Would these discussion be aided by a clearer conception of an equality ideal?
3. Why does the notion of harm depend on social equality? (You may want to refer back to Chapter 9.)
4. Does social equality differ from treating individuals equally? In answering consider a society with gender and race equality. Is it possible that an individual could be unequally treated in such an equal society? If so, does this suggest that an ideal of social inequality is inadequate?
5. Suppose the claim is made that we can only tell whether individuals

are treated equally in a socially equal society. What does that claim mean? (Consider the claims made by people who believe that they were not given a proper raise or the right job because of their sex or race.)

6. In your well-reasoned judgment, whose conception of equality comes closest to the proper equality ideal: Dworkin's, Walzer's, or Tawney's? (Before answering consider carefully the requirements of an equality ideal.)

7. Is preferential treatment consistent with social equality?

10.5 The Lessons from Exemplars and Ideals

Moral ideals are often overlooked by philosophers as well as social critics because they appear to represent impractical utopian thinking. Yet we are influenced by ideals and exemplars. We have reverence for people like Mother Teresa, Martin Luther King, Jr., and Elie Wiesel. We are taught about historical figures and religious leaders. All of these come close to ideals. We may even think of people in our families as nearly ideal. Moral ideals help to make moral thinking more concrete, to set a direction, and to understand the extent to which our environment is far from the ideal.

When philosophers speculate on proper virtues, correct rules and principles, they often write as though full compliance exists. If everyone behaves properly, then the rules work well. But when we are not in full compliance, when the world stacks the cards against many of us, an apparently adequate moral rule may add to disadvantage. Marx believed that morality itself is part of the oppression caused by economic class inequality. An answer to these charges partly rests in the power of moral ideals, including political ideals. Western political ideals—human rights, freedom, justice, and equality—provide a way to think through genuine moral needs. They guide us on a path toward the genuinely equal application of moral rights and duties.

Achieving a better society is not easy. Social life is complex, always waiting to validate Rae's claim that attempts to do better have a way of making things worse. This means that care must be taken. We know that good jobs, low unemployment, good education, good police protection, and progressive taxation help move us toward a more equal society. Progress toward an ideal matters. When we find that attempts to approach an equal society lead to more inequality and more misery, something else should be attempted. Perhaps this is the value of social and individual ideals: when properly designed, they give us a way of knowing when we are failing and when we are succeeding.

Further Reading

The essays in Volume 13 of the *Midwest Studies in Philosophy*, *Ethical Theory: Character and Virtue*, edited by Peter A. French, Theodore E. Uehling, Jr., and Howard K. Wettstein, introduce a variety of issues about character ideals.

Each of the following offers a different, yet plausible, conception of equality: Amy Gutmann, *Liberal Equality* (Cambridge: Cambridge University Press, 1980), Chapter 1; and Kai Nielsen, *Equality and Liberty: A Defense of Radical Egalitarianism* (Totowa, N.J.: Rowman & Allanheld, 1985), Chapter 3. Amartya Sen, *On Economic Inequality* (New York: W. W. Norton, 1973); and Ronald Dworkin, "What Is Equality? Part 1: Equality of Welfare," *Philosophy & Public Affairs*, 10 (3) (1981): 185–246, and "What Is Equality? Part 2: Equality of Resources," *Philosophy & Public Affairs* 10 (4) (1981): 283–345.

Endnotes

1. J.O. Urmson "Saints and Heroes," *Essays in Moral Philosophy*, ed. A. I. Melden (Seattle: University of Washington Press, 1958).
2. Ibid., p. 200.
3. Susan Wolf, "Moral Saints," *The Journal of Philosophy*, 79 (8) (August 1982): 419–439.
4. Ibid., p. 419.
5. R. B. Adams, "Saints," *The Journal of Philosophy* 81 (7) (1984): 392–401.
6. Ibid., p. 396.
7. Lawrence A. Blum, "Moral Exemplars," *Midwest Studies in Philosophy* 13 (1988): 196-211.
8. Ibid., p. 199.
9. Douglas W. Rae et al., *Equalities* (Cambridge: Harvard University Press, 1981).
10. Ronald Dworkin, "What Is Equality? Part 1: Equality of Welfare," *Philosophy and Public Affairs* 10 (3) (1981): 185–246, and "What Is Equality? Part 2: Equality of Resources," *Philosophy and Public Affairs* 10 (4) (1981): 283–345.
11. Ibid., p. 331.
12. Michael Walzer, *Spheres of Justice: A Defense of Pluralism and Equality* (New York: Basic Books, 1983).
13. Ibid., p. 108.
14. R. H. Tawney, *Equality*, 4th ed. (London: Allen & Unwin, 1952), p. 49.

11

Roles and Practices:
Solving Moral Problems

11.1 Introduction

We have already examined, and found partly acceptable, various ways to resolve moral problems. Most philosophers agree that we should not violate moral rules or moral principles, especially when these are stated as prohibitions, and that we can sometimes rely on a virtuous disposition, perhaps a caring disposition, to know the right thing to do. Seeking maximal happiness or universalizing our actions sometimes deserves moral praise and is often morally required. We have also seen that moral praise is typically deserved for actions that seek to bring about justice, freedom, and equality. Finally, we saw that ideals and exemplars may helpfully guide us in character development and in solving some moral problems.

In this chapter we take a different look at moral problem solving. The position we present concentrates on social practices. On a day-to-day basis you and I act under obligations based on our roles in social practices, such as being a student, an instructor, a nurse, a parent, or a police officer. Many of our obligations come from these practices, and practices often motivate behavior. In fact, roles in practices tend to establish who has what obligation to do specific kinds of good. In effect, practices help to specify how we can, or who has the obligation to, pursue welfare, harm-avoidance, freedom, and justice. For example, a firefighter has a special moral obligation to help to prevent harm. Thus, through practices, with their established roles, we can provide a fuller interpretation of moral principles and moral rules. The principle "Prevent harm" is partly, perhaps largely, interpreted through roles within practices. However, many practices, if not all, are far from ideal, and may be reformed through the use of moral principles, rules, and ideals. So while roles and practices help to interpret moral principles, moral principles help to evaluate roles and practices.

This chapter, although abstract, is mainly about how moral problems are solved when they occur in practices, and how practices may be reformed through the application of other aspects of moral experience. Behind this examination we assume that practices do have a moral standing, that they have a pervasive effect on and power over our lives, and that many crucial moral problems today involve the reform of social practices.

11.2 Social Roles

Sometimes it seems as though real moral problems do not arise in day-to-day living. Most of us have roles to perform, and we do the things we need to do. A student or a teacher gets up, goes to class, does needed out-of-class work, and treats others properly. Moral problems arise when something disturbs our lives. We may find that a promise conflicts with another obligation, or we realize the need or desire to cheat or lie, or, more tragically, we face an unwanted pregnancy or the decision to remove a parent from a respirator. But we may go for long periods of time without confronting such problems. In reality, most of us, most of the time, do things out of habit, following established practices. This may be a morally proper thing to do, even if not the morally best we can do. Recall from Chapter 4 that Richard Brandt suggested that current practices are a good approximation to the correct set of moral rules.

Each of us occupies a set of roles within various practices. We are students, teachers, parents, children, firefighters, lawyers, grocers, citizens, and so on. Typically, we behave according to the basic tenets of these social roles. We know that a parent has special obligations to his or her children. Part of coming of age in a given society involves learning what those special responsibilities are. Usually, people follow those rules, at least up to minimum requirements. When parents are caught leaving young children to go on a vacation, the event is newsworthy, suggesting that such gross neglect is relatively uncommon—though probably more common than we would like to believe. Most of the parents we know would not leave their children unattended for long periods of time; when things like this happen more frequently, as they seem to today, conventional role assignments change. Day care is an increasingly available alternative, yet the realities and demands of parenting are changing more quickly than society's response.

Let's return to Joel Feinberg's view, which we examined in Chapter 9: that acting to prevent harm, when it can be done at little personal cost, is required in a way that is morally equivalent to the prohibition against directly doing harm. Feinberg concludes that a society may organize to prevent harm through the social allocation of benefits and burdens aimed at the reduction of harm. Society gives a firefighter a special burden that may involve risk. But that firefighter is specially trained and usually compensated to do the job. We socially assign that job, with the understanding that saving property and lives requires special equipment, training, and compensation. Now the firefighter is assigned a moral obligation that you and I do not have; he or she, while on the job, is morally required to help others even when helping involves significant time, effort, and even risk.

Think of the difference between your or my failure to respond to a fire and the same failure on the part of the firefighter. When a house burns down, no one is going to fault you or me for not putting out the fire, assuming the blaze was serious. We did not cause the harm, and we have no special obligation, moral or social, to put it out. But a negligent firefighter, say one asleep on the job, may be faulted, morally, with the loss of life and property. A social role, as Feinberg suggests, assigns responsibilities that extend the nonharm principle. Preventing harm is the special responsibility of people from elementary school teachers to auto mechanics. If this is correct, then one way of specifying who has what responsibility under the basic but vague moral principle "Prevent harm" is through the social process of assigning roles.

Basic negative principles at first sight require no special action. "Do not harm" and "Do not interfere with the freedom of another" are easy enough to uphold: do nothing. We have just seen that, in the case of the firefighter, this is incorrect. Some people have assigned roles that require action: the teacher may be required to control a class to ensure freedom to speak; a parent or a child may have the obligation to provide opportunities, medical care, and food in ways that promote the freedom of family members. Negative obligations and positive obligations are brought together in social roles.

We started this section by claiming that people go through day-to-day life without facing many major moral decisions. This is true partly because society often does effectively assign duties through roles. College teachers face few moral decisions about how to grade because the practice is more or less well established. We are not tempted to give a better grade to a student who does not deserve it whenever the student complains that a poor grade will hamper his or her efforts to get into medical school. Without a well-established social practice, college professors might face such decisions daily.

Finding reasons to support the action of the professor is easy. Harm is done, agreements are violated, unfairness thrives, professors gain new and undelegated power unless they follow the established rules. The example of the professor suggests not only that ordinary behavior is rule-bound, but that the rules of social practices can have a moral standing in our moral experience, and may fit in, although not tightly, with basic moral viewpoints—for example, with the utilitarian's concern to avoid harm and the Kantian's emphasis on universality.

Let's imagine that Professor Jones disagrees with the grading system.

Jones thinks that students should participate as equals with the professor in pursuit of genuine knowledge. In light of this belief, Jones refuses to give grades and causes an uproar on campus, with ungraded students suffering because of her beliefs. They rightly protest that Jones is causing them to fail to meet the requirements of the university, with the result that many students lose grants or tuition reimbursement. Jones's violation of this social practice comes at a price, even if she is right about a proper education. In this case, the practice socially establishes the way to do things, and Jones has been assigned, through an elaborate process of social selection, the role of a professor. She is not morally free to pursue her individual views on education without good reason.

We may characterize Jones's responsibility in two ways: (1) she has a *prima facie* obligation to give grades, and (2) she has *burden of proof* in her claim that the obligation is improper. Jones has a prima facie moral obligation to act in accordance with the well-established social role she has taken; it is a prima facie obligation because it is not strictly binding. It is one that holds unless good reasons can be found, in particular cases, to act otherwise. For example, the requirements of a social role may conflict with other moral requirements, such as the obligation not to harm another. In this way the requirements of the role might be rejected and another, more morally compelling, action performed.

In moral reasoning a simple appeal to another moral requirement need not be conclusive. Professor Jones may believe that she is required to maximize happiness by giving students the best (ungraded) education possible. This, Jones's individual belief, goes against Jones's well-established role. In this case, a heavy burden of proof is on Jones. When the burden of proof occurs in moral reasoning, the position with the burden of proof must present *compelling* reasons. Finding a reason not to comply is not enough. Even if Jones has a good point about the value of ungraded study, that point is not enough to overcome the burden of proof; the case against the obligation must be more compelling then the original obligation. Jones's reason is not compelling given that it is offered against the moral authority of a well-established and publicly endorsed practice.

This leads to the problem of how can we know that a practice is binding, prima facie, and that the practice establishes a strong burden of proof. This is a difficult issue over which philosophers will disagree. But consider the following list of standards pointing to the binding status of a social role. Fulfilling the requirements of a role establishes a weightier burden of proof when the role is (1) publicly well known and democratically supported; (2) crucial, in general, as a way to avoid harm or promote a well-established good; (3) supported by basic moral principles and basic moral values; and (4) generally thought of as morally binding. Finally, (5) the obligations of the role are weightier, other things being equal, when its requirements are well defined and necessary for the successful function of a practice.

All of these standards are not likely to be met. When most of them are, or some are clearly and fully met, the burden of proof becomes stronger. When the burden of proof is weak, the prima facie obligation succumbs more easily to other moral obligations, but a strong burden of proof makes the prima facie obligation harder to defeat by requiring more serious reasons for violating it. The more the requirements listed are met in an exemplary way, the greater the strength of the obligation. The role of the professor giving grades meets these standards, but the role of the auto salesperson who lies in order to sell a car does not. For example, the role does not make clear whether a auto salesperson is supposed to lie about a car. The prima facie moral obligation to follow such a role would be weak.

Many of our daily decisions are made according to the dictates of the roles we occupy. This should not be habitual or unthinking because roles may not meet the standards listed above, and so actions according to roles may involve improper behavior. But practices do have some moral standing, and, when the standards are met, a strong moral standing. Nevertheless, practices are social creations that may be changed so that they can fit into our moral experience with less conflict.

Study Questions 11.2

1. List some roles, similar to the role of a teacher, where moral obligations are strong, and some, like the auto salesperson, where obligations are weak.
2. Can a utilitarian support the prima facie obligation generated by a well-established social role? A Kantian?
3. Suppose a role involves doing evil, e.g., a government secret agent who is required to perform political assassinations. Does this role convey prima facie obligations?
4. Does a firefighter have a prima facie moral obligation to show up for work when he or she doesn't feel like it?
5. To what extent do people actually have additional moral responsibilities due to the practices in which they participate? In answering, be sure to include practices like family life and professions of various sorts, and include some with codes of behavior, like medicine and law.

11.3 Changing Role Obligations

Suppose Professor Jones is not so reckless. She agrees to give grades, but still believes that they are, on balance, socially harmful. You may think that Professor Jones is not morally true to herself, because she assigns grades despite her belief that they cause harm. This is not the case. Professor Jones understands that a social practice is established through the cooperation of many people often over a long period of time. She may rightly defer to a well-established practice because it has moral standing, and she properly acts in accordance with a role despite her opposition. For example, we want police to enforce laws even if some police officers believe those laws create more harm than good.

However, Professor Jones does not need to stop here; she may seek to change the practice. Jones may think action designed to change the practice is morally obligatory and may, for example, attempt to convince the faculty to expand the use of satisfactory-unsatisfactory grading. She may study the few colleges in the United States that do not give grades and propose them as models to her colleagues. Surely Jones has a difficult task ahead, and is likely to fail in the short run, but she may have some influence and be able to change the practice over time. When faced with a practice we do not believe to be morally optimum, or one we believe to be morally wrong, we may be morally obliged, perhaps by moral principles, to use whatever moral power we have to change that practice.

Under what standards do we seek change? We may decide to seek changes that make a practice more efficient, more effective, or more economical. Such changes are not typically thought to be changes required by moral obligations. But when we seek change designed to reform practices under the guidance of moral principles, moral values, or moral rules, we may be under a moral obligation to seek change; at least our attempts may be morally encouraged. We may believe that a practice is not fair, not free enough, or harmful. We may believe that more welfare would be produced by different role requirements. Or we may believe that a practice encourages violation of moral rules.

Most understand that moral rules and principles ought to guide moral behavior. Lying, deliberately harming, stealing, and killing are morally improper. We also have some moral requirement to prevent harm and help others. A practice that violates any of these should be changed. But many of our obligations are vague, making it difficult to determine that a practice violates a principle. Who should we help, how can we prevent harm, and when are we harming another? Many of these questions are answered through social practices: a parent harms a child by failing to provide a proper environment; you and I are not responsible for the child of another in the same way as the child's parent. Society assigns a parent a special moral obligation in relation to his or her own children. Similar statements can be made about a doctor, a lawyer, or a teacher. The way we assign obligations in practices is morally vital because practices help to specify how principles and rules are applied, and they tend, through internal and external rewards and punishments, to motivate people to conform. This is why reforming practices is morally vitally important. But we cannot use the rule that parents should take special care of their own children as a guide to reform a practice. That rule is itself highly practice-dependent. Practices and moral rules have a synergistic relationship, but one that needs to be examined.

Although seeking needed change in a practice is morally encouraged, whether we are required to seek change is a difficult matter. Certainly when power is democratically shared, as it is to a degree among a college faculty, we are obliged to at least vote according to moral rules, principles, and values. But Feinberg's notion, that we are not obliged to do extraordinary things, holds. Professor Jones might not have the time, energy, or skill required to persuade others to change the grading system. Jones may devote her life to change, and this may be morally commendable. Great social reformers, people like Dorothy Day or Mahatma Gandhi, devote entire lives to social causes. Their actions approach the saintly. These are supererogatory commitments; they may be morally praiseworthy but are not thought to be morally obligatory.

However, some roles contain more power than others to effect change. The faculty at a college or university has more power to change the way things are done than the students do. Workers in a factory may have little power over their roles. Although most people occupy roles that are designed to do a task in well-defined ways, some roles are designed to change roles. A government official, a Supreme Court judge, and a senator may occupy roles dedicated to examining and changing roles and practices. Although a judge may be bound by the law, the law may be informed by moral values that help to determine needed changes. A president or a senator, for example, ought to seek changes that conform to moral principles, rules, and values.

The more power built into a role to direct change, the more we expect those holding power to live by positive moral values: the promotion of freedom and justice, and the improvement of welfare. Doing so is often difficult, involving differences of informed opinion about the best approach. When decisions are made ideologically, people judge in a way that is committed to a certain path without careful moral analysis based on moral principles, rules, virtues, and sound judgments. Ideological commitments, in general, involve a hard-to-shake faith that things will get better when the favored approach is taken. Both liberals and conservatives are often guilty of sticking to ideological guns rather than really attempting to ameliorate social conditions, to actually promote freedom, justice, and welfare. Basic moral values are not comfortable with well-intentioned actions that produce bad results.

Study Questions 11.3

1. Suppose the requirements of a role do not make clear whether an action should be taken. Say a parent is not sure whether to punish a child on a particular occasion. How should that decision be made, morally speaking? (Consider using rules, principles, ideals, etc.)
2. In a democracy all voting-age people have some power, even if a small amount, to change the way things are done. Given this power, do people have a moral responsibility to vote? Your answer should include an analysis of the role of a citizen. Also, should moral principles, ideals, values, and rules direct voting?
3. Why should roles that have power to change practices be guided by positive values? In your answer refer to the contention that practices have the task of spreading the burdens of helpful actions.
4. Recently, the practice of parenting has undergone significant change brought about by the demand for greater gender equality and by such social and economic factors as higher divorce rates and more families with both parents working. What changes have occurred in the practice of parenting as a result of these factors? To what extent can you argue that these changes in parenting have been in accord with moral principles, values, and rules? How could the current practice be reformed for the better?

11.4 Moral Conflict

Social roles help us make moral decisions. If a society has roles that are well designed from both a moral and a practical perspective, including motivating structures within these practices, the values underscored by the moral experience will be enhanced. Poorly defined roles tend to be hostile to moral value. If we design the role of a physician to reward and encourage good care for a patient, this is what we likely get. But if the role is designed to place the well-being of the physician ahead of the patient, good care will be secondary. The same is true with parenting, teaching, and auto sales. We know that a premium in university research is placed on public results and truthfulness. This we tend to get, although scandalous exceptions are sometimes reported in the newspapers. If a scientist puts dye on a mouse claiming that some change was genetically fostered, that is cause for national news attention. Consider similar deception in other occupations, such as advertising, where attempts to mislead are frequent and deliberate and certainly not newsworthy. The point is that a good practice promotes morally proper behavior, and a poor practice does the opposite.

Practices and the roles they contain are morally important because they effectively motivate behavior. They come with subtle and not so subtle reward structures. Furthermore, expectations about how to act in a role are often taught when people are children. Actual *moral motivation,* in large measure, comes from well-defined social roles and the pattern of rewards associated with behavior in those roles. The scientific researcher is not necessarily more truthful than people in some other professions. Instead, we get truthfulness because the scientist's profession is structured around truthfulness.

Role morality can become complex. People occupy many roles. That researcher may also be a mother or father, a son or daughter, a volunteer firefighter, a church member, a union leader, or an active member of a political party. All of these are social roles, and sometimes they involve conflicting moral obligations. Moral obligations conflict when we have two obligations, both serious and strong, and fulfilling one involves neglecting the other. This is a *moral dilemma.* Doing a proper job as a researcher may mean neglecting some family obligation. Or a role responsibility may conflict with a moral principle, value, or rule. We may be required to lie in a social role (say as a police detective), yet this violates a moral rule.

Whenever moral conflict exists, we must consider which obligation is more serious, more binding. We can use the standards explored in previous chapters to determine the moral strength of a role requirement. A negative responsibility—not to harm, not to lie, not to violate freedom—is usually more powerful morally than a positive obligation to promote well-being or to enhance freedom and social equality. Yet an obligation that is unique, that only you or I can satisfy, is more serious than an obligation for which many others may be substituted. This is not, however, as clear as we would like. Often promoting welfare involves avoiding harm, and a unique status may conflict with the need to abide by negative responsibilities. (Think of cases in which this is true.)

Unfortunately, moral theorists have not done an adequate job of investigating role responsibilities. Philosophers look for universal obligations, yet social roles are partly arbitrary. Role responsibilities change, and people move from one role to anther. The arbitrariness and variability of roles leads many philosophers to believe that role obligations are less significant than other moral obligations. But this is not what moral experience suggests. In a day-to-day sense, roles create many of our moral requirements. John Rawls, in his examination of the way practices support moral rules, believes that this is so, as does Richard Brandt in his analysis of optimal moral values. And as we have already explored, Alasdair MacIntyre relies on practices in his view on virtue.

Despite the arbitrariness of social roles, much of our moral awareness, our sense of the right thing to do, is established by social roles. By giving explicit attention to how roles provide moral motivation and define positive responsibilities, philosophers might be able to recommend ways to reduce conflict by reforming practices. Moral conflict is most troublesome when conflicting responsibilities are both firm and unyielding. For example, a parent's responsibility to care for a child may conflict with the demands of a leadership role in a union. Practices, however, may be designed so that conflict is minimized. Effective quality day care can free a parent to fulfill the requirements of other roles as well. The provision for substitutes within a role can lift the moral burden from a person once thought indispensable.

However, some moral conflict appears inevitable, perhaps inherent in the human condition. Moral conflict means that one or the other responsibility cannot be kept. When responsibilities conflict, philosophers have taken two basic paths. One is to deny that the conflict is real. Moral responsibilities are binding, *all things considered.* You and I do not have moral responsibilities pure and simple, but we have them in relation to our circumstances. We must take everything into account to determine what we should do. When we take everything into account, including all of our prima facie responsibilities, we will conclude that we have only one actual obligation. All the other prima facie responsibilities are merely potential obligations. We might, however, not know which responsibility wins in a given case. Two or more may appear equally compelling. Under that case the American philosopher Isaac Levi recommends that we suspend judgment and pursue further inquiry.[1] We may need to do one or the other, but that decision is a practical choice. We do not claim that the action we perform is our genuine responsibility until we inquire further. In this way, Levi affirms the notion that we only have one moral obligation, and not a genuine conflict over obligations.

Another view is that we ought to squarely face the fact of moral conflict and our inadequacy to do both required acts. Since we can only do one required act, we must do it with *moral regret,* with a sense of *moral guilt.* This is Bernard Williams's proposal.[2] A person may have two genuine obligations, but because only one can be performed, that person should be regretful that the other cannot be done.

Both views make sense. How can we be obligated to do something we are unable to do? Philosophers frequently hold to the doctrine that *ought* **implies can.** Any obligation assumes capability. Assigning a task, moral or otherwise, to a person who cannot do it is foolish. On the other hand, not fulfilling a genuine moral responsibility means that something wrong or bad happens: harm is done, expectations are frustrated, welfare is lost, or moral rules are violated. Regretting these moral failures underscores the seriousness of moral obligations. The presence of regret shows the good faith of the moral agent.

By their emphasis on current conflict and the resolution of that conflict, both positions overlook a future-oriented perspective in the moral experience.

Morality is not simply about declaring responsibilities, it is also about changing them. Professor Jones may seek to establish a new way of grading. If she does, her sense of moral conflict will be corrected. Moral conflict, in Professor Jones's case, signals the need for reform. This is a more pragmatic, future-oriented approach than those of Levi or Williams. Whenever moral conflict appears, we have reason to believe that some reform is needed, morally speaking. This reform, when possible or practicable, may change one obligation or the other, or it may change the circumstances, or social practices, so that both responsibilities may be fulfilled.

Many philosophers believe that moral values, at least when positively stated, often conflict. The more equality we demand, the less freedom we have. The more freedom, the less our opportunity to achieve greater welfare. Under these conditions *priority orderings* are established. By establishing a priority ordering, a philosopher does not claim that welfare, equality, and freedom are bad things to seek, but instead that one is more important than the others. Using priority orderings, philosophers hope to limit conflicting obligations. If freedom is more important in a priority ordering than welfare, as it is for most Kantians, then if we can achieve more freedom by ignoring welfare, this is what we must do. Similarly, if welfare is given priority, as it is by utilitarians, then when welfare and freedom conflict, gaining welfare becomes the obligation.

Hard and fast priority orderings that are always applicable seem objectionable. Circumstances, when evaluated, for example, by moral principles or by a caring attitude, often determine whether freedom or welfare is morally more important in a given situation. To proclaim one over the other in all cases seems overly rigid and is bound to increase, rather than decrease, moral conflict. (Speculate on why or whether this is so.)

Furthermore, a strict priority ordering may lead us to be content with less of some value, like welfare. Those who put freedom over welfare may tend to accept situations as morally proper where little welfare is present. But by placing equally high general regard on all values, conflicts between values become more likely, and thus call for mediation. Conflict between values arises due to actual circumstances; it is not inherent in basic values. (Do you agree? Why or why not?) The constraints on freedom needed for greater utility depend on social conditions, social practices, social habits, and social laws. These can all be changed. Given that freedom, equality, justice, and welfare are widely respected basic moral values, our moral experience is reluctant to cast one aside in favor of the others. The demand should be for a *mutuality between values,* for an environment in which a gain in one fosters the attainment of more of another. Insofar as feasible, personal behavior, practices, social institutions, and moral theory should be directed to achieve values in mutually enhancing ways. This involves making decisions, in time of conflict and in anticipation of conflict, that reduce the likelihood of future clashes by creating institutions that avoid conflict and by enhancing the mutual correlation between basic values.

We add this *mutuality principle* to moral theory: **Act to establish mutuality in basic value or to avoid conflict among basic moral values.** Sometimes we need to redesign a practice or reinterpret a value, while at other times we need to overcome the constraints on our actions that cause conflicts. For example, if people will not act freely to establish equality, we may have to motivate people or educate them about the cause and consequences of inequalities. In the short run, freedom or welfare may lose, but this may not be necessary in the long run.

Some have argued that freedom subverts welfare because welfare is a particular goal and freedom permits actions that may not yield welfare. This may be the case in many instances, but it is not necessarily true. First, the broader our conception of freedom, the more it is a positive notion involving abilities to act on formal freedoms, the more it seems false that freedom and welfare typically conflict. As long as some people lack welfare, they are not genuinely free. Also, a society may be designed so that free actions often produce greater welfare. This depends, to a large degree, on social practices. Systems of reward, or of moral motivation, may be in place to encourage people to do, freely, the actions that produce more welfare. (Does this allow for genuine freedom?)

Human beings may face natural constraints that militate against the mutual satisfaction of moral values. For example, psychologically, human beings may need great inequalities to contribute to society. Physicians may require large salaries to act in the interests of their patients, not because of individual greed but due to basic human nature. This may be true empirically, but it has not yet been demonstrated. Many professionals do excellent work on modest incomes. Other countries, including Japan, do not have the same inequality structures we find in countries like the United States. This suggests that people can participate in social practices without elaborate rewards that encourage social inequality.

The mutuality principle does not deny the possibility that moral values and moral obligations may continue to harbor conflict despite our efforts. Instead it calls on us to move toward minimizing conflict, where that is feasible. This is the way to embody more of those nearly universally respected values: freedom, equality, justice, and welfare.

Study Questions 11.4

1. List the ways philosophers have approached moral conflict. Evaluate each.
2. List the roles you expect to occupy during your lifetime. Do any of

these roles establish firm moral obligations? Are these roles likely to conflict?

3. (For class discussion.) The mutuality principle suggests a *pragmatic* approach to moral theory. That is, it is against firm commitment to any particular value in the face of moral conflict, and presents a forward-looking response to moral requirements that suggests experimentation and creativity. Is this pragmatic approach different from a utilitarian approach to conflict? Suppose someone is dedicated to freedom over welfare, that is, to a strict priority ordering. What response would that person make to the mutuality principle? Evaluate that response.

4. A basic claim in Section 11.4 is that practices influence behavior. Is this true? Can practices enhance or block the establishment of virtues? What would a virtue theorist say about the need for good practices? How would a feminist respond to the need for good practices? A Marxist?

5. Suppose a student objects to the petition procedure at his or her college, believing it to be unfair because students are not adequately represented on the committees making the decision. Does this student have a moral obligation to try to change the practice?

11.5 Moral Decisions

So far we have claimed that, in effect, on a day-to-day basis many moral decisions are made in advance for us by social practice. (How true is this? Carefully consider roles such as those of a teacher, student, parent, and child.) However, within any practice there is room for decisions that are not specified by the practice. Parents caring for children or children caring for parents frequently face moral decisions that must be made on their own, without guidance from the typical demands of the practice. Should a child be sent to private school? Should a parent be placed in a nursing home? No generally right or wrong answers exist to such questions, yet they do have moral dimensions. Other decisions also involve choice not clearly guided by a role. For example, which role should a person choose? This may be answered by current participation in a role; a parent's responsibilities may lead him or her to decide in favor of a particular profession. But often such decisions are not dependent on a previous role. So even though many actions are guided by our previous roles, in everyday life the way we act, including the roles we select, is often independent of any role.

Role participation does give moral direction, but even role participation ought to be morally evaluated. Moral rules, moral principles, and moral values often directly guide behavior, and may be used to evaluate practices and roles within practices. The mutuality principle also provides crucial guidance. And, as we have seen in previous chapters, ideals and moral exemplars, care, and the need to develop virtues should guide behavior.

Typically, the moral commands closest to the situation are the best guides for moral behavior. If a person is tempted to cheat on a test, the best guide is the moral rule against cheating. To argue in favor of some exceptional reason for cheating typically goes counter to the demands of universalization; making oneself an exception to a rule often involves some sort of special pleading, reasons we would not accept from others. The burden of proof is on the person who seeks to cheat. The practice of being a student, also part of the action and hence close to the case at hand, also stands against cheating. Cheating is not a virtue, and it encourages the very inadequate behavior that may have produced the felt need to cheat. Building the virtue of honesty is part of leading a moral life. In this way, the rule closest to the case, the rule against cheating, is also backed by many other moral considerations.

In making moral decisions the existence of specific moral commands, geared to a particular situation, establishes a strong prima facie obligation. Negative values also establish strong prima facie obligations. The prohibition against doing harm is a principle, not a rule. But it is a more precise principle than the principle requiring the production of welfare. It is also basic in virtually all moral thinking. Like rules, the prohibition against doing harm often provides specific guidance. Nonharm, negative freedom, and basic justice are fundamental in ethics. The burden of proof is on those who argue in favor of violating such principles.

Positive principles and ideals give overall direction and advocate reform; they guide circumstances that are not under other more specific obligations. They usually do not establish a moral obligation, but they recommend behavior and provide a way to evaluate persons, actions, roles, practices, and institutions. However, some people occupy roles that should be guided by positive principles, and for them moral responsibilities may be established by positive principles and positive values. In effect, their roles give them the responsibility to apply positive principles and values just as a firefighter has an added responsibility to help people in need.

This approach to moral decision making is eclectic. By providing for obligations and ways to recommend behavior through positive principles, we are faithful to the full moral range. By guiding the establishment of virtues and practices and by directing and evaluating individual actions, an eclectic approach is faithful to the full moral domain. More restricted approaches have the burden of proof on them. They limit moral experience. Since moral experience is the data for ethical theory and the ultimate court of appeal, a more comprehensive theory should have a higher standing than a less comprehensive one.

Our moral experience is not fully articulated, is contradictory, and often leads to frustration. A theorist gives guidance to moral experience and so may reject parts of it. A good theory accounts for much of it, and brings the parts it accounts for into coherence, one part with another. A theorist may argue that a limited theory does this better than a more comprehensive one. The questions then revolve around the ability of a more comprehensive theory to bring coherence to moral experience, and whether a narrower theory omits too much that is crucial to a proper morality.

The approach I am advocating uses more specific rules and practices as initial guidance. Less specific negative moral obligations provide solid moral guidance, yet less directly than specific rules and practices. Finally, positive moral principles and values and moral ideals give direction by making moral recommendations and moral evaluations. Those with special, reform-oriented roles may have significant moral obligation to conform their behavior to positive principles and perhaps even to be guided by moral ideals.

We can argue for or against this briefly stated view by considering whether it best brings coherence to the moral experience. Using the coherence method makes sense to the degree we think this is valuable to accomplish. If we believe that the moral experience is too filled with conflict, or too provincial, or the result of centuries of prejudice and exploitation, then this approach will not look promising. If we take seriously our moral experience as the only basis from which a moral theory can be developed, then the problem of establishing a point of view from which to solve moral problems will depend on how best to articulate, amplify, and rationalize our moral experience.

Study Questions 11.5

1. How should the following moral problem be resolved? A good student, one who never cheats, decides that a system depending on constant testing is counterproductive, especially to groups of students who have been socially disadvantaged. The student gets good grades, and will benefit from the system, but believes that this benefit is not morally proper. The student considers refusing to take tests. What should the student do?

2. Does the utilitarian believe that utilitarianism is unfaithful to our moral experience? The Kantian? If they both believe their view is faithful to moral experience, can they both be right? If they both can be right, can one theory better reflect moral experience than the other? Is the status of a theory improved when it better reflects moral experience?

3. (For class discussion.) The claim is sometimes made that something is good in theory, but not in practice. Can we have a moral point of view

that is good in theory but not in practice?

4. (For class discussion.) The view suggested in this section attempts to bring moral experience to coherence and order. Is this a subjective or an objective view? The doctrine of *moral realism* claims that moral values are independent of human judgment: people must discover and not invent moral values. Is the coherence view a form of moral realism?

11.6 The Lessons from Solving Moral Problems

Moral problems are often solved by relying on established practices, rules, and negative principles. These may provide solid guidance because they often give guidance applicable to particular cases, and not the broad general guidance found in positive principles, which needs further interpretation. Furthermore, following an established practice allows others to rely on or expect forms of behavior molded by practices. By having good information about the ways other people behave, we all may become more effective in our own actions, including our attempts to secure morally better behavior.

But established practice often leads to conflict. We want a world in which basic values, justice, equality, freedom, and welfare, are realized and secure. Many practices need to be reformed, some basically, so as to avoid moral conflict and promote moral value. To reform practices, a broad, principled moral view is required. Only a broader view can show how conflict may be avoided; positive moral principles, values, and ideals are needed to guide the resolution and avoidance of moral conflict. Reform, even when conflict is absent, may also be needed to foster valued components of the moral experience.

Moral conflict and the desire to attain moral value suggests that a narrow theory of morality is not adequate. We turn to the moral experience for guidance in selecting a moral theory. Although we need to respect the moral value of proper practices and moral rules, we also need to use positive moral principles and moral ideals to guide our own decisions and to guide social reform. But we need to keep in mind that morality is a complex system, with rules and practices helping to interpret principles and principles guiding the reform and application of practices and rules.

Further Reading

Joseph P. DeMarco, in *A Coherence Theory in Ethics* (Amsterdam: Rodopi, 1994), develops a moral theory relating practices to judgments, conventions, rules, and principles. In *Patterns of Moral Complexity* (Cambridge:

Cambridge University Press, 1987) Charles E. Larmore relates personal commitments and requirements in practices to moral principles. Stuart Hampshire, in *Morality and Conflict* (Cambridge: Harvard University Press, 1983), examines the relationship between a particular way of life and broad moral principles. J. L. Mackie develops a theory of moral responsibilities in relationship to special circumstances: *Ethics: Inventing Right and Wrong* (Harmondsworth, England: Penguin Books, 1977).

Endnotes

1. Isaac Levi, "Conflict and Inquiry," in *Ethics* 102 (4) (July 1992): 814–834.
2. Bernard Williams, "Ethical Consistency," in *Essays on Moral Realism*, ed. Geoffrey Sayre-McCord (Ithaca, N.Y.: Cornell University Press, 1988), pp. 41–58. Originally published in *Proceedings of the Aristotelian Society*, supplementary volume 39 (1965): 103–24.

12

Metaethics

12.1 Metaethical Inquiry

Metaethics studies the nature of moral theory: what it attempts to do; how it is properly established; the meaning of basic moral terms, such as "obligation" and "goodness"; and the objectivity of moral inquiry. Many philosophers believe that moral inquiry should begin with metaethical investigation, and some believe that the only proper job of the philosopher is to make metaethical observations; they object to *substantive ethics*, the branch of moral theory that provides guidance about what we ought to do. Much of our inquiry in the previous ten chapters has had a metaethical dimension, although its ultimate purpose is substantive. For example, we asked whether moral rules are proper or whether all moral judgments should be made in relation to particular circumstances. This is a metaethical question; it may be posed without addressing any particular moral values. The particularist need not declare that some particular act is morally right or wrong. Instead he or she may argue, without considering specific judgments, that all moral judgments must be free of the influence of moral rules. Also, much of what we accomplished was definitional. What does freedom mean? How is equality defined? Definitions are part of metaethics. However, as conceptions take shape, moral claims about whether actions are morally right or morally wrong are typically introduced. So our inquiry into basic values spills into substantive ethics.

In this chapter we will explicitly examine metaethical questions. Metaethics is a refined aspect of moral theory because it is pursued abstractly and technically. Further, it is about moral theory, also an abstract approach to morality. Though refined in the philosophical literature, our metaethical views, even if implicit, will influence the substantive positions we accept. So perhaps metaethics should come first in moral inquiry. I have saved it for last because I believe that abstract and refined metaethical theories are most fruitfully and clearly examined when a variety of substantive positions are in view.

Most of this chapter will deal with recent metaethics, views presented in this century mainly by British and American philosophers, many of whom began to argue that the job of the philosopher in moral theory is entirely metaethical. These philosophers believe that we do not have the ability or the authority to give substantive advice. They reject the status of substantive theories like those proposed by Mill and Kant.

Those philosophers who reject substantive theories were typically motivated by a strict *empiricism,* the view that all genuine knowledge is linked, more or less directly, to *observations. Facts* determine whether something is true or false. Since no moral facts exist, according to philosophers such as A. J. Ayer, then the only job of a philosopher is to show that moral statements have no objective status, or are meaningless. In effect, statements about ethics simply appeal to emotions or feelings, much like poetry. Whether poetic statements are true or false is not the point. The way they affect our sensitivities is what counts.

Other philosophers claim that the correct function of a philosopher rests entirely in analyzing language. These *analytic philosophers* also declare that substantive ethics is outside the view of the philosopher. Instead, metaethics properly helps to sort out the use of moral language. It helps decide whether moral statements, such as "doing action X is morally obligatory," follow an implicit logic. That is, if a person makes this claim, can we derive other statements from the speaker's belief? If Jane thinks that action X is obligatory for John, does that imply that Jane should also consider that X is obligatory for Alice, whose situation is similar to John's?

Suppose that when I claim that X is obligatory for person P, I imply that X is also obligatory for all people whose situation is similar to P's. Kant says something like this, except that he goes a step further. When he discovers a universal claim in ethical discourse, he believes that the rule is morally binding on everyone. This binding nature does not derive from an analysis of language. But from a metaethical perspective, a claim is made about the way language is used and what we may conclude from the use of moral language, without making claims that we ought to use moral language or do certain kinds of actions. We do not conclude that Jane ought to think that X is obligatory; we explore what follows *if* she has that belief. Substantive philosophers, including Kant, think they know what we ought to do or refrain from doing. Kant would be willing to say whether Jane's belief is correct. Kant's examination of moral obligation is substantive because he gives direction about our actions and not simply about how we use words.

The distinction here is not completely sharp; after all, when we are told about the logic of moral terms, we are also told how we ought to use them. Jane may be inconsistent if she does not think Alice is obligated to do X. But there is a difference. Kant thought that certain actions, regardless of how we use words or the values we hold, are morally prohibited, but a strict analysis of language simply tells how to use words consistently and how to make moral evaluations depending on the moral claims we make. If I claim that you are wrong to tell a lie, then I may be inconsistent if I also claim that it is acceptable for me to lie in similar circumstances, but whether telling a lie is actually prohibited, as Kant thought, is not a matter that can be resolved by the logic of moral language.

In British and American philosophy, under the dominance of *positivism* (a strict form of empiricism) and analytic philosophy, metaethics took primacy. Today positivism is not the received view among philosophers. Philosophers recognize that gaining knowledge is not straightforward; even scientific beliefs are not as closely related to observations as the positivists believed.[1] Analytic philosophy also became less secure about how to examine the use of language. A close examination of language leads to questions that are substantive because conclusions about the use of language implicitly bring with them substantive claims—for example, that we should be consistent. Problems of philosophy are not merely questions about the use of language, so as philosophers returned to traditional philosophical problems, the dominance of positivism and strict analytic philosophy over substantive ethics faded. Today philosophers, including analytic philosophers, do both substantive ethics and metaethics. Though not clearly distinct from substantive ethics, metaethics is helpful in doing substantive ethics, and substantive ethics helps to clarify and stimulate metaethical inquiry.

In the following sections we study some basic positions on the status of moral claims, the meaning of basic moral terms, and the method that ought to be used to determine morally correct evaluations.

Study Questions 12.1

1. A person may claim that all value judgments, including moral judgments, are merely matters of personal taste. Is this a metaethical judgment or a substantive judgment? Suppose the person thinks that he or she may now do whatever is desired. Does this affect your answer?

2. How important is metaethics in feminist ethics?

3. (For class discussion.) Science is thought to be value-neutral. Others claim that science is conservative: it only accepts observations that are well established. Scientists are skeptical of UFO reports, sightings of ghosts, and the like, even though many people insist they have made the proper observations. Is the conservatism of science a value judgment? If it is, does this affect the arguments of those who claim

that ethics is meaningless because it is not based on observation? Does this conservatism go against the claim that observations are required to make meaningful claims?
4. (For class discussion.) Is relativism a substantive position or a metaethical position? If it is a metaethical position, does it have substantive implications?

12.2 X Is Good

What does it mean to say that some action or some thing is good? In this century, philosophers have paid special attention to this metaethical question. Utilitarianism provides an answer to the question: the action that produces the greatest happiness for the greatest number of people is what we mean by moral goodness. As a definition, this statement seems to make two things interchangeable. Whenever we say "morally good," we are using shorthand for "the action that produces the greatest happiness for the greatest number of people." In this way, these two statements are interchangeable.

But does "good" really mean what the utilitarian claims? Some philosophers might counter by saying that any attempt to define moral goodness is futile because "moral goodness" is literally meaningless, because meaning relates to observations and moral terms do not refer to anything at all. No observations can back up a moral statement. So for some philosophers, like the positivists, the question we began with, about the meaning of goodness, is a waste of time. But this position is mistaken. We do talk and debate about whether actions are morally good, and our statements make sense. If such use of speech about morality is meaningless, we need a solid argument to show that it is. The positivist's definition that all meaning relates to observation defines "meaning" in a way that itself goes beyond observation, and even theoretical terms in science, like "electron," are not determined by observation. (No one has ever seen an electron!) The positivists are asserting their value judgment that value judgment is meaningless. So instead of rejecting the meaning of terms seriously used in ordinary discourse, other philosophers seriously question whether the utilitarians have the right definition of "good."

Utilitarianism is a form of *naturalism*, a theory that centers on natural things, the kinds of things we see around us and explore through our sciences. Naturalism is a *reductionism*. Reduction occurs when one thing is broken down into something more basic and it is claimed that all there is to the more complex thing is contained in the more basic. Naturalism reduces all things, the human personality, morality, and science, to natural events. Psychological states, like willing or believing, might be thought of as the subject of an independent science, but for a naturalist, if we knew enough, we would be able to reduce all psychological statements to statements about physical events, perhaps brain states. This claim would be reductionist: psychological statements are ways of making shorthand claims about physical events. For example, the fact that I now desire another sip of the coffee on my desk is shorthand for all the physical occurrences going on in my body, and, most importantly, in my brain. The reductionist does not believe in some special free will, or a desire that is somehow independent from the physical state of my body. Similarly, naturalism in ethics reduces moral claims to claims about naturally occurring events. In particular, the utilitarian claims that all moral statements ought to be reduced to statements about the pleasures people experience. Many other forms of naturalism can be found. For example, the American philosopher Ralph Barton Perry claims that moral obligations are reducible to human interests.

After the turn of the twentieth century, the British philosopher G. E. Moore examined naturalism in ethics, including Perry's naturalism, to determine whether it contains fallacious thinking. He wasn't especially interested in examining any particular form of naturalism; instead he wanted to examine moral naturalism in general. He concluded that naturalism is incorrect, that "good" could not be defined by reducing it to any natural quality. His argument is simple, yet ingenious. Suppose someone claims that "good" is defined as the action that produces the greatest happiness for the greatest number of people. We can question this. Does "good" really mean the action that produces the greatest happiness for the greatest number of people? Our question makes perfect sense. Yet if "good" really meant what the utilitarians claim, our question would not make sense. Remember that the definition offered is considered to support a substitution: "good" may be substituted for the longer string of words and vice versa. By substitution the definition permits us to claim that we are really saying "Does good really mean good?" (Be sure you understand how this substitution works.) This is not a significant question. (Explain why.) Since this is an insignificant question, and the original question is significant, Moore concludes that the two questions cannot be equivalent. The fact that we significantly question whether "good" means the action that produces the greatest happiness shows a difference in meaning between good and the natural qualities to which good is reduced.

Moral naturalism, according to Moore's *open question test,* fails. This open question, "Is this really what we mean by 'good'?," can be asked about any proposed natural standard. Is the maximal satisfaction of interests really good? Is any supposed reduction of goodness to a natural quality really what we mean by "good"? Since these questions make sense, "good" and any definition using a natural property cannot be interchanged. Any naturalism fails to offer an acceptable definition of good. Moore believed, and many philosophers agreed, that he had successfully defeated all naturalistic positions in ethics.

Joseph P. DeMarco

Moore offered an alternative account of goodness; instead of being reducible to natural qualities, moral goodness is a *nonnatural* quality that cannot be defined. Definitions of one term depend on other terms. But some terms are so basic that they cannot be defined, like the experience of the color yellow. It would be futile to define a color, although we might indicate that the appearance of a color is always associated with a certain reflection of light. We see or *intuit* colors. Moore thought that we intuit goodness much in the way we see colors, but with a nonnatural "sense" instead of a natural sense like sight. Moore thus links his nonnaturalism with *intuitionism* in ethics.

Although philosophers have taken seriously Moore's rejection of naturalism, they show little support for his nonnaturalism. It is a strange doctrine that assumes an ability to detect qualities about which we can say little. People do not intuit goodness much as they see redness, but instead they seem to respond differently to situations as good or bad, depending on their backgrounds, culture, and commitments. Even though differences in how something is seen may relate to a person's background, differences in moral reaction are more pronounced than differences in sensory observations.

Moore started out with the question about the meaning of "good" and, through his analysis, weakened the naturalist attempt to define the word. But he failed to produce a satisfactory solution, and he opened the door for others to speculate about the significance of moral claims. *Emotivists* focused on the fact that people respond differently to situations. They argued that we claim that things are good or bad neither based on some nonnatural quality nor by reducing events to natural qualities; to say that something is good is not to claim that a thing has a quality, natural or nonnatural. Instead, the statement is merely a report of a person's positive feeling. It is about the *emotions* of the user of the word and not about features of events. This steers a course between naturalism and nonnaturalism. But emotivism appears to be false. People call things good despite their apparent absence of positive feelings about these things. They also debate moral opinions in ways that seem to depend on reasons rather than emotions. Emotivism does not offer a compelling account of moral deliberation and debate.

The British philosopher R. M. Hare proposes a more neutral definition. He developed a doctrine called *prescriptivism*. When a claim is made that some thing or some action is good, that thing or action is commended or praised. But more than commendation is involved. *Moral* commendation also implies that others should hold the thing or action in similar high regard. For me to claim that something is good means that I commend it, and you should commend it as well. In effect, by claiming that an action is good, one person prescribes that action to another.

All of this does not get us far enough. On what basis should we commend things? Is a commendation objective or merely subjective? Can one evaluation be more objective than another? In the examination of the meaning of a word, we fail to determine an adequate base for substantive moral judgments.

Study Questions 12.2

1. Suppose we define a circle as a set of points equidistant from some other point. Can a person make sense by asking, "Is a set of points equidistant from some other point really a circle?" Does your answer help you to decide whether Moore's open question test is adequate?
2. Can a person have a negative response to something she or he believes to be morally good? If so, give an example.
3. Is Hare's prescriptivism correct? Can a person call a thing good without intending that others also commend it? Can we call something good without commending it?
4. (For class discussion.) Is moral inquiry helped by having a clear definition of a moral term like "goodness"?

12.3 Moral Realism

Philosophers have moved beyond the debate over the meaning of goodness. That debate helps us to examine the relationship between moral judgment, on the one hand, and intuitions, emotions, commendations, and prescriptions on the other. But none of the proposed answers we examined are conclusively acceptable. We may, instead, view moral theories as elaborate ways to recommend special definitions of goodness, obligations, rights, and so on. We may ask whether these definitions properly define these terms, but that question should be viewed as a call for debate over whether the theory is adequate. We frequently label things as morally good, and we look to theory to order and evaluate sometimes conflicting and vague valuations.

Today the debate focuses more on the status of moral goodness, its objectivity or subjectivity, than on how it is defined. One debated issue is about what stands behind moral judgments, or what they refer to. We claim that to abuse a child, sexually or physically, is morally wrong. Is this our opinion, a socially supported opinion, or a report on some objective property, namely the *fact* that it is wrong to be abusive? *Moral realism* is the doctrine that moral judgments, when correct, refer to something that is objective, independent of our opinions. Moral realists believe that moral facts support many of our moral judgments. This often seems to be the case. Observing a child being abused, we declare that it is morally wrong. If someone objects, claiming that this is simply our opinion, we wonder whether this person has seen the same thing we did. Surely they should be able to observe that the abuse is wrong, period. Many examples of moral judgments seem to be as reliable as examples of judging color. Although some people cannot make proper observations of even the simplest physical event, we claim that this is their deficiency; the event occurred regardless of whether it is properly observed. Likewise, some people cannot make proper moral observations. This does not mean that moral judgments are not based on real properties, but that such people have some deficiency, or perhaps that making the observation was difficult.

This form of moral realism links moral judgment to observations, much as G. E. Moore's intuitionism does. We may respond similarly in critique. Doesn't common need or common cultural conditioning lead us to call the act wrong, and not some sort of observable property? Opponents of moral realism claim that moral facts, the facts required by moral realists, would be odd elements in our ontology. An *ontology* specifies the kinds of entities, broadly conceived, that exist in the universe. In philosophy, for example, some ontologists believe that only physical objects exist, while others hold that many other kinds of things, mental and spiritual, exist. In moral theory, many philosophers argue that objective, independent moral properties are strange and unneeded additions to our ontology; moral theory makes perfect sense, they insist, without an appeal to special moral objects over and above the nonmoral objects. Even though they reject special moral objects, the opponents of moral realism need not claim that moral judgments are subjective. They may claim that we respond with moral condemnation to the abuse of the child because of our nature, our needs, our cultural standards, or our natural sentiments.

The debate goes on. Those favoring moral realism argue that evil can be observed. They maintain that nothing is odd about having moral properties, objective properties, in our ontology. We observe that it is evil to abuse someone. Most people would agree that such an act is evil, and most would agree that it is difficult to watch abuse without observing it as evil. The opponent of moral realism agrees that we "observe" some events as evil, but argues that this can be explained by our psychological disposition rather than by external events.

Moral realism is a general doctrine. It is consistent with Plato's view that morality involves universal, absolute, unchanging moral ideals that may be fully understood only by the wise. As we saw in Chapter 4, others believe that moral standards are in the mind of God, and so are objective. This is another form of moral realism. However, many philosophers contend that even if God proposes moral standards, we may reject them. If God wanted us to do something evil, we would know that it was evil. Even if God wills only the good, the fact that we can judge what God wills suggests that the reality of moral standards is not simply in God's mind.

The American philosopher Stephen Boyd recently proposed some simple tests to confirm the truth of moral realism.[2] Moral reasoning must start with approximately true moral beliefs. True beliefs must have some relation to observations. Finally, moral terms require natural definitions. Boyd outlines a theory he thinks conforms to these demands, *nonutilitarian consequentialism*. This theory centers on human needs such as friendship, cooperation, autonomy, and physical recreation. These human goods often occur together, and, in proper balance, they are mutually supporting. Moral decision making is concerned with achieving the proper balance, through enhanced psychological and social mechanisms, so as to strengthen the bond between human values. Boyd's theory presumes that we have true moral beliefs relating to these human needs, but this is far from clear. Human needs do play a key role in ethics, but other issues, of freedom, justice, and equality, go beyond basic human needs. Boyd's defense of moral realism rests too heavily on a form of naturalism that relates to an overly restricted part of moral experience.

Moral realism depends on identifying some objective moral standards that do not vary from place to place. So far this attempt appears futile. While relativism is a debated option in ethics, it is not in the natural sciences (although some *philosophers* do debate the issue). If moral realism were true, and observed moral properties were as basic as many current moral realists claim, like observing the evil of a child being abused, we would most likely have made more progress in basic moral theory than we have over the last 2,000 years. On the other hand, if moral realism affirms some recondite property, like Platonic ideals, then moral progress is unlikely. (Explain why.)

As we saw in the previous chapters, morality involves many things, including conventions, social practice, and moral principles, that are not easily reduced to some basic, objective moral properties, as the moral realist would hope. Observations, however they are made, may play a role, but the role is not as fundamental as it is in the sciences. Moral realism may remain true even if we are ignorant of objective moral qualities, but if we are ignorant, then the support for moral realism is more a hope then a well-established belief. We have no way of showing conclusively that moral realism is false. The problem we must face, whether or not we support moral realism, is to show how proper moral judgments can be made. Although moral realists refer to objective facts, because these facts are often unknown, realists frequently fail to show how they aid moral decision making.

We have already explored moral relativism, one of the ways of doing ethics that conflicts with moral realism. Moral relativism rejects objective features in morality. In our examination of moral standards, we determined that objectivity need not refer to a real, external thing. We can also be objective by giving good reasons, or by basing views on some universal aspect of human cultural evolution. In the next sections we explore some views about moral theory that claim to offer objective perspectives without appealing to real, external properties.

Study Questions 12.3

1. Is a utilitarian a moral realist? Is a Kantian?
2. (For class discussion.) How would a moral realist explain the fact that there is so much disagreement today over correct moral values? Do you believe that much disagreement exists today?
3. Does moral realism entail a "strange" ontology?
4. Is G. E. Moore's nonnaturalism a form of moral realism?

12.4 The Basic Value Approach

Moral realism commits itself to the existence of external, independent moral properties. The *basic value approach,* which we examine in this section, does not. It is typically neutral about the independent existence of any moral property. Instead, this approach flows from an examination of the moral experience, or some aspect considered central to the moral experience. This is how Kant proceeded. He wanted to know what makes an action morally good. A good will, doing something because it is the right thing to do, is for Kant the central aspect from which moral theory flows.

Other basic values come to mind. The American philosopher Alan Gewirth considers moral debate, the attempt to determine the right thing to do, as central. Debate presupposes free participation. In this way freedom becomes the moral value around which all moral experience flows.

Another philosopher, David Gauthier, focuses on *rationality.* Rationality, as we have seen, is often thought to involve self-interest. Gauthier attempts to develop a moral theory that all rational people can accept by using self-interest as a nonmoral central value. Selecting a nonmoral value as central is difficult because the theorist must then show how a moral obligation flows from a nonmoral concern. This is what Moore's open question test really amounts to. Why are we morally obliged to seek some nonmoral value like pleasure or individual rationality? The problem is that leaving the central value undefended is unsatisfying. It is a difficult approach to accept if it requires us to support, on faith or from our limited experiences, the global importance of the central value. We want good reasons for reliance on a central value from which to derive all moral obligations. But if the value is defended, the defense likely will involve other values that then compete with the central value for importance. Gauthier resorts to values like autonomy in defending his conception of rationality. Free people should be allowed to follow their own interests. We may approve of autonomy, but when mentioned it becomes another value in the system, not easily derived from the basic value. Suppose individual rationality conflicts with an environment that promotes autonomy. The basic approach, with rationality as the central value, is then lost because rationality has no proper defense— the defense autonomy was intended to provide.

Suppose, instead, that a moral value is selected as the central value. One problem is eliminated; the value already has connotations of moral responsibility. But the second problem remains. If the central value is defended, other values start to play a coequal role, militating against the central value approach.

Even if these problems can be avoided, the use of a central value presents a restricted morality. It violates the notion that our moral experience is broad and supplies the test of any moral theory. Moral experience is the raw data of moral theory; we must show that a theory either conforms to moral experience in some way or another, or that much of moral experience is improper or may be derived and ordered by a central concern. When much of that experience is excluded, the burden of proof is on the central value theorist. It is unlikely that the theorist will meet that challenge.

Yet, the attempt to base morality on a central value is worthwhile. Theories are helpful even when they are not the whole truth. Gauthier tries to spell out what a "rational" ethical theory would be like. Other theories violate his conception; for example, to be utilitarian, from an individual perspective, is not always rational. Insofar as this is the case, Gauthier shows us that something is wrong because we prefer a world in which being a utilitarian does not entail self-sacrifice. We might not be able to resolve the problem—the conflict between individual rationality and gaining welfare generally—but the mutuality principle, explained in Chapter 11, requires that we try or that we take note of the significance of the problem in the hope that someday it may be resolved. Rejecting Gauthier's concern, that much of moral theory is hostile to individual interests, is not the answer. Instead we need a more inclusive theory, but one that takes Gauthier's concern seriously.

Study Questions 12.4

1. Is Gert's system of rules a central value theory? How about Noddings's care theory? (Keep in mind that in a central value theory all moral obligations are derived from one value, moral or nonmoral.) If so, what are the central values in these systems, and how are they defended? Does the defense include any values other than the central

value, and, if so, does this show that the main value is not basic?
2. Of all the values we have so far examined, such as freedom, justice, equality, welfare, and rationality, which would you argue for as the most effective central value?
3. Suppose you believe that freedom is the central value from which all moral values can be derived. How would you defend that view? Do you use other values in your defense? Does this use of other values weaken your defense? Can those other values be derived from freedom?
4. Consider several moral decisions you have made recently. Do those decisions have anything in common? If so, can that common note be made into a central value from which many moral obligations can be derived? Or does that common factor come from some other value or concern? Relate your own experience to the use of a central value as basic in moral theory.

12.5 Intuitionism

Intuitionism is the metaethical doctrine that maintains that moral principles, rules, or judgments are clear and obvious truths that do not need to be supported by argumentation. G. E. Moore was an intuitionist when he claimed that we have the nonnatural ability to observe moral properties. Moore believed that moral knowledge about particular values is much like sense knowledge, but this is not necessary to intuitionism. An intuitionist may claim that principles, rules, or judgments appeal to our sense of reasonableness, or that we cannot imagine them to be false. Such truths may be thought of as *self-evident*. As soon as we understand a statement, the statement may appear undeniable, not because we argue in favor of it, but because we can't understand what it would be like for the statement to be false. In this way general principles may be intuitively supported.

In this sense, a utilitarian might be an intuitionist. As soon as we understand the utilitarian principle, it may make such good sense that we believe it cannot be sensibly denied. One way to defend utilitarianism is to claim that its truth is self-evident, just as the truth of basic geometrical claims was thought to be self-evident. The truth of the utilitarian principle could be considered clearer, more evident, than the truth of any supporting claims. A proper defense of utilitarianism should not contain claims even more controversial than the defended doctrine. But such support for utilitarianism seems not to be available; everything we say to support it may seem less evident than the basic utilitarian principle. Thus, no argument can offer additional support, but an argument might help another person to appreciate the truth of the principle. Peter Singer similarly claims that any moral theory must stem from self-evident basic principles, which he calls *fundamental axioms:*

> . . . search for undeniable fundamental axioms; build up a moral theory from them; and use particular moral judgments as supporting evidence, or as a basis for *ad hominem* arguments, but never so as to suggest that the validity of the theory is determined by the extent to which it matches them.[3]

Intuitionism is an unpopular doctrine in metaethics, and for good reason. Claiming that a moral judgment or principle is intuitively correct is easier when everyone holds the same beliefs. The more anthropologists teach us about the moral views of people in other places and other times, the more we see that what appears self-evidently bad to us may appear good to others. Philosophers supporting intuitionism may claim that such people have some moral disability. But this argument won't work. It is ad hoc and chauvinistic. Furthermore, we know from the history of geometry that the self-evident status of intuitions about the distance between two points is disputable. In geometry, intuitions no longer hold validity. The starting point of a geometry is best considered to be arbitrary, from the point of view of its truth. In mathematical thinking, the power, usefulness, and elegance of the system are what counts, not the self-evident status of its basic axioms.

We don't need to go into the history of mathematics. We do need to say that some of the most secure intuitions—e.g., that the shortest distance between two points is a straight line—are now in dispute. Geometrical intuitions are less controversial than moral intuitions. So when geometry is no longer based on self-evident truths, basing a less rigorous discipline like ethics on self-evident truths is difficult to accept. Whether we appeal to basic intuitions about principles and values or to intuitions about particular judgments, we are faced with the same problems, that so-called intuitions vary from person to person or group to group, and what appears to be self-evident to one person is not so to another. Basic beliefs and judgments in ethics are debated. Reasons are given, whether they are nonmoral reasons or reasons based on other moral values. The appeal to conflicting intuitions runs the risk of hindering interpersonal debate. Morality involves the regulation of social behavior, so any appeal that short-circuits agreement over moral values is not helpful.

The strength of intuitionism is that it appeals to the fact that some moral beliefs stand so firmly that they take on the look of data. That it is wrong to murder or to abuse a child seems more true than Kant's theory, or any other theory. The intuitionist labels such judgments as intuitions. And they certainly appear to be immediate judgments. We don't need to give reasons about them. Yet coming to an immediate judgment can be consistent with giving reasons, or with entering into debate with those who reject our views.

Judgments about murder and abuse are supported by basic moral principles and values. They have intuitive appeal, but such judgments may arise because of socialized sympathy with others, or from basic moral education.

Study Questions 12.5

1. (For class discussion.) Suppose that basic moral judgments spring from human sentiments that are implanted in us by God or produced by a long evolutionary process, and that these sentiments are as invariant as basic human biological functions. When we encounter an event that involves abuse, our sentiments lead us to declare that the abuse is wrong. If this happens, should we claim that we have an intuition that the abuse is wrong? Based on this sentiment, could we intuit that the utilitarian principle is correct? How could we argue for and against the existence of such an sentiment?
2. Two arguments are offered above against the claim that intuitions are the fundamental support for moral theory: that people have very different moral views, and that in mathematics intuitions or self-evident truths no longer play a role. Are these good reasons to reject the existence of intuitive support for a moral belief?
3. Are particularists intuitionists? Explain your answer.

12.6 Conventionalism and Social Contract Theory

Conventionalism is the doctrine that moral beliefs are not objective and universal but are adopted by social choice or by historical custom. A convention, like driving on the right side of the road or keeping a promise, may be serious and well-established. It may be based on human needs or on basic human desires. Nevertheless, it depends on some agreement among people, either explicit or implicit, based on actions if not on words. Or, like many laws, it is based on an initial agreement or consensus followed by social enforcement. Conventionalism in ethics claims that all moral views are conventional and have as their basic support the social agreement that originally produced the belief.

Moral relativism, which we explored in Chapter 4, is a form of conventionalism. In relativism, different groups of people may establish different moral views. Relativism points to the conventional feature of moral views and argues that, indeed, people do have fundamentally different points of view. But conventionalism is not bound to the doctrine that a plurality of moral views exists. It is consistent with the view that only one correct moral view exists. This is the position taken in the *social contract* tradition.

The social contract tradition views morality as properly flowing from an initial unanimous agreement. Morality is not imposed from without. We only act morally when we, personally, intend that our actions follow from proper moral principles. We may tell the truth out of fear, but this deserves no moral praise. Only when we accept a moral principle is that principle morally binding on us, and only then are we properly praised for acting in conformity with that principle. Social contractarians oppose any moral authority imposed by the state, God, the family, etc. Such authority may play a moral role, even a central role, but only when it is validated by the initial approval of all. We are, together, to unanimously establish our moral base, even if that base involves public laws and public policies.

Contractarians must squarely face the problem that what looks like consent to a moral position may in fact involve social or individual coercion. We may be propagandized to accept a moral rule, or we may accept it because those we love have unduly influenced us, especially when we were children. People often accept their own nation's, group's, or family's way of doing things because that is how they are accustomed to acting. We do not really accept those traditions in any philosophically pure sense. We might not know or fully appreciate other ways of doing things. Since social contractarians demand a philosophically pure acceptance of a moral position, they speculate on what people might accept if they were not dominated by current institutional practice, with its current power structures and socialized habits. They propose that we consider not what people actually accept, but what they would accept from a privileged vantage point.

The *original position* or the *state of nature* is the vantage point from which we should decide what people would accept in a way that makes their judgments morally binding. This vantage point must not contain those aspects of life that make us wonder whether a decision is autonomous. For example, in cases of unequal power, we may question whether people are making free decisions. Consider children still under the influence of their parents or teachers. We doubt that they really accept the moral judgments they pronounce. So contractarians insist that the original position is a place of freedom and equality, without social structures, social roles, and social power relations.

Contractarians usually insist that the original position must be free from any source of prejudice. A prejudiced decision does not provide a base for an acceptable morality. When prejudices are allowed, then the decision is not a moral decision, but a idiosyncratic decision. Thus, by using a privileged point from which to judge consent, social contract theory moves away from the notion that we must internalize a moral view, or accept it as our own. We do not need to actually accept the view; it is enough to claim that unprejudiced people in a properly defined original position would accept certain moral obligations. This means that agreement in social contract theory is not actual agreement but a philosophically purified agreement, usually among hypothetical people. Social contract theorists want to use the original position as a way to determine an uncontaminated morality, one that is not influenced by anything that would give us reason to doubt that a moral position is fully acceptable from the vantage point of unbiased and uncoerced people.

John Rawls presents his social contract theory of justice as a kind of game, although a most serious one. He defines people in an original position so that they may make pure moral decisions. The people are hypothetical, so we must decide what they believe. (This is where the game aspect comes in.) If the people in the original position are well defined, we can think through them to derive morally acceptable principles. This means that the description of the imaginary people must be rich enough so that we can figure out what they would decide, and all their defining features must be morally acceptable traits representing basic moral requirements for a fair, unbiased selection of moral principles. As we have seen, Rawls defines the hypothetical people in the original position as free, equal, and ignorant of their own special traits, including their race, sex, and IQ. They are *self-interested* in that they want as much as possible for themselves but *disinterested* in that they don't care what others have as long as they themselves have the most they can. Furthermore, they are not willing to take risks because the stakes are high in defining basic principles of justice. These principles will be used to organize social life, on which depend our goods, our freedoms, and even our self-images.

Based on these defining traits, Rawls claims that we can reason as if we are among the hypothetical people. We know they would not be racists, because they don't know their own race and want more for themselves. (What other traits keep them from being racists?) We know that they would protect their ability to gain the goods they want, because they are self-interested. Even though they are self-interested, they must protect all, because they don't know which social position they will occupy.

Rawls argues that no matter what principles such people accept, those principles are the proper principles of justice. When we put ourselves into the position of these hypothetical people, we accept what we do as free, equal, and rational people. This is a philosophically purified consent to moral principles, and so it defends the principles we are morally obliged to accept. If we do not accept the principles that would be selected in the original position, Rawls believes we are acting in some prejudiced or biased way.

A social contract theory has two main features: (1) the description of the original position or the state of nature, and (2) the reasoning supporting the decisions about moral principles made by the occupants of the original position. Disagreements among contractarians occur on both fronts. Many descriptions of the original position can be developed. Why not make the people in the original position altruistic? Why not allow them some jealousy? Rawls claims that the people in the original position do not take risks, but we may believe that some risk taking is reasonable. Hobbes, writing as the initiator of the British contractarian tradition, argued that people in the state of nature are fearful and greedy. John Locke, whose writings influenced the American Declaration of Independence, claimed that people in the state of nature are self-sufficient. Our problem is to decide which characterization of the state of nature gives us the best vantage point, the best sense of a philosophically pure consent.

The second feature of a contract theory concerns the principles people accept assuming that the original position is well defined. This is a genuine problem. We may define the people in the original position so well that we know they would accept one set of principles over all other principles. For this to be the case, the definition of the people must implicitly contain the principles. But this begs the question—it surreptitiously assumes what we want to discover, the proper principles of justice. We want to know what principles would be accepted by rational, free, and equal people. But to get the answer it seems improper to load the principles we accept into the description of the people.

We may define the occupants of the original position loosely and then debate the principles such unbiased people would accept, but then they might not come to agreement. If they did, we might believe that we reasoned incorrectly by allowing people in the original position to support what we believe instead of what unbiased people would believe. This is the case because bias and prejudice are difficult to detect. The whole point of the original position is to purify decisions about principles of judgment so that bias is not a factor. Either way, by defining people in the original position too narrowly or by allowing too many of our initial beliefs to enter, the original position masks our beliefs. In our starting point, we cannot easily avoid what we actually believe, whether or not our beliefs are justified. The initial positions developed by social contractarians may help to make our views clearer or to show better what they entail, but the mere fact that people in some original position would accept some principle does not say we should as well.

Study Questions 12.6

1. Rawls argues that people in his original position would accept (1) equal liberty, (2) equal opportunity, and (3) equal distribution of basic goods like income and wealth unless unequal distribution would maximally benefit the least well-off group of people. Would people in Rawls's original position, as described above, accept such principles?

Would people in the original position believe that liberty and equal opportunity should be equal unless inequality gives more liberty and opportunity?
2. What traits in Rawls's original position help to guarantee the selection of proper principles? Do any defining traits seem to be arbitrary or contrary to the selection of adequate principles? For example, does it help or hurt to make people self-interested? Risk-adverse?
3. (For class discussion.) Is hypothetical consent, or philosophically purified consent, better or worse than actual consent as a basis for acceptable moral judgments?
4. What is the moral significance of consent to the moral rules under which people live? Are moral rules better when people consent to them? (Think of the ways that moral rules might be "better.") Are rules we consent to more binding on us?

12.7 Moral Coherence

The theoretical point of view I have taken in this book is the coherence view. We have attempted to evaluate theoretical positions based on a broad view of moral experience, attempting to find what is correct about each theory and what is incorrect. *Moral coherence* accepts moral experience as the starting point for moral inquiry. Under this view a theorist attempts to develop a moral theory that includes, explains, and purifies as much of moral experience as possible. Theory is used to find the implications of moral experience, to broaden our moral knowledge by changing moral rules, principles, and values so as to get more value and make the world morally better. We have many values, many commitments, but these need to be organized, defended, and explained. A coherence theory attempts to do this.

As we find it, moral experience is not coherent. Rules may conflict with other rules, principles with judgments, and judgments with other judgments, and so on. Bringing moral experience to coherence may involve rejecting some of its aspects, proposing that some aspects take precedence over others, and expanding or restricting the meanings of some moral terms. These theoretical tasks are probably best done by philosophers who have studied moral traditions and understand the variety of aspects found in moral experience. They are trained in reasoning skills so they understand how a moral theory may be developed and presented.

Philosophers, like everyone else, come from personal and cultural backgrounds with sets of individual commitments. Any philosophical theory must go beyond individual concerns. The job is to bring *our* moral experience to coherence, with "our" meaning the largest number and variety of people. This is a public matter. The coherence view accepts the burden of a public presentation of a theory, with appropriate public modification.

The problem remains that more than one way may bring moral experience to coherence. A plurality of theoretical views may be acceptable. These views may all lead to the same decisions, with little harm involved in having more than one theory. Or else they may occasionally lead to different judgments. Different judgments may be instructive, but we may find more agreement over one judgment than the other. That weight of agreement may indicate a superior judgment. Or else the judgment that stands alone, supported by only one theory, may be better reasoned, and may eventually find more support.

A plurality of theories is especially helpful if, as I believe, the coherence view supports a mutuality principle. When different judgments exists, an attempt must be made to accommodate all judgments, perhaps by changing the circumstances producing the disagreement. Thereby theories cooperate to bring greater moral value into the world. For example, a society that is free, equal, and has a high level of welfare is a better society than one that is equal and has a high level of welfare but is not free. The assumption in the coherence view is that all moral values are important, even though some may be more important than others. The burden of proof is on those who limit our moral domain and range.

A broadly based coherence methodology stands the greatest chance of supporting the development of theories that provide a place for the values people have frequently found crucial in social and individual life. A good coherence theory is going to include ideals, basic values, principles, rules, virtues, and individual judgments. It will not propose a moral realism, or an intuitionism, although it need not reject these. Instead, it is based in the values that are already part of moral experience. It does not begin by judging these values but attempts to order and explain them. It only rejects values when forced to by the overall weight of moral experience.

Developing a successful coherence view is difficult. It must involve a plurality of moral values, which entails ample potential and actual conflict. A monolithic moral theory may avoid such conflicts, but at the cost of giving up much of moral experience. A coherence view may produce several independent theories, each with apparently equal legitimacy. Conflict among supported values and conflict among theories are the main weaknesses of a coherence view. Yet conflict is already present. Other points of view also present a multiplicity of theories; for example, utilitarians have supported many different, conflicting conceptions of the good to be optimized. Moral realists understand that we may never discover the correct theory, partly because the reality of the moral realm is often difficult, if not impossible, to detect. Theoretically, moral realism may lead to one correct theory, but this does not help when disagreement over moral values exists; currently disagreement, even among moral realists, seems to be a permanent part of philosophical debate over moral theory.

Moral realism, conventionalism, and intuitionism are not superior to coherence because they believe in the existence of only one correct theory. And they are less able to deal with a multiplicity of moral values and moral beliefs. Moral coherence is a more encouraging way to offer support for moral decisions, and a better way to support the development of practices and conventions that are able to meet different moral needs and desires.[4]

Study Questions 12.7

1. Consider a family dispute in which one decision abridges freedom and the other means more freedom. How would a realist, an intuitionist, and a coherentist attempt to solve this problem? You should make the example more concrete by spelling out the dispute.
2. Moral coherence may seem false because it seems to admit the moral standing of apparently immoral actions, like the brutal and primitive treatment women undergo in some countries by socially supported convention. Is this a good criticism of moral coherence? How would the person supporting moral coherence respond?
3. Using the method of moral coherence, is it possible to give an intuitive judgment more weight than a judgment supported by many other aspects of moral experience? If you think so, give an example of such a judgment. If not, explain why not. (Consider carefully what such a judgment would need to be like if it is going to win out over many other parts of morality, like rules and principles.)
4. Moral coherence may develop theories that are convoluted. This may be necessary to take into account as much as possible of moral experience. A theory that cannot be easily learned is considered to be a improper moral theory. Is moral coherence more susceptible to this charge than moral realism? How would the coherence theorist respond to this charge? (Consider, for example, whether moral theory would need to be more convoluted than scientific theory.)

12.8 The Lessons from Metaethics

Our brief examination of metaethics should give us reason to believe that refining our basic point of view on the status of moral theory is crucial in moral reasoning. If moral judgments are merely emotional, they should be approached much differently than if they are based on a single value. The examination of metaethical views in this chapter indicates that the arguments supporting moral subjectivity are not compelling. Moral realism supports the view that moral values are independently objective, while other views, contractarianism and the basic value approach, suggest forms of moral reasoning that are considered objective.

Moral experience is as varied as views about moral theory and how it should be approached. Moral coherence attempts to deal with the plurality of views by admitting that no one way has yet surfaced as the right way. A more inclusive approach may be able to account for the strengths of various positions, including metaethical positions, and minimize their weaknesses. This is the attempt in the coherence theory. The point is not to win a theoretical battle but to produce better moral judgments, judgments that spawn more value and so make the world a better place. This is our task as moral theorists and as moral beings.

Further Reading

George Sher offers a fine collection of primary sources, many involving the views mentioned in this chapter: *Moral Philosophy: Selected Readings* (San Diego: Harcourt Brace Jovanovich, 1987). Roger N. Hancock provides a convenient, and thorough, survey of contemporary Anglo-American metaethical theory in *Twentieth Century Ethics* (New York: Columbia University Press, 1974). *Essays on Moral Realism*, edited by Geoffrey Sayre-McCord (Ithaca, N.Y.: Cornell University Press, 1988), an anthology of writings by contemporary philosophers, provides examples of philosophical speculation at its best on the question of the ontological status of moral values. Richard DeGeorge, in "Ethics and Coherence," *Proceedings of the American Philosophical Association* (1990): 39–52, explains and defends the use of coherence in ethical theory.

Endnotes

1. For an account of the rise and fall of positivism, see Frederick Suppe, *The Structure of Scientific Theories* (Urbana: University of Illinois Press, 1977).
2. Stephen Boyd, "How to Be a Moral Realist," in *Essays on Moral Realism*, ed. Geoffrey Sayre-McCord (Ithaca, N. Y.: Cornell University Press, 1988), p. 201.
3. Peter Singer, "Sidgwick and Reflective Equilibrium," *Monist* 58 (1974): 517.
4. See Joseph P. DeMarco, *A Coherence Theory in Ethics* (Amsterdam: Rodopi, 1994), for a full development of a coherence position.

Index